PRAISE FOR
WILD POETS OF]

"Can an anthology of poetry be called a
is. For over a century, canonical literature in general and poetry in
particular have been prisoners of an academic posture which elevates the
voices of despair, depression, and alienation to high culture, and relegates
those of optimism, joy, and well-being to the superficial and ill-informed.
D.J. Moores, in a courageous departure from this convention, has crafted
a soaring collection of exuberant, joyful, and ecstatic verse. The general
reader must be grateful to him for envisioning nothing less than a
'Positive Humanities.'"

—MARTIN SELIGMAN, Fox Leadership
Professor of Psychology at the University of Pennsylvania
and former President of the American Psychological Association

"While teaching Dante's Paradiso I kidded the class that I was done
with 'critique.' I wanted to take up 'Paradise Studies.' This anthology is
a lot closer than I thought scholarship and good taste were likely to come
to such studies. Its rendering of the varieties of ecstatic experience is as
thrilling as it is informative."

—CHARLES ALTIERI, Professor of English at the University of
California-Berkeley and author of The Particulars of Rapture

"In a dark time, it is salutary to be reminded of the many varieties of
light still available to us in the work of poets from Homer to the present.
D.J. Moores has given us that gift in this new anthology."

—DON FREDERICKSON, Professor of Film at Cornell University
and Chairman, International Association for Jungian Studies

"Sometimes both ordinary language and the language of science
fail to capture what we experience, what we want to say, to speak of
or about. So it is with ecstatic experience. D.J. Moores has given us a
treasure trove, a book meant for grazing, for feeling one's way into the
poetic language in which, near as we can, commonplace experiences of
unusual positive states of mind can be met, evoked, recalled, and valued
in the ways they deserve in a rich, meaningful human life."

—OWEN FLANAGAN, James B. Duke Professor of Philosophy and
Neurobiology at Duke University, former President of the Society
for Philosophy and Psychology, and author of
The Nature of Consciousness

archive we feel this limit is far from a defeat. It is a vital inspiration, perhaps even the inspiration for ecstatic poetry, born 'standing outside' and vibrating with the relays of its ordinary and extraordinary demarcations."

—SUSAN J. WOLFSON, Professor of English at Princeton University, President of the Association of Literary Scholars, Critics and Writers, and author of *Romantic Interactions*

"Wild Poets of Ecstasy is a rich and fascinating anthology. Moores's introduction provides an illuminating history of the theory and experience of ecstasy and of its expression in the poetic imagination."

—EUGENE GOODHEART, Professor of English at Brandeis University and author of *The Reign of Ideology*

"Is 'ekstasis' (being on the outside of oneself) possible? These poems do not provide an answer, but reveal how the experience of being 'outside one's self' may arise from having never been completely 'inside' one-self to begin with. The wide ranging poems in this volume chart something of the perforated membrane between the inside and outside of being where and who we are (becoming). Ekstasis, as it appears in poetry, presences more than a sensation (the so-called 'ecstatic'): it offers a communal conception of being."

—JONATHAN STALLING, Professor of English at the University of Oklahoma and author of *Poetics of Emptiness*

"Moores's excellent new anthology is a vital gathering of much needed inspiration. In a culture cringing with conformity, Wild Poets of Ecstasy *helps us dream impossible futures and expand the human creature itself. I salute such a brave and splendid undertaking."*

—SUSAN ROWLAND, Professor of English and Jungian Studies at the University of Greenwich, former Chair of the International Association for Jungian Studies and author of *The Ecocritical Psyche*

"This book provides an eclectic selection of ecstatic poetry from the classical period to the present. General readers and specialists alike will find rich and varied manifestations of various mystical traditions from all over the world. A fine achievement."

—ROBERT STANTON, Professor of English at Boston College and author of *The Culture of Translation in Anglo-Saxon England*

WILD POETS
OF
ECSTASY

An Anthology of
Ecstatic Verse

Selected and with a Critical Introduction by

D. J. Moores

PELICAN POND

Published by Pelican Pond Publishing
an imprint of Blue Dolphin Publishing, Inc.
P.O. Box 8, Nevada City, CA 95959
Orders: 1-800-643-0765
Web: www.bluedolphinpublishing.com

ISBN: 978-1-57733-248-0 paperback
ISBN: 978-1-57733-413-2 e-book

Library of Congress Cataloging-in-Publication Data

Wild poets of ecstasy : an anthology of ecstatic verse / selected and with a
critical introduction by D. J. Moores.
     p. cm.
  Includes bibliographical references and index.
  ISBN 978-1-57733-248-0 (pbk. : alk. paper)
  1. Religious poetry. 2. Ecstasy. I. Moores, D. J.
  PN6110.R4W55 2011
  808.81'9382—dc22

                                                          2010045304

Cover art: Leah McNeir
Cover design: Scott Fray

The poem "Much Madness Is Divinest Sense" is reprinted in this anthology
with the permission of Harvard University Press and taken from the following work: *The Complete Poems of Emily Dickinson*. Edited by Thomas A.
Johnson. New York: Back Bay, 1976.

Printed in the United States of America

5   4   3   2

DEDICATION

To all of my students, who have taught me so much.

ACKNOWLEDGEMENTS

Many thanks to the following assistant editors, whose eagle-eyes and countless hours of attentive labor helped to produce a clean manuscript:

Matthew Cavalier
Christopher Guarino
Denise Marando
Christina Walling

CONTENTS

Contents

FOREWORD

Wild Poets of Ecstasy is a perfect holiday from meetings and melt-downs, cell phones and sciatica, bills and Blackberries. No longer a struggle between past and future, time eases into a blissful *now*. These joyful and dynamic poems return us to what's most precious in human life—love, devotion, wonder, gratitude, enchantment—*ecstasy*.

This exuberant collection is a carnival full of mystery, flashing lights, haunting music, and surprise. Reading it is like a roller-coaster ride; once you start, you can't stop. Here you will revel in ancient and modern voices singing in rhapsody from the deepest realms of the soul. Here, with no political or religious schisms, the world's cultures are celebrated and brought together as one: the Papago Indians hum with the singers of Negro Spirituals; the Inuit feast with eighteenth-century Europeans; Sufi and Christian mystics meditate serenely alongside erotic and secular writers.

As readers, we are whirled into ecstasy: these poems speak for and from our very core. Intimate and fresh, they are home—a refuge. Through them, we move from no to yes, from despair to possibility, from isolation to love. In the perpetual spring of this collection, poets sing and spin in a rapturous dance around a ring of fire. The sacred flame they honor burns for you. Read on.

Susanna Rich, Professor of English, poet, and author of *Television Daddy* and *The Drive Home*

Wild Poets of Ecstasy

Once you have flown,
You will walk the Earth
With your eyes turned skyward;
For there you have been,
There you long to return.
                        —Leonardo da Vinci

INTRODUCTION

A View from the Summit

Ecstasy bites deeply into the soul, sometimes leaving those who experience its joys forever transformed, forever unable to return to their previous lives. The ecstatic experience, however it comes about and whatever form it takes on, quite often leaves people with radically altered perspectives. As a result, their values, ideologies, and even conceptions of selfhood transmute, usually for the better. The work of Elisabeth Kubler-Ross, the physician known for codifying the grieving process and founding the hospice movement in America, supports such an idea. Kubler-Ross spent much of her later career investigating the near-death experience (NDE), by which is meant the phenomenon of returning to life from actual, clinical death. In her analysis of some 30,000 such cases, she found that those who are resuscitated often report experiencing such profound bliss that they are sorry to be brought back to life.[1] Regardless of the question of the validity of NDEs, when these people do re-integrate with the world, they often undergo a sea-change in their values and report a richer, fuller human experience. One previously aggressive, competitive, and materialistic man who had such an ecstasy, for instance, began growing day lilies by the hundreds simply to give them away as gifts.[2] The experience of *ekstasis*, the Greek word for standing outside of oneself, can transform the psyche. It can function as a catharsis that expunges diseased psychological patterns and induces growth. Ecstasy both heals and serves as a catalyst for human flourishing.

Before exploring these healing properties, however, it is first necessary to characterize the ecstatic experience. To define ecstasy is a nearly impossible task, since any definition will by necessity reduce the experience to human understanding and ultimately restrict its range of possibilities. Ecstasy has myriad psychological implications, and psychological theories can thus shed some kind of light on its impact on the human psyche. And yet, it would be wrong-

3

headed to reduce the experience to a mere psychological state. Often confounding rationality, ecstasy is beyond language, no doubt, because it is beyond reason itself. The greatest ecstatic poets have left us a veritable treasure chest of verse in their attempts to capture in language this ecstatic layer of being beyond the mind, but they have also washed their hands of the difficult task of *fully* articulating what they were trying to capture. As Whitman says in "Song of the Rolling Earth," "I swear I see what is better than to tell the best, / It is always to leave the best untold" (103-04). Words, even from those with the greatest facility with language, fail to describe the ecstatic experience in its fullest sense. Scholars of mysticism, a variety of ecstatic experience, have long held that one of the principle characteristics of mystical states is their ineffability. They are beyond language and cannot be put into words.

The term *description*, rather than definition, is probably better served because the latter will always be susceptible to criticism on various grounds, whereas the former will allow for a greater range of configurations. Implied in this "range of configurations" is that ecstatic experiences exist on a spectrum of possibilities that spans feelings of oneness with nature, euphoria while dancing, deep contentment, being in the "zone," and the like, to life's most fulfilling moments, such as intense bliss, deep gratitude, overpowering awe, the joys of love, and the many varieties of spiritual experience. The purists will invariably object at this inclusivity, arguing for a more exclusive definition. Real ecstasy, they will say, is not mere happiness, and, what is more, there are genuine differences among ecstatic experiences. Indian *samadhi*, Japanese *satori*, shamanic visions, Christian mystical illuminations, sexual ecstasy, and a lovely day spent communing with nature in the woods are all in some ways very different experiences. The value of scholarship that points to such differences cannot be overstated in that it demonstrates nuanced variability and highlights the role of cultural determinants in conditioning ecstatic states. To hold fixedly to distinctions, however, is to miss recognizing a whole species by fixating on the differences among its members.

These two approaches—one sees difference while the other sees similarity—are mirrored in the prevailing approaches to the study

4

of mystical states. On the one hand, scholars such as William James, Evelyn Underhill, F. C. Happold, and Aldous Huxley are called *perennialists* because, for them, the experience crops up perennially, again and again, seemingly in every time and place throughout history. On the other hand, *historicists*, such as Jess Byron Hollenback, Henri Delacroix, Steven Katz, and others, emphasize the importance of history and context and the different ways in which these condition the ecstatic experience. As in so many fundamental debates, both camps seem to have a measure of truth, but in raising it to absolute status, it becomes a falsehood. The perennialists are guilty of essentializing the experience by overlooking important differences in cultural determinants, while the historicists perhaps make so much of differences that they prevent cross-cultural connections and a fuller understanding of what is a global phenomenon. Yet, both have something valuable to contribute to our understanding.

So what is the core experience? Ekstasis is a Greek word that means to stand (stasis) outside (ek) of oneself. Its opposite is *enstasis*, or to remain fixed within oneself. It is possible to experience ekstasis in a variety of emotional states. A few years ago, a friend of mine said that, when he lost his father, he felt as though he were being "swallowed in a sea of grief." He was experiencing ekstasis, however tragically, in feeling overpowered by his loss. The expression, "I was beside myself with anger," is also an example of ekstasis, which can be present in any moment in which we act in ways that seem contrary to our self-definitions. To be ecstatic in this etymological sense is simply to experience in any variety a feeling of being other than oneself. Experiences of this kind can result in horrible circumstances, as in killing one's best friend in a drunken rage. Ancient Norse warriors, called *berserkers*, knew this type of ecstatic experience quite intimately. The trance-like states of fury they entered before battle empowered the berserkers to fight with the ferocity and savagery of wild animals, the symbolism of which was captured in the animal pelts they wore.

Ekstasis can result in a simply neutral experience of feeling estranged from one's normal sense of self. While on a trip through Mexico a few years ago, for instance, I awoke in a strange hotel room and for about fifteen seconds could remember neither where I was nor who I was. I had uncannily forgot myself, and it took some gentle self-coaxing for me to remember the arbitrary markers by which I define myself—male professor named Don, on vacation to explore the Mayan ruins—before I came back from my otherwise emotionally neutral, *ekstatic* experience. The term *ekstatic* can thus refer to any experience of feeling outside of one's normal bounds, the enclosure normally referred to as ego, selfhood, and/or subjectivity. In many cases this self-transcendence can seem like a form of self-completion rather than the uncanny feeling of otherness. Regardless, the experience carries with it a transformation of one's sense of selfhood, however this alteration manifests.

As a term, however, *ecstasy* has evolved over time to signify a more positive experience, one accompanied or followed by such feelings as joy, bliss, rapture, euphoria, or *any* intense positive emotion. A student recently told me of an interesting ecstatic experience she had that speaks to the point: While in a supermarket, she had a strange moment of defamiliarization in which "the walls of the enormous store seemed to stretch away from me and I felt as though I could see everything contained within them all at once." She was consequently overwhelmed with "profound" feelings of wonder and gratitude for the abundance of food available for purchase. Although she did not feel joy or bliss per se, she experienced the moment ecstatically, that is, her sense of self was altered in a moment of overpowering positive affect—in this case, gratitude and wonder.[3] The downstream effects of the experience were highly positive, as she claims to have become more of an optimist who realizes she now has a choice in how she responds to ordinary moments. She also reports a greater degree of agency in being able to overcome ingratitude, self-pity, and irritation. Ecstasy is thus not so much an emotion as it is a range of positive affective possibilities, any one of which can catalyze, accompany, and/or follow a moment of standing outside of self. It is thus necessary to distinguish between the terms *ekstatic* and *ecstatic*, the former referring to any experiences of self-transcendence—positive, negative, or neutral—and the latter signifying an *experience of standing outside of self accompanied or at least immediately followed by an intense degree of positive affect*. The two elements—

intense, positive emotion and a feeling of being outside of one's normal bounds—must be present for an experience to be called an ecstasy. One without the other, as in the cases of joy with no sense of self-transcendence or feelings of otherness with no accompanying or following positive affect, is not ecstasy. While the former is simply a strong emotion, the latter is ekstasis but not ecstasy per se.

Such a definition is problematic, however, for it is entirely possible to cite experiences that do not fully align with the benchmarks I have established. For instance, a student recently told me of an out-of-body experience in which he saw himself objectively in a rather strange moment of perception. Although he was able to see himself with greater clarity, he did not like what he saw, as the experience gave him a glimpse of unpleasant aspects of self he felt he needed to transform in order to flourish. The ekstasis was accompanied by negative affect, in this case a feeling of disappointment over not having lived up to one's potential. According to the definition I have articulated, this experience would not count as an ecstasy. Still, it led to highly positive downstream effects, for he locates in the ekstatic moment the beginnings of a highly positive self-transformation. As he puts it, "I really credit this experience—that is, the out of body experience and being able to see myself removed and objectively—with changing my entire life."[4] So is this an ecstasy or an ekstatic experience that later led to a larger and more integrated conception of self? While the experience was accompanied by negative affect, it also resulted in positive affect and a constructive reorganization of the psyche after it ended. In one sense this experience meets the criteria I have established for ecstasies, but in another sense it does not, for the presence of negative affect is a complicating factor. A definition of ecstasy that applies in all circumstances is thus an impossibility. The "definition" I have put forth is merely functional and will serve only as a reference point and organizational principle. Ultimately, the ecstatic experience is unrepresentable and will always manifest in ways that confound those trying to understand it.

Ecstasy is also not synonymous with joy and happiness, as Adam Potkay demonstrates in his award-winning study *The Story of Joy*. Potkay offers a helpful discussion of joy and happiness, and in doing so he sheds considerable light on ecstasy. While happiness can refer "either to a mental disposition or an ethical evaluation," joy "refers primarily to a mental state."[5] However, it can also be used to signify one's disposition, as in the case of a *joyous* person, a designation Potkay acknowledges is in some ways synonymous with being a *happy* person. The distinction is helpful, nevertheless, and points to the generality of happiness and the particularity of joy, which carries connotations of intensity and specificity that happiness does not. When joy intensifies to an extreme degree, it metamorphoses into ecstasy, according to Potkay. Given the previous discussion, however, it seems necessary to expand the definition to include the intensification of *any* positive emotion. Ecstasy is thus not an emotion in itself, although it has come to be associated with joy or bliss and understood in such terms, but a space beyond affective limits, the point at which any positive emotion reaches its climax, much like an affective orgasm. The difference between simple positive emotion and ecstasy thus lies in the "fullness" of the former and the "absence" or "annihilation of embodied agency and surrender to the not-I" found in the latter.[6] "Joy, at least on this side of ecstasy," Potkay argues, "is about return and fullness, not about standing elsewhere and hollowing out." In the ecstatic experience, the "self (in some sense) is cleaved away from the body, the senses annihilated; absence becomes fulfillment."[7] By no means faulty, Potkay's distinction nonetheless rests on a strictly Western understanding of ecstasy, which is informed by Orphic and Christian notions of the separation of soul and body. It is necessary to point out, however, ecstasy for myriad African and other nonwestern cultures is fundamentally a bodily experience inseparable from its basis in physicality. Even the ancient Dionysian cult in its earliest form sought to facilitate ecstasy through a celebration of the body, not through an escape from it. In his earliest manifestation, Dionysus was a vegetation and fertility god associated with the phallus, procreation, and the natural cycle of birth, death, and rebirth.[8] Sexual ecstasies, moreover, are often accompanied by feelings of self-transcendence as a direct result of erotic joy and physical union, not of bodily escape. Still, Potkay's separation of ecstasy and joy is extremely helpful because it points out the *ekstatic* nature of ecstasies, the self-transcendent aspect of which is generally not found in joy and other forms of positive affect (or only in an attenuated form) and proves to be problematic for happiness. Happiness in the tradition of Aristotelian *eudaimonism*, as he further demonstrates, is opposed to the loss of self found in ecstasy and in some forms of intense joy. Happiness in this tradition "is a technology of the self, a fashioning and indemnification that elevates inner integrity, constancy and wisdom over external mutability, loss, and death."[9] Happiness is protective of the self and serves to help one to resist its transcendence. The problem with Aristotle's conception, however, is that happiness is so frequently the result of ecstatic experiences; peaks in so many cases result in the quintessence of human happiness. Aristotelian notions of happiness, then, carry a self-preserving impulse and in one sense prove inimical to ecstasy, but happiness more broadly defined allows for both the protection and transcendence of the self.

Marghanita Laski, one of the first researchers of secular ecstasies, observed that they occur most frequently in the following domains of experience: observance of or immersion in nature, sexual love, childbirth, exercise or movement, participation in religion or spirituality, creating or appreciating art, and introspective recollection.[10] In courses on ecstatic poetry I frequently teach, I usually ask students to brainstorm their best moments, peak experiences, most exquisite joys, most savored memories, defining experiences, optimal performances, and instances of intense positive emotion. In many cases students who claim they never have had any ecstatic experiences begin to fill pages with brilliant examples of ecstasy. Here is one such example, taken (with permission) from a student's journal:

> It came completely out of the blue and for no reason at all. It actually happened last summer on the Atlantic City beach of all places. I was walking on the boardwalk and decided to walk down by the water. At some point, completely out of nowhere, I realized that everyone I saw was beautiful, and I felt dazzlingly happy. When it hit me, no matter where I looked I saw profound beauty in every single person. It was a sudden and pure state of bliss and I knew that I loved everyone I saw and that I loved myself and loved being alive ... It was undoubtedly the most powerful (and probably the most enjoyable) experience I've known.

9

Here are some additional examples of both religious and secular ecstasies, taken from a variety of scholarly sources:

1. Sometimes I have concentrated myself, and driven away by continued will all sense of outward appearances, looking straight with the full power of my mind inwards on myself. I find "I" am there; and "I" do not wholly understand or know—something is there distinct from earth and timber, from flesh and bones. Recognizing it, I feel on the margin of a life unknown ... on the verge of powers which if I could grasp would give me an immense breadth of existence.[11]

2. The first thing I saw when I awoke in the hospital was a flower, and I cried. Believe it or not, I had never really seen a flower until I came back from death. One thing I learned when I died was that we are all part of one big, living universe. If we think we can hurt another living thing without hurting ourselves, we are sadly mistaken.[12]

3. I realized a great scene was about to unfold within myself. I actually shook and shuddered at what I felt. A tremendous earthquake feeling was building up in me. There was a tremendous force, and I saw a glorious beauty of space unfold before me, of light, color, and of song and music, and not only of one thing good and beautiful, but of a oneness in fellowship, a wanting to belong to this greatness of beauty and goodness that unfolded before my eyes ...[13]

4. I was feeling more and more peaceful and calm, and my experience seemed to acquire incredible depth and breadth. I had an increasing sense that my consciousness had a distinctly oceanic quality until I felt that I actually became what can best be described as the consciousness of the ocean.[14]

5. I sat there and knew again the oneness of all things by the sounds of the restless sea, the mournful clang of the buoy bell, the cry of the seagull as it flew ahead of the storm, but no one of these was alone. They were each part of the whole. So am I. Nothing exists anywhere which I am not a part of, and which is not part of me.[15]

6. Then and there came on me the hour of revelation ... Scents, sights, and sounds blended into a harmony so perfect that it

transcended human expression, even human thought. It was like a glimpse of the peace of eternity.[16]

7. The thing happened one summer afternoon, on the school cricket field, while I was sitting on the grass, waiting my turn to bat. I was thinking about nothing in particular ... Suddenly, and without warning, something invisible seemed to be drawn across the sky, transforming the world about me into a kind of tent of concentrated and enhanced significance. What had been merely an outside became an inside. The objective was somehow transformed into a completely subjective fact, which was experienced as 'mine,' but on a level where the word had no meaning; for 'I' was no longer the familiar ego.[17]

8. Then I was standing on the highest mountain of them all, and round about beneath me was the whole hoop of the world. And while I stood there I saw more than I can tell and I understand more than I saw; for I was seeing in a sacred manner the shapes of all things in the spirit, and the shapes of all things as they must live together like one being.[18]

These examples serve to illustrate the two common elements, self-transcendence and positive affect, found in ecstatic experiences. In all cases self and the world are radically transformed in a moment of intense positive emotion. In all cases, the experience culminates in a perception of unity that is cosmic in proportion and leaves the individual with a profoundly altered sense of self.

Ecstasies can also manifest in other, less spectacular forms, and can occur during seemingly any activity. There are countless reports of ecstasies occurring at weddings, engagement dinners, sporting events, yoga classes, and musical performances. Ecstasy can also occur while cleaning the house, solving math equations, reading exquisite poetry, walking on a spring day, playing chess, viewing a natural wonder, stargazing, being silly, savoring a memory, doing volunteer work, relaxing after an intensely stressful period, and many other activities and moments of passive receptivity. There are many comical stories in Zen literature of *satori* occurring where it is least expected, that is, while cleaning the toilet, visiting a prostitute, walking in the fish market, and the like. Although Abraham Maslow, the famous psychologist known for his "hierarchy of needs," distinguished peakers, or those who have frequent ecstatic experiences, from non-peakers, he believed that peak experiences characterize nearly every human life, not just a privileged few. Peakers are simply those who know how to relish and replicate the experience. Maslow also observed that peakers are found evenly distributed across the population. Ecstasies thus occur not only among artists, hippies, musicians, and new-agers but also among dock workers, insurance executives, engineers, politicians, and scientists.[19]

Ecstasy comes in an endless number of varieties. Sometimes these involve the physical world of nature or the material world in which we live, and sometimes they offer a transcendent glimpse of the otherworldly beyond. Ecstasy can manifest in either a sober form, as in many varieties of Buddhist enlightenment, experiences amidst tranquil natural settings, and in calm moments of blissful serenity. Or it can manifest as drunkenness, as in the divine intoxication of African shamans, Dionysian revelers, whirling Sufis, and modern "ravers" gyrating to trance-dance music. Ecstasy can be an intensely personal, introspective experience, involving a journey within one's deep, mysterious interior, as in so many forms of mysticism. Or it can be shared among individuals as a collective phenomenon, as in the early Hebrew prophets, Christian Gnostics, concert goers, participants in tribal dancing rites, sports fans, and any group of people sharing an experience of self-transcendence and intense positive affect. Emile Durkheim, a pioneer in the field of sociology, called this last form of group ecstasy "collective effervescence," and he believed it was the essence of all religion.[20] Victor Turner, an anthropologist, called it "communitas," because he saw such group ecstasy as a form of social cement that binds members of a group or society together.[21] Ecstasies, needless to say, come in a variety of forms.

Scholars have argued extensively in their hair-splitting attempts to offer taxonomies of ecstasies. Such scholarship has proven to be of inestimable value in our understanding of this universal experience, bringing attention as it has to the nuances of what was previously regarded as a single experience. Dan Merkur's sophisticated analysis of hallucinogen-induced ecstasies is a case in point. Prior to his research, it was well known that psychedelics such as LSD-25, peyote, psilocybin, mescaline, iboga, and others often yielded profoundly meaningful religious experiences.[22] Merkur has identified not only seven distinct phases of hallucinogenic ecstasies but no less than

24 types of unitive phenomena that have been associated with such experiences.[23] The type of unitive ecstasy Sigmund Freud called the oceanic is but one of Merkur's 24 types.[24] The matter of ecstasy, it seems, is far more complex and varied than we previously thought.

However insightful such taxonomies may be, they are also susceptible to criticism on various grounds, not least of which is the problem of objectively identifying what is a deeply subjective experience. Scholars working in the field of mystical studies have been at loggerheads over a variety of issues precisely because of the seemingly insurmountable problem of classifying and pigeonholing a range of experiential perceptions whose boundaries are frequently blurred. William Wordsworth, one of the poets featured in this anthology, saw through such artificial boundaries, when in his famous work, *The Prelude*, he wrote

> Of that false secondary power by which
> In weakness we create distinctions, then
> Believe our puny boundaries are things
> Which we perceive, and not which we have made. (2.216-19)

The ecstatic experience is beyond our full comprehension, and while it may manifest differently from culture to culture, as well as from person to person, it is important to remember that the differences we see in its manifestations are due to the limitations of our own perspectives. No doubt, cultural determinants do play a significant role in shaping these experiences, but there are also several characteristics that ecstatic states share in common, and an exclusive focus on difference will surely inhibit an understanding of the experience. Scholarship, nevertheless, is highly valuable and entirely necessary if we are to characterize and better understand ecstasies.

To further complicate the matter of describing ecstatic experiences, the question of the nature of self must be addressed. What is the self? If the self is transcended in moments of ekstasis, then is the perspective from which we perceive in such experiences not part of the self? An answer to the latter requires an explanation of the former. Since human beings have pondered the question of human identity from time immemorial, it is unlikely that I will be able to offer any kind of solution to this knotty problem and offer compelling answers to the nagging questions it raises. The ultimate nature of the self is an absolute mystery whose depths we can never fully explore intellectually, since those depths contain the mind. In other words, the psyche is not simply a construct of the mind; the reasoning intellect, rather, emerges from and is a part of something larger than itself. What that *something* is, however, cannot be put into words, for to do so would be to put limits on what Martin Heidegger believed cannot be contained in language, that is, being itself.[25]

Nearly all people, nevertheless, have a sense of self, without which they could not function. Jungian depth psychology calls this sense of self "ego," which is an illusion that must, nevertheless, be protected and preserved if we are to avoid our fate in the padded room at the state mental institution. The ego is only the tip of the iceberg, as Freud put it, and emerges from psychological depths that transcend the conscious will. The human psyche consists of a totality of energies that includes the ego and much more. As Jung argued, however, ego-differentiation, the process by which one comes into possession of a sense of individual selfhood, is a vital component of psychological health and is responsible for conscious-ness itself. "The resistance of the conscious mind to the unconscious and the depreciation of the latter," he wrote, "were historical neces-sities in the development of the human psyche, for otherwise the conscious mind would never have been able to differentiate itself at all."[26] The opposite of ego-differentiation, ego-dissolution, is healthy in moments of ekstasis but over a prolonged period goes by the name of psychosis. Jung claimed that the mystic and the madman both plunge into the same ocean. The difference is that the mystic knows how to swim and ultimately makes it back to shore, whereas the madman chokes on the divine waters and drowns. The self referred to in "ekstasis" thus corresponds to ego in depth psychology, and its temporary transcendence is immensely beneficial. To let go of the willing ego, to lose one's sense of self in a moment of positive affect, is the mark of a healthy psyche.

For researchers of secular ecstasies such as Maslow and Laski, as well as most scholars of mysticism, ecstatic experiences thus can-not be willed. It is not possible to decide to have an ecstasy simply because one desires it. Laski cites a number of common triggers that seem to be present in the ecstatic experience (these correspond exactly to the domains of experience I listed previously), but she also points out that these are correlative and not causal.[27] The trigger does not cause the ecstasy but is frequently present before or during the experience. In other words, it seems to serve as the tipping point, or the culminating factor in a series of elements that combine to create the experience. It is thus quite possible to desire ecstasy, to hike to a majestic mountain peak or to listen to a brilliant piece of music or to make passionate love and still not have a fully ecstatic experience. It is likewise possible to do everything wrong—as in the case of Elisabeth Kubler-Ross, who admitted that her carnivorous diet, cigarette habit, and refusal to meditate or pray made her a very strange mystic indeed—and still have a lifetime of ecstatic experiences. Triggers are by no means causal, but statistically they seem to be conducive to ecstasy.

Laski lists four "anti-triggers"—the presence of other people, reason, language, and commerce—that serve as inhibitors of ecstasy.[28] Some of the anti-triggers seem to contradict the triggers. People frequently report feelings of ecstasy, for instance, in the presence of other people. Though there are exceptions here in Tantra and Kundalini yoga, it is unusual to have a sexual ecstasy without another person involved. Once again, anti-triggers are not causal but simply correlative. A student in one of my courses objected to Laski's anti-triggers by declaring that he once had an ecstatic moment while sitting in a noisy bookstore café amidst garrulous book buyers and reasoning intellectuals. His point was well taken, as his ecstasy occurred despite the presence of all four of Laski's inhibitors. There are no hard fast rules in ecstasies, and the complexities of each person's state of consciousness serve as the real determinants of the experience.

In a certain sense, then, ecstasy happens to people, and people do not make ecstasy happen. It seems to come inexplicably and sometimes at random, and by no means does it ever seem to happen when one is expecting it. To the contrary, expectation, as any seasoned meditator will affirm, might reasonably be considered another inhibitor of the experience. As an aspect of the will, expectation proceeds from the willing ego, the confines of which must be expanded or outright transcended if ecstasy is to bestow its gifts on someone. And yet, a study of ecstatic cultures and their practices clearly shows a plethora of ecstatic "techniques" used to induce ecstasy. Some of these include chanting, visualizing, drumming, dancing, contemplating, whirling, fasting, enduring climatic extremes, sleep deprivation, breath manipulation, prolonged gazing, lucid dreaming, ingesting hallucinogens, praying, singing, and various spiritual exercises. All of these activities have been used by various cultures as a means to induce the ecstatic experience, but it is important to remember that inducement does not equal cause. Here, too, as in Laski's triggers, the techniques used only make someone receptive to ecstasy; they do not cause the experience but perhaps serve as catalysts in a complex reaction of a number of elements that results in ecstasy. Such experiences do not happen randomly, and they are not bestowed willy-nilly by some capricious god of ecstasy. Rather, a number of factors, foremost among which is the relinquishment of the will, must be present for the appropriate reaction to take place. In ecstasy, one must let go.

In his interesting research, Mihalyi Csikszentmihalyi rejects some of the claims of Maslow and Laski and asserts that optimal experience, by which he means *enjoyment* of experience, does not just happen by accident. "Happiness," he argues, "is a condition that must be prepared for, cultivated, and defended privately by each person."[29] Csikszentmihalyi has conducted extensive research on optimal states of being, most of which "are reported to occur within sequences of activities that are goal-directed and bounded by rules—activities that require the investment of psychic energy, and that could not be done without the appropriate skills."[30] People usually claim the highest levels of positive experience, according to Csikszentmihalyi, when no less than eight factors are present: (1) a chance of completing the task; (2) intense concentration; (3) clearly defined goals; (4) immediate feedback; (5) deep but effortless involvement that removes from awareness the worries and frustration of everyday life; (6) exercise of control over actions; (7) loss of a sense of self, which nevertheless emerges more strongly after the experience is over; and (8) alteration of time (that is, time is either lengthened or shortened).[31] Csikszentmihalyi calls this state of being "flow," because so many of his subjects used the term to describe their moments of optimal experience. Flow is a state of consciousness that requires cultivation; it does not just happen.

Csikszentmihalyi's objection is well taken, since people do have a hand in preparing for and having intensely enjoyable experiences. As he argues, in flow there is a measure of control, as people in some way direct the activity. Yet, his seventh characteristic—"concern for self disappears but re-emerges more strongly after the experience is over"—clearly speaks to the idea that flow is made possible only when we get out of our own way, so to speak.[32] Consciousness of self chokes the flow. Anyone who suffers from extreme self-consciousness will attest to its paralyzing effects. Consciousness of self is a bell that tolls one back from ecstasy. The problem implied in Csikszentmihalyi's objection can be resolved by a simple appeal to the Taoist concept *wu wei*, which translates as "effortless action." To be in accord with the Tao is to be in *wu wei*, a state in which one walks the razor's edge between exercising the will but not so forcefully that self serves as a stumbling block to itself. Musicians, artists, athletes, speakers, skydivers, writers, and practitioners of the techniques of ecstasy know this state quite well.

In yet another distinction between flow and Laski's ecstasies and Maslow's peaks, Csikszentmihalyi makes it clear that in most examples of flow there is no affect present. The positive emotions associated with the experience manifest later when the sense of self re-emerges. He does acknowledge that sometimes people report "a feeling of ecstasy for no apparent good reason."[33] In most cases of flow, however, the individual is too focused and immersed in the moment to experience positive affect, which follows the state of flow. This is clearly different from the states of euphoria so often present *during* ecstasies. To resolve the problem raised by Csikszentmihalyi's objection, I would suggest that examples of flow in which positive affect is present are indistinguishable from ecstasies. When the affect follows, however, the state of flow serves to function as an ecstatic technique, at the end of which comes the ecstasy. A close examination of the various activities used to induce ecstasies would thoroughly support this statement. The state of flow, as Csikszentmihalyi describes it, is thus synonymous either with ecstasy or ecstatic technique, depending on the presence or absence of positive affect.

Ecstasy can thus be characterized in myriad ways and finds configuration in a variety of forms. However the experience manifests, it seems to contain two core characteristics—self-transcendence accompanied or followed by positive affect—that, nevertheless, manifest kaleidoscopically in a variety of culturally determined permutations. More nuanced definitions invariably seem to run the risk of overstatement and thus distortion of the elusive nature of what is ultimately a mysterious experience. In some ways it is better to leave ecstasy a mystery and simply stand rapt in ecstatic awe before its wondrous power to transform the psyche.

The Ecstatic Cure

Human beings seem to sense at an intuitive level these transformative properties. In Toni Morrison's *Beloved*, for instance, the character, Baby Suggs, organizes ecstatic gatherings for newly freed slaves as an attempt to heal them from the traumas of being subjected to racial hatred and the horrid material conditions of enslavement. These "whoops," as they are called, involve festive singing and dancing in a circle. Although appearing in a work of fiction, Baby Suggs' whoops are a replication of the "ring-shouts" that often took place in early African-American culture. A ring-shout, an example of which is included in this anthology, is a similar ecstatic activity in which participants beat time with a broomstick and dance in a circular formation, sometimes for hours, while repeating some inspirational word or phrase. This use of ecstatic practice for healing purposes is very ancient and can also be found among the *Orpheotelestae* of ancient Greece. The *Orpheotelestae*, adherents of the Orphic mysteries, which taught people how to make ecstatic out-of-body journeys,[34] offered cures by performing circle dances around the afflicted. Native Americans, the !Kung of Africa, Moroccans, Christian Ugandans, and many others engaged in similar ecstatic activities to heal sick people.[35]

Such an intuitive understanding of the value of ecstasy finds support in recent research. Andrew Newberg, a neurologist at the

University of Pennsylvania medical center, has conducted some interesting neurological studies on the brains of groups of people who engage in various types of ecstatic practices. His conclusions support what people seem to have intuitively known: ecstasy is good for us. Among those whose brains Newberg has mapped are praying nuns, meditating Buddhist monks, and Pentecostal Christians who engage in an old ecstatic practice called *glossolalia*, or speaking in tongues. These fascinating studies show observable differences in the types of brain states resulting from each ecstatic activity.[36] Ecstasy is not merely "in the imagination." The common thread in all of these practices, moreover, is neurologically, psychologically, and physiologically beneficial states that enhance well-being and thus optimize human experience. The altered brain waves that result from such states, as he concludes, lead to positive beliefs, which themselves not only stimulate the immune response but also result in lower levels of cortisol, a hormone related to stress.[37] Such states also result in a sense of the loss of time, the result of which is a central ingredient in human happiness—losing oneself through total immersion in the moment.[38] Given the well known mind-body connection, which today finds the clearest endorsement in what is called *integrative* medicine, Newberg's findings highlight the value of cultivating ecstatic states of being. Ecstasy positively alters the brain and beneficially impacts the body.

Other studies of the brains of people who engage in an age-old ecstatic technique, meditation, scientifically support the value of ecstasy. In one study, for instance, practitioners of Yoga Nidra, a form of meditative visualization, exhibited a 65% increase in dopamine levels over non-meditating controls.[39] The neurotransmitter dopamine, a chemical produced naturally in the brain, is responsible for feelings of well-being. When such levels are low, human beings are often miserable. Even in monkeys, low dopamine levels result in a "multifaceted misery that in human beings is labeled neurotic."[40] Responsible for observable optimal states of mind, ecstatic techniques help us to achieve high levels of positive affect. In another study meditators were shown to have a decreased activation of the autonomic nervous and endocrine systems, both of which are intimately involved in stress management.[41] The same study also observed significantly better attentional control and lower emotional reactivity in meditators. When shown a violent movie clip, meditators exhibited lower levels of emotional arousal than non-meditating controls, the implication of which is that they have better control over their emotions.[42] Several other studies show that meditators often demonstrate lower levels of negative emotion, higher levels of positive affect, increased neural response, increased immune response, enhanced endurance to affective challenges, and improved psychological coping.[43]

A recent meta-analysis confirmed that there is a large body of scientific literature attesting to the value of meditation, which has been demonstrated to be an effective treatment for depression, anxiety, psychosis, borderline personality disorder, and attention deficit hyperactivity disorder.[44] The same meta-study also pointed to irrefutable evidence of immediate and long-term changes in the brain as a result of meditation. Most compelling is the brain mapping research that clearly shows a greater cortical thickness in the brains of meditators, particularly in the regions responsible for processing positive emotions.[45] This positive effect of ecstasy is no wonder, given the affective content of the experience, which is often described in such highly positive terms as joy, transport, rapture, euphoria, elation, exhilaration, bliss, exultation, felicity, jubilance, glee, mania, excitement, intoxication, and overpowering happiness. An encounter with such an intense concentration of positive emotion is a call to growth and also facilitates psychological development, a refinement of one's values, attitudes, and relationships, and a clearer sense of one's occupation, goals, and purpose in the world. To stand outside of oneself in the experience of ecstasy, then, is highly beneficial and generally conducive to growth.

What is more, there is a need for ecstasy in the human psyche. Findings from research on the importance of love, the greatest ecstasy, have validated this last statement. It is well known that married people are healthier and live longer than their single counterparts. Cardiac patients who own dogs have significantly fewer additional heart attacks than those who have no canine companionship during their recovery.[46] Love, says modern neurology, is responsible for the creation of important neural circuitry, without which humans could not adapt and survive. Children deprived of love will often simply die, or if they do survive they will display serious psychological and even physiological disturbances. Researchers have learned this truth from a variety of sources: (1) Friedrich II famously attempted to ascertain the natural language he stupidly believed all human beings would speak if they were not spoken to at birth. The basic needs of the babies he enlisted in his horrible study were met, but the children themselves were never spoken to or verbally interacted with. They all died. (2) The sterile nurseries of the 1949 and 1950s—orphanages that provided for basic needs but denied children any kind of loving touch out of fear of disease—reported a mortality rate of 75% to 100%. The majority of their children simply died, unloved and emotionally abandoned. (3) Feral children, who are raised in the wild or locked in a closet and denied all human contact, seem to be developmentally stymied for their whole lives, and they are further beset by other challenges, such as learning disorders, speech problems, and social ineptitude. (4) Monkeys separated from their mothers display all of the characteristics of human neurosis.[47] Love is a central ingredient in the recipe for human development.

The kind of ekstasis that love makes possible, moreover, is responsible for one of the most sophisticated processes in which the human brain can engage—feeling empathy for someone or something outside of ourselves. This kind of empathic reaching out of ourselves into someone (or something) else's world, says neurologist Gerard Huther, "requires a tremendously refined level of perceiving and processing."[48] It is this capacity, he claims, "that sets the human brain apart from all other nervous systems."[49] The need for ecstasy, then, is possibly explainable in such terms, for its gratification results in a sophisticated level of neurological development. Ecstasy, it seems, completes us by facilitating our growth.

Maslow's work thoroughly bolsters the assertion that human beings have a developmental need for ecstasy. Maslow demonstrated that we have a number of inherent psychological needs that, if gone unmet, result in neurosis and psychological disease. He arranged such needs in a hierarchy because he also claimed that higher needs such as the urge to express oneself creatively and the desire for social recognition are not activated until the lower needs for physiological sustenance and safety are met. In other words, human beings are not even aware of the higher needs if the lower ones are not gratified.

We cannot be cognizant of our need for social acceptance if we are hungry or physically imperiled. Maslow's hierarchy, then, is a prioritization of human needs, and it says that certain needs (the lower ones) have stronger claims over others (the higher ones). Yet, the higher needs must be met if we are to reach our full human potential. At the top of his hierarchy, Maslow placed "self-actualization," or the need for personal growth and the cultivation and fulfillment of potential. What led him to value self-actualization as the highest need were his investigations into the peak experiences of psychologically super-healthy people.[50] Maslow observed that super-healthy people often reported states of intense bliss, joy, and sometimes even rapture in moments when the boundaries that divide the self from the other are dissolved. He used the words "ecstasy" and "peak" synonymously to describe such experiences, and their investigation occupied a prominent position in his research throughout most of his career.

"The term peak experience," Maslow wrote, "is a generalization of the best moments of the human being, for the happiest moments in life, for experiences of ecstasy, rapture, bliss, of the greatest joy." Such peaks are often associated with but not limited to "profound aesthetic experiences such as creative ecstasies, moments of mature love, perfect sexual experiences, parental love, experiences of natural childbirth, and many others."[51] Maslow believed human beings became fully human when, once their lower needs were met, they could allow themselves to become conscious of their need for ecstasy and begin moving towards a full cultivation of their potential. Peak experiences were for Maslow both indicators and facilitators of mature psychological health.[52] The circularity of this last point is not tautological, for it says that peaks are not only effects but also causes. To experience an ecstasy causes a realization or further activation of the need for such states of being, which, once experienced, enable human beings to function optimally.

The assertion that ecstatic states of being represent a need and serve as inducements to psychological growth also finds support in contemporary psychology. In the last decade the discipline of psychology has undergone a sea-change in its focus on positive states of emotion. In the field called *positive* psychology, scores of researchers have now begun rigorously examining the impact of positive affect on psychological development. One of the leading figures in positive psychology, Martin Seligman, a researcher at the University of Pennsylvania and one-time President of the American Psychological Association, has made the forceful claim that positive emotions are not mere *epiphenomena*, or effects of some prior cause.[53] They are, rather, phenomena, or causal agents that exert a beneficial impact on psychological growth. According to Seligman, who bases his assertion on the brilliant work of Barbara Fredrickson, positive emotions "broaden our abiding intellectual, physical, and social resources, building up reserves we can draw upon when a threat or opportunity presents itself."[54] In other words, they undo all of the harmful effects of negative emotions, and they also serve as a healthy, mature defense against unhappiness and the potentially hazardous internalization of the world's many woes.

This current acknowledgment of the value of positive emotion is a long time in the making, coming as it does after a century-long focus on psychological disease. Most of the dominant schools in psychology have fixated on pathology and have even pathologized positive states of being. Sigmund Freud, despite his brilliant contribution to the discipline of psychology in providing the first systematic codification of the unconscious and its dynamics, seems to have established a pattern from which psychology has only recently begun to free itself. Freud's model of the psyche was entirely disease-focused, and he interpreted nearly all psychic states and traits in terms of underlying neuroses and unresolved, unconscious complexes.

Freud's crude reduction of "oceanic" experiences is a case in point. When asked by a friend, Romain Rolland, to explain "spiritual" experiences in which the ego seems to dissolve and flow outside of itself, Freud first declared that he could not discover this oceanic feeling in himself. He then went on to interpret such experiences as symptoms of neurosis, claiming that "pathology has made us aware of a great number of states in which the boundaries between ego and the external world become uncertain."[55] For Freud, the oceanic feeling is merely the result of a narcissistic regression to an earlier phase of psychological development before ego had fully dissociated itself from the objects of its perceptions. His theory, focused as it was on what was wrong with the human psyche, could make no sense of ecstatic experiences, nor could it enable him to recognize their value. What is more, he did not believe happiness was really possible, and he dismissed as folly all attempts at achieving it through the appreciation of art, religion, love, and beauty. The happiness that seems to result from ecstatic experiences was itself a naïve illusion from which individuals would do well to free themselves.

With his negative focus on disease, Freud seems to have set the twentieth-century standard for most of mainstream psychology, or what Seligman calls "business-as-usual psychology," by which he means the type of research that focuses exclusively on disease and ignores wellness and positive states of being such as those found in and resulting from ecstatic experiences. What is more distressing is the tendency among such scholarship to interpret highly beneficial, positive states and experiences through the lens of disease. One example of such reductive interpretations is found in the work of scholars who have pathologized shamanic experiences, classifying as schizophrenic what is perhaps human consciousness at its absolute best. Mircea Eliade, the famous scholar of religion and myth, forcefully refuted this interpretive paradigm and argued for trying to understand shamanic experiences with a more open mind.[56] Another example is found in the similar diagnoses by some twentieth-century psychiatrists of C.G. Jung, Freud's greatest student and later rival, as psychotic. Just as many of Jung's peers could not understand him, so have even modern scholars suggested that his bizarre, ekstatic states of consciousness were symptoms of an underlying psychological disturbance. In a thorough but rather negative biography, for instance, Ronald Hayman implies that Jung was a borderline schizophrenic whose visions could be explained in terms of psychiatric models of disease.[57] Such assertions do no justice to ecstasy, born as they are out of ignorance, fear, and a tendency to interpret any abnormal state of consciousness as a symptom of pathology.

A meta-analysis cited in the *New York Times* on the types of studies published in psychology journals proves the point that there has been little focus on healthy states of mind: from 1968 to 1998 researchers published over 45,000 articles on depression and only 400 on happiness.[58] There is something clearly wrong with this ratio, which amounts roughly to 100:1, as it speaks volumes about where our focus has been and where it needs to be. As Seligman and other positive psychologists argue, it is undoubtedly necessary to investigate psychological pathology, but it is equally necessary to learn about optimal states of psychological well being by identifying and studying models of health. The new positive psychology does not call for an end to the study of pathology, as this would prove disastrous for human development. It does point out the woeful imbalance in our focus on disease states, however, and it calls for a redirection of scholarly energies through the careful examination of the optimally functioning psyche. Seligman's tenure as the APA President inspired a whole new wave of researchers, and the brilliant work he has catalyzed has caused a major paradigm shift in psychology and thus legitimized the value of studying states of mind associated with the ecstatic experience.

Positive psychology thus represents the latest major turn in the discipline of psychology. This turn towards the positive is in one sense only a decade or so old, but in another sense it is a natural outgrowth of a whole series of developments in psychology. Not all of the pioneers of psychology, for instance, were entirely pessimistic and disease-focused. Early in his career, Jung rejected his mentor's narrow focus on pathology and his reduction of all psychological states to neurotic sexuality. Jung accepted many of the psychodynamics of the Freudian model of the psyche, but he also believed the unconscious was not merely a repository of disagreeable traits and socially unacceptable impulses. To the contrary, the unconscious for Jung represented the promise of growth and the possibility of self-renewal through ekstasis, or ego's engagement with the mysterious depths of the human psyche. In his work with clients, Jung discerned that an encounter with the *collective* unconscious, or the deeper psychic levels beyond the Freudian personal unconscious, usually carried with it a numinous[59] quality. The *numinosum* for Jung is the mysterious aspect of the unconscious, the *imago dei* (God-image) in the human psyche, the part of the unconscious that seems spiritual to those who experience its joys and terrors. Although he made no professional claims to the absolute validity of the spiritual aspects of the unconscious, he did recognize the transformative value of an encounter with their numinous depths:

25

No matter what the world thinks about religious experience, the one who has it possesses the great treasure of a thing that has provided him with a source of life, meaning and beauty that has given a new splendour to the world and to mankind. He has pistis[60] and peace. Where is the criterion by which you could say that such a life is not legitimate, that such experience is not valid and that such pistis is mere illusion?[61]

Jung so highly valued numinous experiences that he encouraged his clients to cultivate religiosity, not simply by attending church services but through an experiential engagement with a spiritual path. Jungian psychotherapists thus encourage a deep involvement with spirituality because psychotherapeutic methods can only take one so far. As part of their therapy, many Jungian analysands become intimately engaged with various types of experiential spirituality such as Buddhism, Yoga, Sufism, Christian Gnosticism, Kabbala, and the like.

Another influential psychologist, Erich Fromm, insightfully theorized about the most important of all ecstasies—love. For Fromm, the need to overcome through ekstasis the isolation of the ego is the central drive in the human psyche:

This awareness of [man] as a separate entity, the awareness of his own short life span, of the fact that without his will he is born and against his will he dies, that he will die before those whom he loves, or they before him, the awareness of his aloneness and separateness, of his helplessness before the forces of nature and society, all this makes his separate, disunited existence an unbearable prison. He would become insane could he not liberate himself from this prison and reach out in some other form with men, with the world outside.[62]

This reaching beyond the self is achieved, according to Fromm, in mature, unconditional love, not only in its erotic form but also in its platonic varieties. The ecstasy of love, in its manifestations as *eros*, *philia*, and/or *agape*, represents the completion of human development and signifies the meaning of human life. Fromm's ideas found further development in the work of Rollo May, who believed that love is the antidote to the general Western "condition," in which we are detached from our deeper selves, our emotional lives, and our guiding intuitions in an all-pervasive, schizoid malaise that stands in the way of human development and happiness.[63] Only love, according to May, can heal this kind of diseased, neurotic ekstasis.

William James, the father of American psychology and one of Freud's contemporaries, recognized the value of what he called "healthy-mindedness," or the refusal to embrace a negative emotion or state of mind. In his study, *The Varieties of Religious Experience*, a foundational work in the fields of religious studies and the psychology of religion, James expressed admiration for those who consciously reject unhappiness and embrace an optimistic outlook on life. He claimed that the "religion of healthy-mindedness," or the loose confederation of self-help groups and ecstatic spiritualisms that existed in his day, was "anything but absurd" and actually systematized the strategy all humans use to a greater or lesser degree to protect their happiness.[64] This refusal to succumb to despair—or stated more positively, the deliberate choice to preserve positive states of emotion in the face of negative outward circumstances—is a survival strategy human beings have used for time immemorial:

> We find such persons in every age, passionately flinging themselves upon their sense of the goodness of life, in spite of the hardships of their own condition, and in spite of the sinister theologies into which they may be born ... It is probable that there never has been a century in which the deliberate refusal to think ill of life has not been idealized by a sufficient number of persons to form sects, open or secret, who claimed all natural things to be permitted.[65]

Human beings intuitively seem to know that in order to preserve their sanity, they must (to some extent) shut out the miseries of the world and take refuge in their own self-cultivated, inner bowers. To function optimally as a human being, it is necessary not to give in to despair and to cultivate in consciousness the positive states and emotions that characterize happiness. The most potent weapon against unhappiness, it seems, is happiness itself.

This last statement is deceptively simple, but a closer look at its implications suggests an oft-overlooked profundity: happiness is not something that simply happens to us; happiness does not come by happenstance but by cultivation and effort. The experience of

Victor Frankl, another precursor to positive psychology, attests to the notion of choice in happiness. Frankl was a Jewish doctor and researcher—interestingly, one of the first investigators of the out-of-body experience—who survived the horrors of Auschwitz. While in the camp, Frankl realized that the Nazis could take everything from him, as they did, but they could not take from him what he came to regard as the most prized human possession—his freedom to choose how he let the outer circumstances of his confinement and the loss of nearly all of his loved ones affect him. He observed that when his fellow inmates relinquished this freedom by succumbing to victimhood and despair, they would die almost invariably within forty-eight hours. Frankl developed a whole new type of psychotherapy called logo-therapy as a result of his observations at Auschwitz.[66]

Yet another important school that valued positive states of being was humanistic psychology. Carl Rogers and Abraham Maslow in some ways provided the first layer in the foundation of positive psychology. Although humanistic psychology was generally distrustful of the scientific method as a viable means of uncovering important insights about the human psyche, its focus on health over disease provided a model that positive psychologists have thoroughly embraced. Christopher Peterson, another founding member of the positive school, acknowledges the contributions of Rogers and Maslow, and several others who made positive psychology possible.[67] He claims there is considerable overlap in the general programs of positive and humanistic psychology, but he distinguishes the new psychology from the older humanism in that the former is still firmly committed to the scientific method, an emphasis on statistical reliability, and the need to replicate findings.

Positive psychology thus did not originate in a vacuum, and many important thinkers in the twentieth century have made possible the exploration of its signature premise—namely, that "what is good about life is as genuine as what is bad and therefore deserves equal attention from psychologists."[68] So, thanks to some daring and forward thinking individuals, there is a new psychology in the new century, a field of legitimate academic inquiry that sees immense value in positive states of being and even says that we have a choice in their creation. Csikszentmihalyi, yet another founding member of the positive school, thoroughly endorses the idea of a willful cultivation of such positive states. The key, according to his theory, is how we utilize our attention. Csikszentmihalyi claims that "the information we allow into our consciousness becomes extremely important; it is, in fact, what determines the content and quality of life."[69] According to this idea, our state of being is determined by the thoughts we allow into our minds and by the emotions we cultivate as a result. The value of ecstasy here rises immediately to the foreground. Intense bliss is not just so much fluff, as twentieth-century cynicism and pessimism would have it, but proves to be of inestimable value as both a marker of and a catalyst for psychological development.

The Divine Madness

Given that ecstasies have been reported for time immemorial and occur across cultures, it is safe to say that they are not only a private affair but also a social issue. What, then, is the relationship between ecstasy and society? Once again, this is a difficult question to answer, since it depends entirely on the values, mores, and structure of the society in which the ecstasy occurs. Another element to complicate the matter is whether we are referring to individual or collective ecstasy, since both have social ramifications but in different ways.

One of the functions of group ecstasy, according to Barbara Ehrenreich, is to keep the structure of a society "from becoming overly rigid and unstable by providing occasional relief in the form of collective excitement and festivity."[70] In her downright fascinating book, *Dancing in the Streets*, Ehrenreich explains the function of group ecstasy in terms of Turner's concept of *communitas*, or "the spontaneous love and solidarity that can arise within a community of equals."[71] *Communitas* is highly effective in fostering social cohesion and can thus be considered, from a strictly anthropological perspective, the endpoint of ecstatic rites in tribal and egalitarian communities. By serving as a kind of pressure relief value that eases tensions and restores social balance, collective ecstasy binds people together. In overly rigid, hierarchical, and/or dogmatic societies, however, ecstasy does not fare too well. As Ehrenreich points out, "hierarchy is antagonistic to the festive and ecstatic tradition."[72] Collective ecstasy, in the forms of carnival celebrations, Roman bacchanalia, music festivals, and the like can pose a challenge to authority, since it levels class distinctions and dissolves ethnic, racial, and gender boundaries. In communal ecstasy, everyone is the same and belongs equally to the same collective social body, a serious problem in a society hyper-conscious of its social divisions.

An example of group ecstasy as a challenge to hierarchy is found in the American counter-culture of the 1960s. Today, America has more or less become tolerant of hippie culture, however marginalized it still is. But in the formative days it was a major social problem precisely because of its ecstatic nature. Characterized by non-courtship trance dancing, wild hair whipping, egalitarianism, communal joy, and loss of self in highly rhythmic music, the counter-culture replicated many of the features of ecstatic rituals and practices found in cultures all over the world, as Ehrenreich observes. Its values questioned authority and called for the liberation of the oppressed and a re-examination of social distinctions based on race, ethnicity, class, gender, and sexual orientation. The counter-culture adopted as its chemical agent of choice a drug not coincidentally called "ecstasy" (LSD-25), which was the vehicle through which nearly a generation of people defied the roles prescribed to them by what they saw as an overly rigid hierarchy and woefully outdated value system. LSD, with the ecstatic experience it offered, was for the counter-culture the path to self-transformation and societal re-configuration.

How did the hierarchy respond to such group ecstasy?—with extreme violence in many cases. More relevant to our discussion, LSD was rendered illegal in America and most other parts of the West. Why did the hierarchy ban a well studied, relatively benign drug, the natural derivative of which occurs naturally in flora all over the world, causes no chemical dependency, and poses no overdose dangers, when a toxic drug such as alcohol continues to be legal and thus responsible for some 50,000 deaths annually? No doubt, a thoughtful answer here would require more space than I have the luxury to fill, and I do not mean to ignore that recreational use of all mind-altering substances poses challenges to any society. At least part of the reason for the ban on LSD, however, is that the ecstatic values of the counter-culture it spawned challenged the materialistic foundation of American society. One of the value-shifts that often seems to occur as a result of ecstatic experiences, whether they are chemically or naturally induced, is the favoring of a more meaningful human experience through deeper emotional bonds and self-fulfillment, neither of which the acquisition of material goods and status markers can provide. Given this value shift, various hallucinogens have even been used as a treatment for alcohol and narcotic addictions.[73] Maslow speculated that LSD's efficacy in helping alcoholics recover from addiction lay in its ability to induce, by chemical means, a peak experience.[74] Its possible benefits notwithstanding, LSD posed a threat to the social hierarchy because those who ingested it often came to reject the shallowness of materialistic living, the foundation of American life.

The subtext here is that we can tolerate the alcoholic who destroys his own life, ruins the lives of family members, and even accidentally kills a few people on the highway, because he poses no danger to foundational American values. But if young people begin ingesting a chemical agent that causes them to see the rigidity of social stratification and the hollowness of societal values, then the drug must be banned, which indeed it was. I am by no means making a plea for recreational drug use of any kind here. Albert Hoffman, the chemist who created LSD, has explored the problems posed by the recreational abuse of LSD and other hallucinogens and the obstacles this placed in the way of valuable research. To the contrary, I am merely pointing out the politics of ecstasy as a social phenomenon,[75] as well as the utter irrationality of allowing the use of a toxic, addictive, harmful drug that annually ruins the lives of tens of thousands of people and banning a benign agent that offers, through carefully designed research controls, an interesting window into the mysteries of human consciousness. Incidentally, the U.S. Government has recently approved clinical trials involving psychedelics, and in the last few years there have been several studies conducted in places around the country, including Harvard University, the institution that fired Timothy Leary and Richard Alpert back in 1963 for their research on hallucinogens.

Group ecstasy is thus a problem if a hierarchy is too rigid or too insecure about its foundational values. In some cases the ecstatic experience will prove to be such a problem to certain hierarchies that it will be deemed madness and banned. The Romans, for instance, for all their enthusiastic embrace of Greek culture, could not tolerate the Dionysian festival called the *Bacchanalia*, outlawing it in 186 B.C.E., an early date in the development of the empire. To be sure the ecstatic festival would not continue, the Romans killed roughly 7000 Dionysian worshippers in one of the bloodiest crackdowns in religious history.[76] The Romans found the Bacchanalia threatening in part because its energies represented a madness that threatened the state.

Insanity is a fitting label in some ways. Ecstasy, after all, is also a synonym for madness. This linguistic connection can be traced back to the god of ecstasy, Dionysus, who was also the god of madness. The experience he bestowed, depending on whether one accepted or rejected the god, was either a blissful, divine intoxication in which the soul might even leave the body in joyous flight or a horrible and sometimes violent loss of all restraint. In either case, however, the resulting experience was to go temporarily out of one's mind—that is, to go mad. The ecstatic experience renders access to deep layers of the psyche that normally remain inaccessible to the illusory self we call ego. If a person is unprepared for an engagement with the unconscious *other* self, it is entirely possible he or she can end up temporarily or even permanently mired in a psychotic state. According to Jung, an encounter with unconscious depths should only occur "if [one's] conscious mind possesses the intellectual categories and moral feelings necessary for their assimilation."[77] Otherwise, the result is likely madness, an experience that can so thoroughly destabilize and de-center a person's inner landscape as to render him or her unfit to return to society.

Even if the individual does not go clinically insane, it is possible that he or she could become at least incongruous with mainstream society. The Sufi poets and masters, for instance, often spoke of the *matzoob*, one who directly experiences the joys of Allah. The *matzoob* in Sufi literature is a social outcast, a pariah who has glimpsed God-realization and thus can no longer function in society. In India, as well, there is a tradition of the wandering yogi who re-

32

nounces all ties to normal life to seek the state of *samadhi,* or blissful intoxication in which the perceiver cannot distinguish himself from the objects of his perceptions. The attainment of such intense, ego-dissolving bliss renders the yogi unfit for societal re-integration, and he thus spends his days wandering on the fringes of life. How do you come back from a psycho-spiritual experience so intense that it dissolves the puny boundaries of the ego? How do you go from the glorious heights to interacting with people who are so weighed down by survival challenges that they believe that to soar on the wings of ecstasy is self-indulgent folly?

In most cases, however, ecstatic experiences do not result in an individual being banished to the far cliffs, condemned to live a life of solitude because he or she has dared to speak the unintelligible language of joy. Nor do they usually result in incarceration in the state mental hospital, though this is a real possibility. Yet, they do leave one with social challenges. Maslow observed that transcenders, or self-actualizers who experienced multiple ecstasies, seem less happy in some ways because their peaks leave them with radically altered perspectives. Such transcenders "can be more ecstatic, more rapturous, and experience greater heights of 'happiness,'" he wrote, "but they are as prone or maybe more prone to a cosmic-sadness ... over the stupidity of people, their self-defeat, their blindness, their cruelty to each other, their shortsightedness."[78] In other words, because they see the lack of actualization of potential in most people, self-actualizers often no longer fit well into society. No doubt, they can and frequently do adapt and adjust to the stupidity, blindness, self-defeat, and shortsightedness of others, but they often spend their lives feeling as if they are in some ways fringe-dwellers.

Ecstasy and society thus do not always mix well together. To be a functioning member of society is to be well adjusted, but as Freud observed in his seminal work, *Civilization and Its Discontents,* social adjustment often requires that we turn our backs on parts of ourselves. This is in some ways the essence of socialization itself. The problem here is that it is thoroughly possible to be well adjusted, to make lots of money, to have a family, and to embody all of the markers a given society values but also be utterly miserable and neurotic. In "The Unknown Citizen," W.H. Auden brilliantly explores this idea in his description of a deceased man who the bureau of statistics says had everything that should result in happiness. As the speaker claims, the man "was fully sensible to the advantages of the Installment Plan / And had everything necessary to the Modern Man" (19-20). The poem's closing irony, however, drives home the point that the appearance of social markers of happiness does not equal happiness itself: "Was he free? Was he happy? The question is absurd: / Had anything been wrong, we should certainly have heard" (28-29).

Jung once saw a client who closely resembled Auden's subject, a successful, well adjusted engineer with a family and all of the outward appurtenances of a successful life. When he began analyzing the man's dreams, however, Jung discontinued therapy because he saw in them a latent psychosis. Jung was afraid that had he continued prompting the man to engage the unconscious through dream work, he would end up in an irreversible psychosis. The man's social adjustment was compensatory to a potentially destabilizing, latent psychosis. Maslow lamented that our older ideals of the sage, the knight, the prophet, the hero, and the like have all given way in the modern age to the mere "well adjusted man." But adjustment does not equal psychological health, as Auden's poem and Jung's anecdote both demonstrate. Depending on society or at least one's immediate environment (spouse, family, friends, teachers, co-workers, etc...), sometimes being well adjusted can mean turning one's back on ecstasy, which is tantamount to closing the door on psychological health and self-actualization. The key element here is the social group to which one belongs and whether it is conducive or hostile to ecstatic states. In a brilliant poem Emily Dickinson captured this idea of the role a given society or social group plays in determining reason and madness:

Much Madness is divinest Sense—
To a discerning Eye—
Much Sense—the starkest Madness—
'Tis the Majority
In this, as All, prevail—
Assent—and you are sane—
Demur—you're straightway dangerous—
And handled with a Chain—

If ecstasy is deemed valuable by the collective, as it was in so many ancient cultures, then it will be considered divine sense. If, however, society finds ecstasy problematic, as so much of the modern world generally has, then it will be seen as the starkest madness. The mob rules on this issue.

In his famous work, *Madness and Civilization*, Michel Foucault traced the history of madness from the Renaissance through the eighteenth-century and offered a detailed analysis of the central idea found in Dickinson's poem: madness is in some ways a social construct and changes according to a society's values and needs. According to Foucault, the specter of *unreason*, reason's other, begins to bulk large on the European horizon at the end of the Middle Ages. Madness and the madman "become major figures" in this period, and how they are treated (first sent away from society in the famous ship of fools and then later confined in the hospital) signifies Europe's desire to distance itself from and then to repress unreason.[79] Foucault never explains why madness becomes such a central concern from the Renaissance onward, confining himself principally to the eighteenth century. One way to account for this phenomenon is to interpret it as a symptom of the West's troubled relationship with ecstasy. According to Robert Johnson, a Jungian analyst who argues for the value of ekstasis, unless we temporarily go out of ourselves in the healthy madness of ecstasy, we will go insane, or at least become neurotic as a result of denying ourselves moments of self-transcendence. The uneasiness over and preoccupation with madness in the Renaissance is thus in some ways reflective of the West's problematic encounter with and denial of ecstasy over the centuries. Central to the issue are Western religious doctrines, values, and attitudes. Let us turn, then, to an examination of the religious implications of ecstasy.

The Devil's Work

Across the ancient world, people practiced ecstatic forms of spirituality, either individually or collectively, by losing themselves in divine intoxication. In rural China, even in the sober Confucian era, there were festivals in which people worked themselves into a state of ecstasy while dancing "to the sound of clay timbrels." Those who took part in such activities, according to Marcel Granet, "were all like madmen."[80] The Aryan invaders of India brought to the sub-continent the worship of their god of ecstasy, Soma, whom they honored by imbibing a hallucinogenic drink by the same name. The Aryans encountered in India the cult of the ecstatic dancing god, Shiva. Scholars have not agreed on a date for the origin of Shaivite worship, but the evidence suggests that it predates the Indo-European invasions and probably stretches back at least to the Indus Valley civilization of Mohenjo-Daro (2600 B.C.E.) and probably further into history.[81] The cult of Shiva, as some scholars have maintained, is likely the ultimate origin for the Dionysian practices found all over the ancient Mediterranean world.[82]

Other influences on the Greek form of ecstatic worship include multiple Near Eastern cults, such as those of Isis, Baal, Asherah, Cybele, and Anat. These cults, themselves characterized by ecstatic practices, are likely responsible for the ecstatic character of early Hebrew worship, which was marked by celebratory dancing and singing the praises of God. In Africa ecstatic drumming and dance was, and still is in many parts of the continent, an inseparable component of religious life. In Oceania the historical record attests to countless varieties of ecstatic forms of spirituality. The archeological remains of the pre-Columbian Americas suggest ecstatic practices used for healing and religious rites. In Europe ecstatic practices bearing a shamanic character can be found among the Celtic, Druidic, and Norse cultures. In Central Asia and Siberia, religious life centered around the shaman, whose primary function was to engage in out-of-body journeys to the heavens or to the underworld either for the purpose of healing, retrieving a lost soul, and securing a revelation, or simply for joy alone. Ecstatic spirituality, it seems, is the oldest form of religion and can be found nearly everywhere in the ancient world.

And yet, for all its ancient ubiquity, ecstasy has found a hostile reception in the modern era, particularly in the West but also in other parts of the globe, including Africa, the Middle East, and Asia. In China the older ecstatic rites were eventually prohibited, perhaps because civic authorities and priests of the state religious cult saw them as a challenge to the hierarchy. By the time of the great ancient empires, "all orgiastic elements were strictly eliminated," according to Max Weber, because religious authorities deemed them "as dangerous as the Roman nobility once considered the cult of Dionysus."[83] In the Near East the advent of monotheism, with its later global impact, proved to be a fatal blow to ecstatic spirituality, serving as a means of repression of ecstasy in nearly every culture where it spread its doctrines.

The relationship of monotheism to ecstatic spirituality is not simple and clearly defined, however, and it certainly cannot be viewed strictly in the terms of the former's outright hostility to the latter. After all, the three monotheistic faiths—Judaism, Christianity, and Islam—were founded as a result of ecstatic experiences. The ancient Hebrew patriarchs, Abraham and Moses, communed ecstatically and thus directly with God. Jesus experienced the divine during his baptism, when the spirit came to him as a white dove. Muhammad, during his famous meditations in his mountain cave, Gare Hira, heard a mystical tinkling of bells that later resolved itself into the sacred words that he dictated to scribes, who wrote them down as the *Qur'an*. Muhammad also made his famous night journey from the Dome of the Rock in Jerusalem through the heavens, a shamanic journey, according to David Leeming,[84] that rendered Jerusalem the third holiest city in Islam (after Mecca and Medina). All of these pivotal founders had some kind of ecstatic experience that served as the foundations of their respective faiths. Monotheism, in some ways, would not be possible without ecstasy.

What is more, all three monotheistic faiths tolerated and even participated in ecstatic spiritual practices. The oldest Hebrew prophets operated in prophetic guilds, or bands of holy men, who, with the help of music and dancing, would work themselves into a "form of collective, self-induced ecstasy" and lose themselves in a "sea of divine intoxication."[85] The ecstatic prophetic guilds exerted such a considerable influence over the Israelites that they played a pivotal role in the transformation of Saul from man to first king of Israel. The prophet Samuel tells Saul that before he can become king, he must endure the kind of ecstatic transformation that the guilds effected in people. Samuel sends Saul on a journey and prophesies that he will meet "a company of prophets coming down from the shrine, led by lute, drum, fife, and lyre, and filled with prophetic rapture." Then, says Samuel, "the spirit of the Lord will suddenly take possession of you, and you too will be rapt like a prophet and become another man" (1 Sam. 10: 4-6). Saul becomes king as a result of his ecstasy, an experience Israelites so thoroughly cherished that their participation in ecstatic cults was widespread.

Although Muhammad and his followers destroyed the many ecstatic cults that worshipped at the sacred Kaaba stone in Mecca, Moslems retained some features of the pagan cults they positioned themselves against, foremost among which is the circumambulation around the Kaaba in a counterclockwise direction. The *tawaf*, as it is called, seems clearly to be a sober variant of the circle dance found throughout so many ecstatic cultures, as Ehrenreich observes. Islam also spawned a rich ecstatic tradition in Sufism, the mystical variant of Muslim spirituality that honors, as a kind of first principle, the ecstasy of knowing God directly.

Early Christians were so influenced by the ecstatic Dionysian cult that their version of Jesus was a variant of Dionysus. Scholars have long noted the striking similarities between the two gods: both are sons of a major deity; both are born of virgin mothers; both survive being killed as infants; both perform miracles to inspire faith; both battle evil forces; both return to their birthplaces only to be rejected; both are strongly associated with wine and turning water into wine; both suffer wounding, death, and resurrection; both descend into the underworld; both attain to immortality; both evangelize their messages and establish cults; and both pose challenges to social barriers and class/gender distinctions.[86] Such similarities attest to the pervasive influence of the Greek form of ecstatic religion—after all, the early Christian world was a Greek world—and thus the ecstatic character of early Christian spirituality.

For all of this participation in ecstatic spirituality, however, monotheism also found ecstasy to be a troubling challenge. Early Hebrews participated heavily in ecstatic religious cults, both Near Eastern and Greek, to such an extent that later priestly and prophetic reformers saw this as a violation of the first four commandments. The Hebrew Bible is rife with the pattern of the Israelites breaking their covenant with Yahweh and then being punished for bowing down to other gods. Foremost among these was the Greek god, Dionysus. The origins of the prophetic guilds is unclear, but scholars have found coins, funerary objects, and building ornaments in Palestine (modern day Israel) clearly showing that ancient Israelites worshipped Dionysus, sometimes alongside Yahweh, despite Biblical prohibitions.[87]

A detail in the story of Saul's transformation would also indicate a connection to Dionysus: Samuel tells Saul that before he meets the band of prophets he will encounter three young men carrying, among other things, *three goats* (1 Sam. 10:3). The goat was strongly associated with Dionysus and served as the god's ritual stand-in during rites. A baby goat, or kid, in particular, was often boiled in its mother's milk at the sacred meals of Dionysian and Orphic rituals and celebrations. Such practices, as Max Radin points out, shed light on the mysterious injunction (which appears three times in the Bible) against seething a kid in its mother's milk. Radin notes that it appears twice in Exodus (23:19 and 34:26), along with a list of other *ritual* prohibitions, and once in Deuteronomy (14:21) as a *dietary* prohibition. The prohibition against boiling a goat in its mother's milk is, in effect, a ban on Dionysian worship.[88] The Deuteronomist, however, a priestly reformer, misunderstood the injunction and placed it in a list of dietary regulations, perhaps because by the time he wrote Dionysian participation had been significantly curtailed. It seems that a foundational element in Jewish dietary laws—the prohibition against having meat and dairy in the same meal—is based on a misunderstanding of a Biblical injunction, which was itself based on an attempt to prohibit participation in an ecstatic pagan cult.

Robert Johnson sees the Biblical injunction as the pivotal moment when the Hebrew religion turned its back on ecstasy.[89] His point is bolstered by the fact that many Jews who desire spirituality continue to identify with Judaism culturally but also turn to Buddhism, Sufism, Vedanta, and the New Age for the promise of direct ecstatic experience. Still, it must be remembered that Judaism as a faith has not entirely closed the door on ecstatic experience. The Jewish mystical tradition, informed by the many ecstatic cultures

Jews encountered over the centuries, stretches back to well before the Christian era and has persisted throughout the ages in the form of esoteric Judaism, or Kabbala. Today, there is even a resurgence and popularization of Kabbala, particularly in America, with many non-Jewish adherents turning to its ecstatic doctrines. Two of the most notable of these are former Catholics, Madonna and Alex Rodriguez. In general, however, the ecstatic principle has not fared too well in mainstream Judaism.

Islam, too, has received ecstasy problematically. No doubt, Muslim mysticism, or what is called Sufism, the essence of which is the cultivation of ecstatic inner experiences, has a long history stretching back to the beginnings of Islam. With its ecstatic practices of meditation, recitation of God's many names, fasting, sleep deprivation and the like, Sufism bears a striking resemblance to the other ecstatic traditions—Buddhism, Shaivism, Dionysian and Orphic Mysteries, Gnosticism, Zoroastrianism, and Christian mysticism—that Muslims encountered in the cultural exchanges necessary to building their empire. Yet, although Sufism is still alive today as a rich and vibrant worldwide movement, Sufis have been marginalized in many parts of the Muslim world. Sufism arose in ancient Persia, an area comprising present-day Iran and parts of Afghanistan.

The Shi'a of Iran, however, have found Sufi practices to be of dubious value. Interestingly, the Ayatollahs of the fundamentalist government are well known for their mystical writings—the Ayatollah Khomeini even penned a book of Sufi poems before his death and Iranians claim the rich tradition of Sufi writing as their own. The poetry of Rumi and Hafiz, selections of which are included in this anthology, have achieved a kind of scriptural status in Iran, valued as they are just beneath the *Qur'an* and the *Hadith*. The theological narrow-mindedness and intolerance of the Iranian Shi'a, however, have driven practicing Sufis out of Iran. To be called a *dervish*, a once revered title used to designate a follower of a Sufi order, is now pejorative in Iran and signifies "a term of contempt suggesting idleness, drug use, immorality, and every other sort of evil."[90] While "expelling living dervishes, Iranian Ayatollahs claim the cultural mantle of safely deceased Sufi saints."[91] Such a distancing enabled "the religious hierarchy of Iran to eliminate possible rivals to their authority while appropriating those Sufi doctrines which they admired."[92] The fundamentalists of Iran, it seems, have their cake and eat it, too.

The Sufis of Afghanistan have not fared much better. The type of spirituality that today characterizes Afghanistan, as well as many other parts of the radicalized Muslim world, is called *Wahhabism*, after the fiery and puritanical eighteenth-century reformer, Abd al-Wahhab, who believed the ecstatic Sufis were infidels. Wahhab's legacy is the violent persecution of Sufis in the form of the destruction of shrines and tombs and the elimination of Sufi worship in much of the Muslim world. Wahhab was something like the John Calvin of Islam, as Ehrenreich observes. He interpreted the ecstatic variety of Muslim spirituality as "a rivalry between competing authorities"—a problematic power struggle that stood in the way of his version of a "pure" Islam—and reacted violently to Sufism.[93] In 922 c.e. in a similarly intolerant, fundamentalist climate, the famous Sufi teacher, Mansur al-Hallah was crucified and then beheaded for daring to challenge the religious authorities of his day by sharing the Sufi concept of cultivating ecstatic inner experiences directly with the people. Wahhab's crackdown was thus by no means unprecedented and served as a resurfacing of the ongoing tension between exoteric and esoteric spirituality that has characterized the world's religious history.

Despite Wahhabism, the Sufis enjoyed a safe haven in Turkey, the final resting place of the great poet Rumi, until Mustafa Kemal Ataturk rose to power in 1920. In his attempts to secularize and westernize Turkey and free it from Ottoman models of governance, Ataturk waged a war against Islam in general by replacing Muslim laws with secular legal codes, closing religious schools, and restricting the building of Mosques. Because the Sufis were quite influential in Turkey, they bore the brunt of Ataturk's reforms, which resulted in the confiscation of all Sufi meeting places and the banning of all Sufi activity. The most significant blow came with the illegalization of Sufism. To the present day, Sufis are legally restricted from operating in Turkey. The ecstatic variety of Muslim spirituality has proven to be problematic for the two major forces at odds in the world today—fundamentalism and secularism. Yet, the Sufis do enjoy significant freedom to operate in the rest of the secularized Western world, Turkey notwithstanding. Today, Sufism is more of a Euro-American phenomenon than a Middle Eastern one. Rumi's immense popularity in the Western world, particularly in America, where he is the best-selling poet more than 800 years after his birth, attests to the enthusiastic embrace of Sufi doctrines in the largely Christian West.

The turn to Sufism by many former Christians has much to do with Christianity's own troubling relationship with ecstatic spirituality. No doubt, Christianity has a rich tradition of mystics whose experiences are quintessentially ecstatic. Yet, like the Iranian mullahs who claim Sufi doctrines from a safe distance but then distance themselves from actual Sufis and their practices, so have Christians proudly claimed their mystics but also found them a challenge. St. Theresa of Avila, for instance, was almost brought up on heresy because of her "diabolical" ecstatic visions. Shortly after her death, however, she was canonized as a saint and later named a Doctor of the Church, two very high honors indeed. Meister Eckhart, with his mystical doctrine of the soul's interchangeability with God, was also almost charged with heresy in his day. Today, however, he is fondly claimed by Christians as a much revered, mystical theologian.

This after-the-fact praise suggests that there needs to be a safe enough temporal distance between the ecstatic experience and the Church hierarchy for a given mystic to be brought into the fold. Because the Catholic Church serves as a mediator between God and believer, mystics and their claim of direct experience prove to be a highly problematic challenge that threatens the authority of the priesthood, liturgy, and sacred texts—elements that serve as the foundation on which the Church authority rests. Despite the tradition of the mystics, Catholicism has effectively turned its back on ecstasy in its attempt to build and then preserve the ecclesiastical structures erected on the foundation of Christ's own ecstatic experience. The antagonism among early Christians, characterized in part by the debate over the selection of books that would later be called the *New Testament*, was centered in some ways around the issue of ecstatic experience. Whereas the Gnostics advocated the cultivation of direct spiritual experience, claiming in various texts that all people could attain the states of consciousness Jesus experienced, the more ecclesiastical Christians favored texts that supported the importance of mediators of spiritual experience, such as the papacy, the priesthood, and the liturgy.[94] The latter group won the day, obviously, and Gnostic texts were banned from the Biblical canon, in some cases lost in obscurity until their rediscovery in 1945 at Nag Hammadi in Egypt.

The early Church did tolerate some of the vestiges of ecstatic practices in allowing as part of the Mass wine drinking, circle dancing, speaking in tongues, and *enthusiasmos*, or becoming filled with God.[95] Over the centuries, however, the Church began to sober up and became much less tolerant of such Dionysian elements. At the end of the fourth century, this sobriety found its finest expression in the words of John Chrysotom, whom Ehrenreich calls the "fiery and intolerant" archbishop of Constantinople. Chrysotom's pronouncement on the matter of dancing in the Church serves as a barometer of the age: "For where there is a dance, there is also a Devil."[96] In 400 c.e. this verbal venom was accompanied by the wholesale destruction of Eleusis and its sacred precinct, as well as the killing of its priests, by Romans who had by now formally adopted Christianity as its official and only religion.[97] Eleusis, long the seat in the ancient Mediterranean world of the Greater Mysteries, which provided an initiatory experience culminating in a mystical revelation induced by the ecstatic practices of fasting, dancing, and imbibing a hallucinogen, proved to be a threat to Christians who saw themselves alone as mediators between God and the soul.

From this point onward the Church grew increasingly more hostile to the ecstatic and festive traditions, despite the Church-sanctioned Feast of Fools, a festival held between Christmas and New Year's Day involving an inversion of Church norms, cross-dressing, and the mockery of religious authorities. The practice of ecstatic dancing in Catholic churches, moreover, continued through the late Middle Ages. In the thirteenth century, however, the Church could tolerate no more. "Catholic leaders," according to Ehrenreich, "finally purged the churches of unruly and ecstatic behavior" by banning dancing inside churches and listing it as a "confessable sin" in a directory of sins published in 1317.[98]

Christianity, like Islam and Judaism, found ecstatic practices too problematic and purged them from the list of admissible behaviors within the confines of a house of God. What was once sacred activity for so many ancient cultures thus became unacceptable to the sober Church fathers, who sufficiently demonized it that to this day direct spiritual experience is viewed by many Christians suspiciously and skeptically. Despite a few notable Protestant exceptions, such as tongue-speaking Pentecostals, rapturous Baptists, ecstatic Evangelicals and Born Again believers, Quakers who meditate on the inner light, and Catholics who fuse Christianity with African and Native American religious practices, ecstasy has come to be synonymous with the devil's work in the collective Christian psyche.

Unspeakable Rites

This suspicion informed the attitudes of many European Christians who, in their missionary and imperialistic endeavors, encountered countless ecstatic practices in Africa, Oceania, and aboriginal North, Central, and South America. The bringers of Christian light to the dark and shadowy recesses of far flung, darker-skinned parts of the world often encountered the ecstatic practices that had once been a central feature of their own religion. Their response, however, was to demonize and often attempt to eradicate such practices in countless acts of religious chauvinism. As Ehrenreich observes, "*grotesque* is one word that appears again and again in European accounts of such events; *hideous* is another."[99] Though it is a work of fiction, *Heart of Darkness*, a novella by Joseph Conrad, clearly demonstrates this negative reception. Conrad's narrative is a warning against the "midnight dances" and "unspeakable rites" in which his protagonist, Kurtz, participates. Kurtz is a European "emissary of light," who, nevertheless, is seduced and seemingly destroyed by the allure of dark, ecstatic rites performed in the jungle. Marlow, the narrator through whom Kurtz's story is filtered, himself speaks of the allure of the "weird incantations" of ecstatic practices, which he ultimately resists, likening them to "the responses of some satanic litany." He also notes the "narcotic effect" produced by the big African drums, the hypnotic "throb" of which he similarly resists. This ability to retain one's European sense of self-consciousness and self-possession in the face of rituals that serve as an alluring call to ecstasy is not confined to Conrad's work of fiction. To the contrary, the encounter, as it is configured in *Heart of Darkness*, is highly characteristic of the whole history of European confrontation with and refusal of ecstatic rites and experiences.

In general, therefore, the West has not recognized the need for ecstasy, even antagonistically positioning itself against ecstatic experiences. An example of such antagonism is found in the so-called Black Mass, or Witches' Sabbath, of the Middle Ages. Until fairly recently, scholars believed the Black Mass—a supposed nighttime gathering of witches and Satan worshippers who fly to the woods on broomsticks or animals, conjure the dead, kiss a goat on the anus, renounce the Christian faith, and engage in dancing and a sexual orgy—was merely an imaginative fiction created by overly zealous inquisitors. To a great extent, the elements of the Black Mass were imaginative colorings offered by cruel, Catholic inquisitors whose creative tortures would encourage confession to the most outrageous of scenarios. But in his book, *Ecstasies: Deciphering the Witches' Sabbath*, Carlo Ginzburg makes a sophisticated case for modifying the total dismissal of the Black Mass as fiction. Some of the activities were, in fact, actual practices, remnants of older ecstatic forms of pagan spirituality. Through an exhaustive analysis of historical documents, Ginzburg compellingly demonstrates the presence of shamanic and/or ecstatic elements in various versions of the Black Mass, particularly the flight, coded fertility rituals, nighttime dancing, and orgies—all of which strongly indicate the persistence of ancient ecstatic practices that predate the Christian era.[100] The witch hunts, it seems, were a battle in the West's war on ecstasy.

Another example of the West's antagonism toward ecstasy can be seen in its internalized devaluation of the wildness of ecstatic celebrations and states of mind. The physical world correspondent of the ecstatic state of mind is the *wilderness*—a wild, untamable, natural locale beyond the strictures of society and its values, morality, prohibitions, and hierarchies. As Jung and the post-Jungians have made clear, the wilderness in the collective Western psyche is a source of anxiety, intimations of which can be seen in a variety of sources. Ancient Hebrews in their scapegoating practices would ritually load all of the tribe's sins onto two goats, offering one as a sacrificial slaughter to Yahweh and sending the other away from the tribe into the wilderness where it could scatter the Israelites' transgressions.[101] The psychological subtext here is that untamed nature, or wildness, is associated with sin and transgression, an idea that finds repeated expression in Western literature. So many of the pagan Canaanite divinities who represented the natural wilderness in various manifestations became demons in the Hebrew Bible and later New Testament. Christians demonized two of these ecstatic, pagan goat-gods, Pan and Dionysus, amalgamating them and using the image as a visual representation of Satan himself. In the *Divine Comedy* Dante's Pilgrim thus strays from the "True Way" of the Christian path into the "Dark Wood of Error" and needs a journey through hell in order to be cleansed of his transgressions.

This anxiety over wilderness, with its threat to societal order and morality, is in some ways well founded, for early humans by necessity needed to recognize the dangers of the natural wild and thus band together to form rudimentary societies for the sake of survival. In another sense, however, the demonization of the wild comes at the expense of an estrangement from one's own nature, that is, the body. Ecstasy, although it can take on the form of transcendent, otherworldly visions, is also a corporeal experience of the flesh and the senses, as Robert Johnson observes.[102] One of the implications of the repression of ecstatic forms of worship, therefore, is that physicality, or the sensuous life of the body, is also denied. This association between the body and ecstasy can be seen in countless ecstatic cults, such as those of Dionysus, Asherah, Shiva, Tantrism, and many others, in which sacred sexuality in the form of female fertility and/or phallus worship features prominently. The much-commented-upon mind/body split in Western consciousness clearly indicates that the body, despite its promise of ekstatic renewal, is a source of anxiety in the collective Western psyche.

Ehrenreich cites as another example of this antagonism toward ecstasy the West's over-emphasis on rationalism, which served to exclude from consciousness the Dionysian principle. In Delphi, the most sacred religious site in the ancient Mediterranean world, Dionysus, the god of ecstasy, and Apollo, the god of reason, were both worshipped together, the former during winter and the latter during the rest of the year.[103] The Greeks seemed to know intuitively that one without the other results in psychological imbalance. She also charges Calvinism, with its profound distrust of direct spiritual experience and its reliance on blind faith, with being an influential and pervasive force that greatly contributed to the widespread Western prejudice against ecstasy. The fullest expression of Calvinism, Puritanism, proved to be a relatively joyless form of spirituality that H.L. Mencken comically defined as "the haunting fear that someone, somewhere, may be happy."[104] The Puritan legacy, with its cold sneer at joy and its version of an angry, punishing God who frowns on human sinners, still stares America and parts of Europe angrily and disapprovingly in the face.

Despite ecstasy's place at the top of Maslow's hierarchy of needs, the West has not proven to be very conducive to ecstatic experience. Although these negative attitudes about ecstasy permeate Western culture, the need for ecstasy in the human psyche continues until it is met in one form or another, whether constructively or destructively. As Robert Johnson points out, ecstasy needs can be met through high-grade forms, such as cultivating the state of consciousness necessary for the ekstasis of joy; through attenuated forms, such as sporting events and political rallies; or through low-grade forms such as drug-use. An example of the manifestation of the psychological need for ecstasy is found in the birth of the European carnival. Ehrenreich observes that almost precisely when the Catholic Church banned festivities as a worship activity and sent them out into the streets, carnival was born.[105] The festival came to serve as a secularization of what was once a deeply religious/spiritual practice. Carnival, as Mikhail Bakhtin observed, should not be confused with mere holidays or other state-sanctioned festivals, since its origins are in the people themselves. Carnival started from the ground up and stemmed "from a force that pre-exists priests and kings and to whose superior power they are actually deferring when they appear to sanction carnival."[106] With its masks, hierarchical inversions, celebration of joy, and classless ethos, carnival served to ease social tensions and to prevent political hierarchies from becoming overly rigid—functions previously served by ecstatic rites.

Carnival also served, and continues to do so in many parts of the world, as a vehicle of the celebration of the repressed bodily other.

As I previously noted, ecstatic states are intimately related to the body and the senses. Carnival, with its privileging of what Bakhtin calls the *grotesque*, celebrates "the lower stratum of the body, the life of the belly and the reproductive organs."[107] Grotesque literary forms are thus concerned with "acts of defecation and copulation, conception, pregnancy and birth."[108] Carnival, with its foregrounding of the lower bodily stratum, served as a healing balm for the mind/body split that occurred when the West turned its back on ecstatic experience. In all of its grotesque forms, carnival carried with it the theme of madness, the virtue of which, as Bakhtin observed, was that it enabled people to look at the world with different eyes. Such madness, with its "gay parody of official reason, of the narrowness of official truth," allowed people to extend beyond the confines of self in a communal, celebratory setting.[109] For Bakhtin, as for the followers of the Dionysian and Orphic Mysteries, madness functioned positively by facilitating ecstasy and thus offering a release from the confines of a self too narrowly defined. However sad it may be, since the advent of carnival, there have been literally thousands of acts of legislation passed throughout Europe to ban or to curtail its festivities.[110]

A more recent example of the cultural manifestation of the psychological need for ecstasy is found in the modern "rave" scene, itself a variant of the carnival. Ecstasy needs are met so poorly in the West—usually through the euphoria of shopping, the thrill of the sports contest, the joys of eating, or the pleasures of alcohol—that young people in the 1980s began to have parties that on the surface seemed like the celebratory folly of youth but on closer inspection proved to be a resurfacing of the old demon—the ecstatic rite. Rave culture, a more recent version of the ecstatic hippie scene, consists of groups of people ingesting a mind-altering, mildly hallucinogenic drug not coincidentally called "ecstasy," dancing to the hypnotic rhythms of music classified in the genre of "trance-dance," and losing themselves in the joys of ekstasis through sexual and platonic bonding with other ravers.[111] In another era the rave would be considered a highly sacred practice and given a prominent position in the priorities of society. In the contemporary West, however, it is deemed an embarrassing sub-cultural activity or dismissed as a youthful descent into sex, drugs, and music. Regardless, the need exists in the human psyche and will be met in one way or another.

Any unmet psychological need, if denied gratification for too long, will result in neurosis and disease. Foucault's observation about the rise of the madman and madness as central concerns in the European renaissance thus speaks to the West's denial of ecstasy, the effects of which returned in the early modern period after a centuries-long neglect in the form of uneasiness over and a neurotic preoccupation with madness. With our hyper-rationalism and extreme self-consciousness, we in the West will continue to be haunted by the specter of our repressed ecstatic needs until perhaps we learn to recognize the inherent value of ecstasy and begin to foster social and institutional structures that will facilitate its realization. It is a sore that still festers.

On the Wings of Poetry

Another manifestation of the need for ecstasy can be found in a long-standing tradition of ecstatic verse that extends throughout the ancient world and into the contemporary era. The poets in this tradition celebrate human beings in their best moments—"the soul at the white heat"—to use Emily Dickinson's line. Ecstatic poets affirm the value of happiness, human connections, festivities, sexuality, and relatedness to the divine; they praise the goodness of life, the abundance of nature, and the intimate interrelation of the whole cosmos; and they configure in their verse peak states of being and positive, life-affirming emotions, such as serenity, awe, hope, wonder, rapture, gratitude, and love.

Such poetry and its accompanying poetics of ekstasis (poets composing in a state of rapturous possession) are found ubiquitously among the writings of the Hindu rishis and Zoroastrian poet-prophets; among the Celtic bards and the Norse warrior-poets; among the work of the great Sufi saints and Christian mystics; in the songs of the nebi'im of ancient Israel and the rhapsodes, lyric poets, and performers of the dithyramb of ancient Greece; in the work of the *nahuatl* poet-kings of pre-Columbian Mexico and the

Buddhist writers of India, China, Korea, Tibet, and Japan; and in a large body of verse chanted and sung by poets in Oceania, Africa, and native North, Central and South America. Ecstatic verse, found in nearly every culture in the ancient world, is perhaps the oldest poetry on the planet.

Following is an explicit typology in the form of a list of twenty-two characteristics of ecstatic poetry. Such verse

1. configures peak experiences, spiritual "illuminations," states of flow, and ecstasies
2. configures moments of growth and clarity, epiphanies, and consciousness expansion
3. expresses the life force, the inherent will-to-health, the desire for constructive change, the cultivation of potential, and well-being—Aristotle's *eudaimonia*
4. configures intense positive affect, such as bliss, overpowering joy, intense happiness, awe, rapture, love, and the like
5. conveys images of intoxication as revelry and as sacred inebriation
6. configures "sober" positive emotions and states of being, such as gratitude, wonder, hope, serenity, peace, and contentment
7. views the world positively and optimistically but in sophisticated, mature ways that eschew naïve and misguided thinking and neurotically avoidant coping strategies
8. turns its back in healthy and constructive ways on the negative and represents a mature psychological defense mechanism
9. affirms the interconnectedness of all life
10. affirms humankind's rootedness in the physical body and celebrates the joys of eroticism
11. takes delight in the abundance and goodness of the natural world and its flora and fauna
12. expands the self (through ekstasis) beyond its normal bounds, often into unconscious depths, in constructive ways
13. holistically incorporates sundered aspects of the psyche, trending toward wholeness rather than fragmentation
14. mimics in form and/or content the "trance" states, or poetics of ekstasis, out of which it is born

15. calls upon the reader's sympathetic response and serves as a formal invitation to positive experience and well-being
16. orients itself positively toward the "sacred" in various manifestations and generally, though not always, opposes exoteric religious forms
17. lends itself to speaking, chanting, incantation, music, and/or singing
18. inspires dance and movement
19. celebrates festivities and hilarity
20. suggests images of flight and outward movement, transport, soaring—the winged life
21. exists as an actual aesthetic in historical traditions and also as a mood found spontaneously in nearly all literary corpuses
22. rivals the poetry of pessimism and despair in its complexity and sophistication

Of course, not all of these characteristics are ever found in one poem, but by and large they underpin, in their entirety, the ecstatic poetic tradition.

This tradition, though stifled throughout the ages in various cultures, continues to erupt perennially in different forms. European Romanticism, American Transcendentalism, Beat poetry, and the modern spoken word movement are all variants of the ecstatic impulse. Such poetry is alive and well in the twenty-first century and can be found in Asia, the Indian sub-continent, parts of the Middle East, Africa, and Oceania in various forms (for a more complete discussion, see my forthcoming book, *The Ecstatic Poetic Tradition*). In America, the best-selling poet is Rumi, a thirteenth-century Sufi writer whose ecstatic verse has widespread appeal in a culture that does not highly value poetry, or ecstasy for that matter. Rumi's popularity in America is due in part to Coleman Barks's rather creative and poetically beautiful paraphrases of the dry and dusty (but more accurate) scholarly translations. Another, perhaps deeper, reason for the Rumi phenomenon, as well as for the global appeal of ecstatic verse in general, is that it expresses the inherent human will-to-health, the demand for ekstasis and its transformative functions. The positive turn that has taken place in psychology and some of the hard sciences makes it irrefutably clear that positive emotions have played an integral role in human survival. Our evolutionary human ancestors who descended into pessimism and despair were no doubt easy prey for the hungry predators of the African plains. The ancestors who passed their genes on to us did so because in the face of adversity they cultivated optimism and other positive states of being, all of which served to broaden and build their psychological resources and equipped them with the creative means necessary to deal with their survival challenges. A symptom of the demand for ecstasy in a not-so-ecstatic world, the ecstatic poetry phenomenon serves to express and catalyze such broadening and building emotions and thus represents the enduring human insistence on thriving and flourishing.

Although there is clearly a global ecstatic poetic tradition in the historical sense, it is also possible to view such verse as an example of an aesthetics of ecstasy that poets configure in various forms. Based on the foregoing discussion, it should be clear that ecstatic states are not reserved for the select few. To the contrary, any poet can experience a moment of ecstasy, or any other state of being, and then attempt to capture its spirit by reconstructing it in verse form. Poets who are not known to be particularly rhapsodic, therefore, can write ecstatic poetry. Emily Dickinson, for instance, known principally and perhaps stereotypically for her brooding poems about death, left a body of poetry that covers the full range of human experiences, not least of which are her many depictions of ecstatic states of being. Even the Puritan poet, Anne Bradstreet, despite her theological narrow-mindedness, sounded an ecstatic pitch at times in her verse. Despite its hostile reception and repression throughout the world, the need for ecstasy has never gone away and finds expression and fulfillment in the poetic tradition.

No doubt, the tradition has suffered, particularly in the West. Nietzsche, in his famous work, *The Birth of Tragedy,* lamented the moment in history when the Greeks eliminated the chorus from their tragedies, because it signaled to him the loss of the Dionysian principle that provided the theatre with its initial, fiery impetus.[112] Theatre, and by extrapolation much of later Western literature, became more Apollonian—that is, cooler, more rational, less exuberant, less vital, more cerebral, less *ecstatic*. This loss has resounded throughout so many works in the Western canon, much of which is indeed characteristically Apollonian. And yet, the Dionysian tradition has survived to the present day. My principal purpose for organizing and editing this anthology is to demonstrate the existence of this tradition.

The Apollonian turn that Nietzsche identified in late Greek drama, nevertheless, is pervasive and has influenced not only literature but literary criticism and the various theories used in its service. Today, the theories currently in vogue do not enable a literary critic to assess the positive, Dionysian aspects of the human psyche as they appear in various works. To illustrate this problem, let me first use a Dionysian analogy: Imagine the wine connoisseur who intimately knows about all aspects of the making of a given wine—the type of grape used, the soil and climate in which it was grown, the date of manufacture of the oak casks in which it is stored, the economics of the bottling process and the market demographics, ideologies, and sexual orientations of those who will purchase it. Imagine that the connoisseur knows all of this but has absolutely no taste for discerning the various nuances in the wine itself. Wine critics must know about the wine-making process, but they must also have refined palates. In literary criticism today, scholars focus on everything but the literary equivalent of the nuances in wine, that is, the aesthetic qualities in a text. There is even a widespread prejudice against discussing those nuances, which are often seen as being complicit in various undesirable discourses, such as classism, sexism, patriarchy, capitalism, heterosexism, racism, imperialism, and the like.

There are psychological theories that enable critics to brilliantly tease out a text's underlying neuroses by revealing that a given character, speaker, or author exhibits oedipal dynamics or wants to fill his lack by serving as a surrogate for his mother's (yes, *mother's*) penis. And there are linguistic theories that can cleverly show that love in a work is really hate, or that any expression of emotion, whether negative or positive, linguistically undermines itself by signifying in opposite ways. The Apollonian turn, I suspect, has caused some scholars to ignore the need to cultivate their literary palates, and in the process they have forgotten the other ecstatic half of the human experience. Much of this theory is immeasurably valuable. As a professor who teaches literary theory, I also employ its myriad ideas in my courses and in my scholarship. My point is simply that such theories, with a few notable exceptions,[113] are almost always put in the service of shedding light on some negative aspect of the human existence. Where is the theory that *positively* accounts for being moved to rapture by beautiful passages of poetry? It was once part of the New Criticism but has since been rendered irrelevant.

One exception here is found in the Indian theory of poetics known as *Rasa*, which is making its way into Western criticism perhaps because it enables an account of the rapturous response. Rasa calls for ekstasis in the reading process in its focus on total immersion in a work. Sophisticated readers, say Rasa theorists, are able to achieve deep levels of self-transcendence through identification with a work of art. The rasa experience, which calls for the kind of cultivation required in refining one's palate for wine tasting, is intended to result in such a high degree of aesthetic relish that there is no distinction between subject and object, reader and text.[114] The sophisticated reader of a text becomes so ecstatically moved that he or she forgets self and enters something like a state of flow, or what Maslow and Laski called an aesthetic peak experience.

The intellectual climate in Western literary studies, by contrast, has caused many professors to be embarrassed by their own love of the arts and the imagination because the rapturous, mystified response to beauty is seen as being uncritical and unsophisticated. I once occupied an office next to a fellow professor of English—a radical, poststructuralist Deleuzean who told me quite seriously on several occasions that he hated literature and that the professor of literature is a "dying paradigm." An untenured, junior faculty member, I would often say nothing but inwardly laugh and cringe at the same time. A legitimate response to a work of literature has now become one that refuses the call to rapturous mystification and reads the text against its grain. No doubt, reading "against the grain" can be an interesting and valuable contribution to literary studies, but it also has its limits. Some scholars read *only* against the grain and never let themselves be mystified and awed by texts. Such critics only know how to demystify literary works by arguing that their truths are merely coded assertions of power and thus patriarchal illusions, or that they are complicit in capitalist values and thus rooted in socio-economic conditions, or that they are neurotic psychological defense mechanisms, or that they are entirely derivative of the culture in which they were produced, or that they are purely linguistic constructions that undermine themselves and unravel in the face of close, intellectual scrutiny.

This refusal to soar on aesthetic wings is rooted firmly in the Platonic tradition of denigrating poetry and privileging reason over the imagination, however anti-rationalist such contemporary critics may claim to be, and regardless of their stated intentions of undermining Platonic logocentrism. Many literary theorists attempt to achieve a mastery over the text, seeing themselves as being more sophisticated than the works they are put in the service of analyzing. This approach reached its zenith in the 1990s with the frequent declaration of the "primacy of theory over literature." No doubt, scholars who made such a statement were suggesting that all reading is governed by theoretical assumptions, regardless of whether one is conscious of these. The psychological subtext of the language in the statement, however, clearly implies a kind of dominating behavior—ego's refusal to surrender to something larger than itself. And literature is larger and more profound than criticism and theory.

Psychologically healthy responses to these forces so much larger than the ego are awe, wonder, and, if we are blessed, ecstasy. Maslow observed that one of the characteristics of his peakers is that they see the world with a sense of awe and wonder, that is, they let go and recognize that life's fundamental mysteries cannot be mastered and must be accepted and even heartily embraced. Without this response, he claimed, human beings become disenchanted and neurotic. He went as far as to say that disenchantment can be a defense mechanism designed to protect a fragile ego, for if one is disenchanted, he or she will never be disappointed.[115] The corollary to this last statement is that the disenchanted will never be able to self-transcend, to experience the joys and benefits of ecstasy. No doubt, literary critics must read texts critically against the grain, and they must teach their students to do the same. If this is all they do, however, and if they never learn to let go and savor the rapture that certain literary texts afford, they will miss the chance of experiencing the peak states that characterize the optimally functioning human psyche.

Where, then, is the theory that says it is not only acceptable to love literature and to have something of an ecstatic experience while reading it, but that such a response is immeasurably valuable and necessary to optimal human experience? The brilliant work researchers are currently conducting in the field of positive psychology, itself built on a much earlier account of the positive aspects of human experience, coupled with some kind of reader response theory such as Rasa or the ideas found in the writings of Wolfgang Iser or Norman Holland, together offer the promise of a new account of the joy, rapture, bliss, and ecstasy so often found in literary works but ignored by scholars. It is a brand new day for literary studies, as we now have the potential for a "positive" turn in literary studies.

About the Selections

I conceived of an idea for an anthology of ecstatic poetry because I love ecstatic verse, and I am not afraid to admit that to read it is an absolute joy in itself, as it often evokes in me the kind of response one might call ecstatic. I first encountered it through the work of two major poets, the Dionysian Walt Whitman and the more sober but equally ecstatic William Wordsworth, both of whom are subjects of my first book, *Mystical Discourse in Wordsworth and Whitman*. I began teaching ecstatic poetry several years ago after I encountered my critical tipping point, Jungian psychology, first through Robert Johnson's excellent little book, *Ecstasy: Understanding the Psychology of Joy*, and then through the utterly brilliant work of C.G. Jung himself. Since then I have designed and taught a number of courses on the topic, and in the process I have discovered a cornucopia of ecstatic poetry from all over the world. There are ecstatic poems in the rich literary treasuries of Buddhism, Taoism, Catholicism, Sufism, Protestantism, Judaism, Hinduism, Sikhism, and African and Native American spirituality, as well as in a large body of secular poetry from nearly every canon. I have tried to represent this tradition as broadly as possible. Surely, there is more such poetry than I have included in this anthology, and future projects offer the promise of a lifetime of discoveries.

Regarding all selections, whether translated or written in English, practical demands required me to confine myself to works lying in the public domain. Copyright laws, which vary from country to country, protect published works and prohibit their reproduction without express authorial consent. For this reason, much of the twentieth-century is conspicuously absent from the anthology, despite that the ecstatic poetic tradition has existed from time immemorial and continues through the twentieth century right up to the present moment.

Clearly, not all of the poets represented in this anthology are wild Dionysian bards who sing of rapturous, intoxicated states of mind. Nor is every poem an expression of wild joyousness. In some cases I have selected wild, Dionysian poets or at least rhapsodic poems from otherwise "sober" poets. In many others, however, there are poets who are neither Dionysian in temperament nor writers of inebriate verse but rather sober poets who configure many of the calmer, more sober states of positive affect. I justify the inclusion of the latter in that they are ecstatic in the sense of being beyond our normal bounds. Although we may have great love for a child or a spouse, life's demands often stand in the way of a complete realization and expression of such love. The feeling of oneness with nature comes not on most days when we are in the office cubicle or the warehouse but in exceptional moments when we make it to a spectacular natural setting. Because they take us beyond the boundaries of our normal sense of selfhood, such moments are as much a part of the ecstatic experience as are the ecstasies of nighttime revelers who dance around a sacred fire and mystics, yogis, and contemplatives who realize God, or spirit, or the Self.

This anthology is thus a collection of poetry that celebrates ecstasy in many of its varieties: intense bliss, soul-lifting rapture, communion with nature, spiritual illumination, ego-transcendence, mind-stilling peace, wild eroticism, perceptual estrangement, overpowering joy, self-renewal, moving aesthetic responses, peak experiences, oceanic moments, sacred encounters, and consciousness expansion, as well as life-affirming emotions such as awe, wonder, gratitude, and, most important of all—love.

I hope you enjoy it.

THE POETS

HEBREW BIBLE
c. 700-200 B.C.E.

Psalm 150

Praise the LORD!
    Praise God in his sanctuary;
        praise him in his mighty firmament!
    Praise him for his mighty deeds;
        praise him according to his surpassing greatness!
    Praise him with trumpet sound;
        praise him with lute and harp!
    Praise him with tambourine and dance;
        praise him with strings and pipe!
    Praise him with clanging cymbals;
        praise him with loud clashing cymbals!
    Let everything that breathes praise the LORD!
    Praise the LORD!

2 Samuel (6:13-23)

So David went and brought up the ark of God from the house of
Obed-edom to the city of David with rejoicing; and when those who
bore the ark of the LORD had gone six paces, he sacrificed an ox and
a fatling. David danced before the LORD with all his might; David was
girded with a linen ephod. So David and all the house of Israel brought
up the ark of the LORD with shouting, and with the sound of the trumpet. As the ark of the LORD came into the city of David, Michal daughter of Saul looked out of the window, and saw King David leaping and

dancing before the LORD; and she despised him in her heart. They brought in the ark of the LORD, and set it in its place, inside the tent that David had pitched for it; and David offered burnt offerings and offerings of well-being before the LORD. When David had finished offering the burnt offerings and the offerings of well-being, he blessed the people in the name of the LORD of hosts, and distributed food among all the people, the whole multitude of Israel, both men and women, to each a cake of bread, a portion of meat, and a cake of raisins. Then all the people went back to their homes. David returned to bless his household. But Michal the daughter of Saul came out to meet David, and said, "How the king of Israel honored himself today, uncovering himself today before the eyes of his servants' maids, as any vulgar fellow might shamelessly uncover himself!" David said to Michal, "It was before the LORD, who chose me in place of your father and all his household, to appoint me as prince over Israel, the people of the LORD, that I have danced before the LORD. I will make myself yet more contemptible than this, and I will be abased in my own eyes; but by the maids of whom you have spoken, by them I shall be held in honor." And Michal the daughter of Saul had no child to the day of her death.

HOMERIC HYMNS
c. 650-550 B.C.E.

To Dionysus

I BEGIN TO SING OF IVY-CROWNED DIONYSUS, THE LOUD-CRYING GOD, SPLENDID SON of Zeus and glorious Semele. The rich-haired Nymphs received him in their bosoms from the lord his father and fostered and nurtured him carefully in the dells of Nysa,[116] where by the will of his father he grew up in a sweet-smelling cave, being reckoned among the immortals.

But when the goddesses had brought him up, a god oft-hymned, then began he to wander continually through the woody coombes,[117] thickly wreathed with ivy and laurel. And the Nymphs followed in his train with him for their leader; and the boundless forest was filled with their outcry.

And so hail to you, Dionysus, god of abundant clusters! Grant that we may come again rejoicing to this season, and from that season onwards for many a year.

To Aphrodite

I will sing of stately Aphrodite, gold-crowned and beautiful, whose dominion is the walled cities of all sea-set Cyprus. There the moist breath of the western wind wafted her over the waves of the loud-moaning sea in soft foam, and there the gold-filleted[118] Hours welcomed her joyously. They clothed her with heavenly garments: on her head they put a fine, well-wrought crown of gold, and in her pierced ears they hung ornaments of orichalc[119] and precious gold, and adorned her with golden necklaces over her soft neck and snow-white breasts, jewels which the gold-filleted Hours wear themselves whenever they go to their father's house to join the lovely dances of the gods. And when they had fully decked her, they brought her to the gods, who welcomed her when they saw her, giving her their hands. Each one of them prayed that he might lead her home to be his wedded wife, so greatly were they amazed at the beauty of violet-crowned Cytherea.[120] Hail, sweetly-winning, coy-eyed goddess! Grant that I may gain the victory in this contest, and order you my song. And now I will remember you and another song also.

To Pan

Muse, tell me about Pan, the dear son of Hermes, with his goat's feet and two horns—a lover of merry noise. Through wooded glades he wanders with dancing nymphs who foot it on some sheer cliff's edge, calling upon Pan, the shepherd-god, long-haired, unkempt. He has every snowy crest and the mountain peaks and rocky crests for his domain; hither and thither he goes through the close thickets, now lured by soft streams, and now he presses on amongst towering crags and climbs up to the highest peak that overlooks the flocks. Often he courses through the glistening high mountains, and often on the shouldered hills he speeds along slaying wild beasts, this keen-eyed god. Only at evening, as he returns from the chase, he sounds his note, playing sweet and low on his pipes of reed: not even she could excel him in melody—that bird who in flower-laden spring pouring forth her lament utters honey-voiced song amid the leaves. At that hour the clear-voiced nymphs are with him and move with nimble feet, singing by some spring of dark water, while Echo wails about the mountain-top, and the god on this side or on that of the choirs, or at times sidling into the midst, plies it nimbly with his feet. On his back he wears a spotted lynx-pelt, and he delights in high-pitched songs in a soft meadow where crocuses and sweet-smelling hyacinths bloom at random in the grass.

They sing of the blessed gods and high Olympus and choose to tell of such an one as luck-bringing Hermes above the rest, how he is the swift messenger of all the gods, and how he came to Arcadia, the land of many springs and mother of flocks, there where his sacred place is as god for Cyllene.[121] For there, though a god, he used to tend curly-fleeced sheep in the service of a mortal man, because there fell on him and waxed strong melting desire to wed the rich-tressed daughter of Dryops,[122] and there he brought about the merry marriage. And in the house she bare Hermes a dear son who from his birth was marvelous to look upon, with goat's feet and two horns—a noisy, merry-laughing child. But when the nurse saw his uncouth face and full beard, she was afraid and sprang up and fled and left the child. Then luck-bringing Hermes received him and took him in his arms: very glad in his heart was the god. And he went quickly to the abodes of the deathless gods, carrying the son wrapped in warm skins of mountain hares, and set him down beside Zeus and showed him to the rest of the gods. Then all the immortals were glad in heart and Bacchic Dionysus in especial; and they called the boy Pan because he delighted all their hearts.

And so hail to you, lord! I seek your favor with a song. And now I will remember you and another song also.

SAPPHO
c. 630/612-570 B.C.E.

To the Moon

THE STARS AROUND THE LOVELY MOON[123]
    Fade back and vanish very soon,
When, round and full, her silver face
    Swims into sight, and lights all space.

The Garden of the Nymphs

Through orchard-plots with fragrance crowned
    The clear cold fountain murmuring flows;
And forest leaves with rustling sound
    Invite to soft repose.

Venus

    Come, Venus, come
Hither with thy golden cup,
    Where nectar-floated flowerlets swim.

    Fill, fill the goblet up;
These laughing lips shall kiss the brim,
    Come, Venus, come.

A Girl in Love

Oh, my sweet mother, 'tis in vain,[124]
    I cannot weave as I once wove,
So 'wildered are my heart and brain
    With thinking of that youth I love.

To a Girl

Like the sweet apple which reddens upon the topmost bough,[125]
Atop on the topmost twig,—which the pluckers forgot, somehow,—
   Forgot it not, nay, but got it not, for none could get it till now.

Like the wild hyacinth flower which on the hills is found,
Which the passing feet of the shepherd for ever tear and wound,
   Until the purple blossom is trodden into the ground.

To Evening

O Hesperus![126] Thou bringest all things home;[127]
   All that the garish day hath scattered wide;
The sheep, the goat, back to the welcome fold;
   Thou bring'st the child, too, to his mother's side.

Cretan Women

Then, as the broad moon rose on high,
   The maidens stood at the altar nigh;
And some in graceful measure
   The well-loved spot danced round,
With lightsome footsteps treading
   The soft and grassy ground.

A Child

I have a child, a lovely one,
   In beauty like the golden sun
Or like sweet flowers of earliest bloom;
   And Cleis is her name, for whom
I, Lydia's treasures, were they mine,
   Would glad resign.

ALCAEUS
c. 620 B.C.E.

Winter

THE RAIN OF ZEUS DESCENDS, AND FROM HIGH HEAVEN[128]
    A storm is driven:
And on the running water-brooks the cold
    Lays icy hold:
Then up! beat down the winter; make the fire
    Blaze high and higher;
Mix wine as sweet as honey of the bee
    Abundantly;
Then drink with comfortable wool around
    Your temples bound.
We must not yield our hearts to woe, or wear
    With wasting care;
For grief will profit us no whit, my friend,
    Nor nothing mend;
But this is our best medicine, with wine fraught
    To cast out thought.

Spring

I heard that flowery spring
    Its glories about is to bring.
Mix therefore wine with great speed,
    A bowl full, as honey sweet.

Summer

Come, wet thy chest with wine: the dog-star[129] now
    Is rising high, the oppressive sultry glow
Of summertime brings parching thirst to all.
    Now from the leaves the locust its loud call,
Its sweet shrill song, pours out from 'neath its wings.
    The blazing heat, which withereth all things,
O'er all the earth is spread; the blooming thistle
    Holds up its head; now womankind doth bristle
With passion most, and man is haggard worn;
    For Sirius his head and limbs doth burn.

In the Afternoon

Let us drink—do not tarry till night.
    Why wait for the lamp's pale light?
But a brief span of life is a day.
    My dear friend, let us drink while we may.
The large figured cups from above
    Take down; for the son of Jove
And of Semele[130] wine gave to man
    To release him from misery's ban.
Do thou therefore mix two and one:
    O'er the brim so it almost doth run,
For us all one large goblet fill,
    And then come with another one still.

At Night

Let us drink, let us drink, let us drink;
For the dog-star is up o'er the brink.

ANACREON
c. 572-488 B.C.E.

The Vintage

MEN AND MAIDS AT TIME OF YEAR[131]
The ripe clusters jointly bear
To the press, but in when thrown,
They by men are trod alone,
Who in Bacchus' praises join,
Squeeze the grape, let out the wine:
Oh with what delight they spy
The new must when tunned[132] work high!
Which if old men freely take,
Their grey heads and heels they shake;
And a young man, if he find
Some fair maid to sleep resigned
In the shade, he straight goes to her,
Wakes, and roundly 'gins to woo her;
Whilst Love slyly stealing in
Tempts her to the pleasing sin:
Yet she long resists his offers,
Nor will hear whate'er he proffers,
Till perceiving that his prayer
Melts into regardless air,
Her, who seemingly refrains,
He by pleasing force constrains;
Wine doth boldness thus dispense,
Teaching young men insolence.

Age

Oft am I by the women told,
"Poor Anacreon! Thou growest old;
Look; how thy hairs are falling all;
Poor Anacreon, how they fall!"
Whether I grow old or no,
By the effects I do not know;
But this I know, without being told,
'Tis time to live, if I grow old;
'Tis time short pleasures now to take,
Of little life the best to make,
And manage wisely the last stake.

Spring

See the Spring herself discloses,
And the Graces gather roses;
See how the becalmed seas
Now their swelling waves appease;
How the duck swims, how the crane
Comes from winter home again;
See how Titan's cheerful ray
Chaseth the dark clouds away;
Now in their new robes of green
Are the plowman's labors seen:
Now the lusty teeming Earth
Springs each hour with a new birth;
Now the olive blooms: the vine
Now doth with plump pendants shine;
And with leaves and blossoms now
Freshly bourgeons every bough.

ORPHIC HYMNS
c. 550-450 B.C.E.

To the Stars

WITH HOLY VOICE I CALL THE STARS ON HIGH,[133]
Pure sacred lights, and daemons of the sky.
Celestial stars, dear progeny of Night,
In whirling circles beaming far your light;
Refulgent[134] rays around the heav'ns ye throw,
Eternal fires, the source of all below.
With flames significant of Fate ye shine,
And aptly rule for men a path divine.
In seven bright zones ye run with wand'ring flames,
And heaven and earth compose your lucid frames:
With course, unwearied, pure and fiery bright,
Forever shining through the veil of Night.
Hail, glittering, joyful, ever wakeful fires!
Propitious shine on all my just desires,
These sacred rites regard with conscious rays,
And end our works devoted to your praise.

To Pan

Strong past'ral Pan, with suppliant voice I call,
Heav'n, sea and earth, the mighty queen of all,
Immortal fire; for all the world is thine,
And all are parts of thee, O pow'r divine.
Come, blessed Pan, whom rural haunts delight,
Come, leaping, agile, wand'ring starry light.
Throned with the Seasons, Bacchanalian[135] Pan,
Goat-footed, horned, from whom the world began;
Whose various parts, by thee inspired, combine
In endless dance and melody divine.
In thee a refuge from our fears we find,
Those fears peculiar to the humankind.
Thee, shepherds, streams of water, goats rejoice,

Thou lov'st the chase and Echo's secret voice:
The sportive Nymphs thy ev'ry step attend,
And all thy works fulfill their destined end.
O all-producing pow'r, much-famed divine,
The world's great ruler, rich increase is thine.
All-fertile Pan, heavenly splendor pure,
In fruits rejoicing, and in caves obscure.
True serpent-horned Jove, whose dreadful rage,
When roused, 'tis hard for mortals to assuage.
By thee the earth wide-bosomed, deep and long,
Stands on a basis permanent and strong.
Th' unwearied waters of the rolling sea,
Profoundly spreading, yield to thy decree.
Old Ocean, too, reveres thy high command,
Whose liquid arms begird the solid land.
The spacious air, whose nutrimental fire
And vivid blasts the heat of life inspire;
The lighter frame of fire, whose sparkling eye
Shines on the summit of the azure sky,
Submit alike to thee, whose gen'ral sway
All parts of matter, various formed, obey.
All natures change though thy protecting care,
And all mankind thy lib'ral bounties share;
For these, where'er dispersed through boundless space,
Still find thy providence support their race.
Come, Bacchanalian, blessed pow'r, draw near,
Enthusiastic Pan, thy suppliants hear,
Propitious to these holy rites attend,
And grant our lives may meet a prosp'rous end;
Drive panic fury too, wherever found,
From humankind to earth's remotest bound.

To Bacchus

Bacchus I call loud-sounding and divine,
Inspiring God, a twofold shape is thine:
Thy various names and attributes I sing,
O firstborn, thrice begotten, Bacchic king.
Rural, ineffable, two-formed, obscure,

71

Two-horned, with ivy crowned, Euion pure:
Bull-faced and martial, bearer of the vine,
Endued with counsel prudent and divine:
Omadius, whom the leaves of vines adorn,
Of Jove and Persephone occultly[136] born
In beds ineffable; all-blessed pow'r,
Whom with triennial off'rings men adore.
Immortal daemon, hear my suppliant voice,
Give me in blameless plenty to rejoice;
And listen gracious to my mystic prayer,
Surrounded with thy choir of nurses fair.

To the Curetes

Leaping Curetes,[137] who with dancing feet
And circling measures armed footsteps beat:
Whose bosoms Bacchanalian furies fire,
Who move in rhythm to the sounding lyre:
Who traces deaf when lightly leaping tread,
Arm-bearers, strong defenders, rulers dread:
Famed Deities the guards of Proserpine,
Preserving rites mysterious and divine:
Come, and benevolent this hymn attend,
And with glad mind the herdsman's life attend.

To Dionysus Bassareus Triennalis

Come, blessed Dionysus, various-named,
Bull-faced, begot from thunder, Bacchus famed.
Bassarian[138] God, of universal might,
Whom swords and blood and sacred rage delight:
In heaven rejoicing, mad, loud-sounding God,
Furious inspirer, bearer of the rod:
By Gods revered, who dwell with humankind.
Propitious come, with much rejoicing mind.

To Licknitus Bacchus

Licknitan[139] Bacchus, bearer of the vine,
Thee I invoke to bless these rites divine:
Florid and gay, of Nymphs the blossom bright,
And of fair Venus, Goddess of delight.
'Tis thine mad footsteps with mad Nymphs to beat,
Dancing through groves with lightly leaping feet:
From Jove's high counsels nursed by Proserpine,
And born the dread of all the powers divine.
Come, blessed God, regard thy suppliant's voice,
Propitious come, and in these rites rejoice.

To Bacchus Pericionius

Bacchus Pericionius,[140] hear my prayer,
Who made the house of Cadmus once thy care,
With matchless force his pillars twining round,
When burning thunders shook the solid ground,
In flaming, sounding torrents borne along,
Propped by thy grasp indissolubly strong.
Come, mighty Bacchus, to these rites inclined,
And bless thy suppliants with rejoicing mind.

To Sabazius

Hear me, illustrious father, daemon famed,
Great Saturn's offspring, and Sabazius[141] named;
Inserting Bacchus, bearer of the vine,
And sounding God, within thy thigh divine,
That when mature, the Dionysian God
Might burst the bands of his concealed abode,
And come to sacred Tmolus, his delight,
Where Ippa dwells, all beautiful and bright.
Blessed Phrygian God, the most august of all,
Come aid thy mystics, when on thee they call.

To Amphietus Bacchus

Terrestrial Dionysus, hear my prayer,
Rise vigilant with the Nymphs of lovely hair:
Great Amphietus[142] Bacchus, annual God,
Who laid asleep in Persephone's abode.
Her sacred seat, did lull to drowsy rest
The rites triennial and the sacred feast;
Which roused again by thee, in graceful ring,
Thy nurses round thee mystic anthems sing;
When briskly dancing with rejoicing pow'rs,
Thou move in concert with the circling hours.
Come blessed, fruitful, horned, and divine,
And on this sacred Telete[143] propitious shine;
Accept the pious incense and the prayer,
And make prolific holy fruits thy care.

To Silenus, Satyrus,
and the Priestesses of Bacchus

Great nurse of Bacchus, to my prayer incline,
Silenus,[144] honored by the powers divine;
And by mankind at the triennial feast
Illustrious daemon, reverenced as the best:
Holy, august, the source of lawful rites,
Frenetic power, whom vigilance delights;
Surrounded by thy nurses young and fair,
Naiads and Bacchic Nymphs who ivy bear,
With all thy Satyrs on our incense shine,
Daemons wild-formed, and bless the rites divine.
Come, rouse to sacred joy thy pupil king,
Our orgies shining through the night inspire,
And bless, triumphant power, the sacred choir.

SOPHOCLES
494-406 B.C.E.

A Fair Euboean Shore

THERE STRETCHETH BY THE SEA[145]
A fair Euboean[146] shore, and o'er it creeps
The vine of Bacchus, each day's growth complete.
In morning brightness all the land is green
With tendrils fair and spreading. Noontide comes,
And then the unripe cluster forms apace:
The day declines, and purple grow the grapes;
At eve the whole bright vintage is brought in,
And the mixed wine poured out.

Praise of Colonus
from Oedipus at Colonus

Stranger thou art standing now
On Colonus' sparry brow;
All the haunts of Attic ground,
Where the matchless coursers bound,
Boast not, through their realms of bliss,
Other spot as fair as this.
Frequent down this greenwood dale,
Mourns the warbling nightingale,
Nestling 'mid the thickest screen
Of the ivy's darksome green;
Or where, each empurpled shoot
Drooping with its myriad fruit,
Curled in many a mazy twine,
Blooms the never-trodden vine,
By the god's protecting power
Safe from sun and storm and shower.
Bacchus here, the summer long,
Revels with the goddess throng,
Nymphs who thus on Nysa's wild,
Reared to man the rosy child.

Here Narcissus, day by day,
Buds, in clustering beauty gay,
Sipping aye, at morn and even,
All the nectar dews of heaven,
Wont amid your locks to shine,
Ceres fair, and Proserpine.[147]
Here the golden Crocus gleams,
Murmur here unfailing streams,
Sleep the bubbling fountains never,
Feeding pure Cephisus river,
Whose prolific waters daily
Bid the pastures blossom gaily,
With the showers of spring-tide blending,
On the lap of earth descending.
Here the Nine,[148] to notes of pleasure,
Love to tread their choral measure,
Venus, o'er those flowerets gliding,
Oft her rein of gold is guiding.

Now a brighter boast than all
Shall my grateful song recall;
Yon proud shrub, that will not smile,
Pelops, on thy Doric isle,
Nor on Asiatic soil,
But unsown, unsought by toil,
Self-engendered, year by year,
Springs to life a native here.
Tree the trembling foeman shuns,
Garland for Athena's sons,
May the olive long be ours,
None may break its sacred bowers,
None its boughs of silvery gray
Young or old may bear away:
Morian Jove,[149] with look of love,
Ever guards it from above,
Blue-eyed Pallas[150] watch unsleeping
O'er her favorite tree is keeping.

Swell the song of praise again;
Other boons demand my strain,

Other blessings we inherit,
Granted by the mighty Spirit;
On the sea and on the shore,
Ours the bridle and the oar.
Son of Saturn old! Whose sway
Stormy winds and waves obey,
Thine be honor's well-earned meed,[151]
Tamer of the champing steed:
First he wore on Attic plain
Bit of steel and curbing rein.
Oft too o'er the waters blue,
Athens, strain thy laboring crew;
Practiced hands the bark are plying,
Oars are bending, spray is flying,
Sunny waves beneath them glancing,
Sportive Nereids[152] round them dancing,
With their hundred feet in motion,
Twinkling 'mid the foam of ocean.

ANACREONTEA
c. 50 B.C.E.-550 C.E.

To Spring or Summer

THERE TO STROLL IS A DELIGHT
Where luxurious grass is growing,
Where o'er meadows, sweet and bright,
Gentle Zephyr's[153] breath is blowing.

I delight in Bacchus' shade
'Neath a leafy vine to tarry,
Talking with a lovely maid,
E'en whose breath doth Cypris[154] carry.

A Love Song

The dance of Bacchus I admire,
In sportive mirth abounding;
With youthful friends to hear my lyre
At drinking-bouts resounding.

Howe'er, with wreaths of hyacinth gay
My festive head to cover,
And then with charming maids to play,
Of this I am most a lover.

My heart bleak envy knoweth not;
At drink I hate all quarrels;
The darts by tongues abusive shot
To shun—these are my morals.

With blooming maidens I desire
To banquet and to revel,
And, dancing to the tuneful lyre,
To keep life free from evil.

To the Rose

The rose, which red with Cupid's glow,
With vines we'll interlace;
The beauteous-leaved, the fragrant rose
We'll o'er our temples place;
Of joyful laughter let us think,
And let us cheer our hearts with drink.

Thou, rose, which of flowers dost most delight,
Spring's favor hast thou won;
The gods take pleasure in thy sight,
And Cytherea's son,[155]
With Graces[156] dancing, e'er doth crown
With wreaths of rose his hair's soft down.

Now wreathe me too—I'll play the lyre,
And with a maid, whose gown
In deep folds falls, do I desire
In Bacchus' shrine to crown
With wreaths of rose again my hair
And in hilarious dancing share.

To Himself

I now am very old, 'tis true,
Yet more I drink than young men do,
And when to dance I would commence,
    Then I will rush
    Into the crush,
Then like Silenus will I dance.
A wine-bag then my staff shall be;
For nothing means a wand to me.

The one to whom 'tis dear to fight
May ever fight with all his might.
To me a cup be brought by thee
    O boy, I enjoin,
    Sweet honeyed wine

Mix in it and bring here to me.
I now am very old, 'tis true,
Yet more I drink than young men do.

To a Lover of Drink

When Bacchus here is present,
My cares are put to sleep;
Like Croesus' riches pleasant[157]
Is my contentment deep.

With ivy o'er my temples,
I'll sing a graceful song;
My mind on all things tramples.
Pour in—to drink I long.

A cup do to me carry:
Than lying dead, my boy,
'Tis better to be merry,
And lie one's drink to enjoy.

To Dionysus or to Wine

Whenever Bacchus, son of Zeus,
Lyaeus, who our cares doth loose,
The giver of wine, my spirit reaches,
Then he to me blithe dances teaches.

But something gladsome also is mine,
I, who a lover am of wine:
Venus me too with song entrances;
Again will I take part in dances.

To Dionysus

That god to us doth now appear,
Who from young lovers takes their fear;
Through him the troubled no more tire,
Whom drink and dancing doth inspire.
To man a wondrous charm he hath shown,
Love to arouse, yet not to groan.
He guards the offspring of the vine,
Which in its fruit hems in the wine
Imprisoned in the clustered grapes.
When once from them their juice escapes,
Then all without disease shall be,
Then sickness shall our bodies flee,
And from our glad minds disappear,
As time flies on year after year.

To Wine

Men and maidens both make merry,
When in baskets grapes they bring,
And them on the shoulders carry,
And into the wine-vats fling.
Men alone the purple grapes
Press, so that the wine escapes.

To the god they sing loud praises,
Vintage songs; upon the juice,
As it bubbles, each one gazes,
At the jars; but through its use
E'en the trembling gray-haired dare
Now to dance and shake their hair.

81

THE ACTS OF JOHN
c. 150 c.e.

Gnostic Round Dance of Jesus

NOW BEFORE HE WAS TAKEN BY THE LAWLESS JEWS, WHO ALSO WERE GOVERNED BY
(had their law from) the lawless serpent, he gathered all of us together
and said: Before I am delivered up unto them let us sing an hymn to the
Father, and so go forth to that which lieth before us. He bade us therefore make as it were a ring, holding one another's hands, and himself
standing in the midst he said: Answer Amen unto me. He began, then,
to sing an hymn and to say:

Glory be to thee, Father.
And we, going about in a ring, answered him: Amen.
Glory be to thee, Word: Glory be to thee, Grace. Amen.
Glory be to thee, Spirit: Glory be to thee, Holy One:
Glory be to thy glory. Amen.
We praise thee, O Father; we give thanks to thee,
O Light, wherein darkness dwelleth not. Amen.
Now whereas (or wherefore) we give thanks, I say:
I would be saved, and I would save. Amen.
I would be loosed, and I would loose. Amen.
I would be wounded, and I would wound. Amen.
I would be born, and I would bear. Amen.
I would eat, and I would be eaten. Amen.
I would hear, and I would be heard. Amen.
I would be thought, being wholly thought. Amen.
I would be washed, and I would wash. Amen.
Grace danceth. I would pipe; dance ye all. Amen.
I would mourn: lament ye all. Amen.
The number Eight (lit. one ogdoad)[158] singeth praise with us. Amen.
The number Twelve danceth on high. Amen.
The Whole on high hath part in our dancing. Amen.
Whoso danceth not, knoweth not what cometh to pass. Amen.
I would flee, and I would stay. Amen.
I would adorn, and I would be adorned. Amen.
I would be united, and I would unite. Amen.

A house I have not, and I have houses. Amen.
A place I have not, and I have places. Amen.
A temple I have not, and I have temples. Amen.
A lamp am I to thee that beholdest me. Amen.
A mirror am I to thee that perceivest me. Amen.
A door am I to thee that knockest at me. Amen.
A way am I to thee a wayfarer.

Now answer thou (or as thou respondest) unto my dancing. Behold
thyself in me who speak, and seeing what I do, keep silence about
my mysteries. Thou that dancest, perceive what I do, for thine is this
passion of the manhood, which I am about to suffer. For thou couldest
not at all have understood what thou sufferest if I had not been sent
unto thee, as the word of the Father. Thou that sawest what I suffer
sawest me as suffering, and seeing it thou didst not abide but wert
wholly moved, moved to make wise. Thou hast me as a bed, rest upon
me. Who I am, thou shalt know when I depart. What now I am seen
to be, that I am not. Thou shalt see when thou comest. If thou hadst
known how to suffer, thou wouldst have been able not to suffer. Learn
thou to suffer, and thou shalt be able not to suffer. What thou knowest
not, I myself will teach thee. Thy God am I, not the God of the traitor. I
would keep tune with holy souls. In me know thou the word of wisdom.
Again with me say thou: Glory be to thee, Father; glory to thee, Word;
glory to thee, Holy Ghost. And if thou wouldst know concerning me,
what I was, know that with a word did I deceive all things and I was no
whit deceived. I have leaped: but do thou understand the whole, and
having understood it, say: Glory be to thee, Father. Amen.

Thus, my beloved, having danced with us the Lord went forth. And we
as men gone astray or dazed with sleep fled this way and that. I, then,
when I saw him suffer, did not even abide by his suffering, but fled unto
the Mount of Olives, weeping at that which had befallen. And when he
was crucified on the Friday, at the sixth hour of the day, darkness came
upon all the earth. And my Lord standing in the midst of the cave and
enlightening it, said: John, unto the multitude below in Jerusalem I am
being crucified and pierced with lances and reeds, and gall and vinegar
is given me to drink. But unto thee I speak, and what I speak hear thou.
I put it into thy mind to come up into this mountain, that thou mightest
hear those things which it behooveth a disciple to learn from his teacher
and a man from his God.

LI PO
701-762

On a Picture Screen

WHENCE THESE TWELVE PEAKS OF WU-SHAN!
Have they flown into the gorgeous screen
From heaven's one corner?

Ah, those lovely pines murmuring in the wind!
Those palaces of Yang-tai, hovering yonder—
Oh, the melancholy of it!
Where the jeweled couch of the king
With brocade covers is desolate—
His elfin maid voluptuously fair
Still haunting them in vain!

Here a few feet
Seem a thousand miles.
The craggy walls glisten blue and red,
A piece of dazzling embroidery.
How green those distant trees are
Round the river strait of Ching-men!
And those ships—they go on,
Floating on the waters of Pa.
The water sings over the rocks
Between countless hills
Of shining mist and lustrous grass.

How many years since these valley flowers bloomed
To smile in the sun?
And that man traveling on the river,
Hears he not for ages the monkeys screaming?
Whoever looks on this,
Loses himself in eternity;
And entering the sacred mountains of Sung,
He will dream among the resplendent clouds.

The Mountain Moon

The autumn moon is half round above the Yo-mei
    Mountain;
Its pale light falls in and flows with the water of the
    Ping-chiang River.
Tonight I leave Ching-chi of the limpid stream for the
    Three Canyons,
And glide down past Yu-chow, thinking of you whom
    I cannot see.

In the Mountains

Why do I live among the green mountains?
I laugh and answer not, my soul is serene:
It dwells in another heaven and earth belonging to no man.
The peach trees are in flower, and the water flows on.

Three with the Moon and His Shadow

With a jar of wine I sit by the flowering trees,
I drink alone, and where are my friends?
Ah, the moon above looks down on me;
I call and lift my cup to his brightness.
And see, there goes my shadow before me,
Hoo! We're a party of three, I say—
Though the poor moon can't drink,
And my shadow but dances around me,
We're all friends tonight,
The drinker, the moon, and the shadow.
Let our revelry be meet for the springtime!

I sing, the wild moon wanders the sky.
I dance, my shadow goes tumbling about.
While we're awake, let us join in carousal;
Only sweet drunkenness shall ever part us.
Let us pledge a friendship no mortals know,
And often hail each other at evening
Far across the vast and vaporous space!

An Exhortation

Do you not see the waters of the Yellow River
Come flowing from the sky?
The swift stream pours into the sea and returns nevermore.
Do you not see high on yonder tower
A white-haired one sorrowing before his bright mirror?
In the morning those locks were like black silk,
In the evening they are all snow.
Let us, while we may, taste the old delights,
And leave not the gold cask of wine
To stand alone in the moonlight!

Gods have bestowed our genius on us;
They will also find its use one day.
Be not loathe, therefore, to spend
Even a thousand gold pieces! Your money will come back.
Kill the sheep, slay the ox, and carouse!
Truly you should drink three hundred cups in a round!

Chin, chin, my friend!
Dear Tan-chiu, too.
To you I offer wine, you must not refuse it.
Now I will sing a snatch of song. Lend ear and hearken!
Little I prize gongs and drums and sweet-meats,
I desire only the long ecstasy of wine,
And desire not to awaken.

Since the days of old, the wise and the good
Have been left alone in their solitude,
While merry drinkers have achieved enviable fame.
The king of Chen would feast in ancient days
At his palace of peace and pleasure;
Ten thousand measures of wine there were,
And reckless revelry forever.

Now let you and I buy wine today!
Why say we have not the price?
My horse spotted with five flowers,
My fur-coat worth a thousand pieces of gold,

These I will take out, and call my boy
To barter them for sweet wine.
And with you twain, let me forget
The sorrow of ten thousand ages!

Before the Cask of Wine

The spring wind comes from the east and quickly passes,
Leaving faint ripples in the wine of the golden bowl.
The flowers fall, flake after flake, myriads together.

You, pretty girl, wine-flushed,
Your rosy face is rosier still.
How long may the peach and plum trees flower
By the green-painted house?
The fleeting light deceives man,
Brings soon the stumbling age.

Rise and dance
In the westering sun,
While the urge of youthful years is yet unsubdued!
What avails to lament after one's hair has turned white
     like silken threads?

ANTAL
c. 750

from **Tiruppavai**

1

ON THIS AUSPICIOUS DAY,
full moon in the month of Markali,[159]
come beloved young maidens
of blessed Ayarpati,[160]
come adorned with jewels,
come all who wish
to bathe in the limpid waters.

Dark-bodied one,[161]
face fiery as the sun,
soft as the moon,
with eyes like pink lotus;
that young lion;
child of Yasoda[162] of beauteous eyes,
son of Nandagopa[163]
ready with the sharp spear,
that Narayana[164] himself
will fulfill our desires.

Come join us in this Markali vow,
all will applaud you.

Fulfill, O song of our vow.

4

Beloved god of rain
you dive into the ocean,
scoop and drink its waters,
you rise into the skies—
do not hold back your wealth.

Your form is dark as the hue
of the primordial lord
of the deluge.
Your lightening flashes like
the brilliant discus in the hand
of Padmanabha[165]
of broad-shouldered beauty.
Your thunder resembles
the resonance of his
Valampuri conch.

Like the stream of arrows
from his saranga bow,[166]
rain upon us, do not delay.
Let plenty come to all
as we joyously dip
in the Markali waters.

Fulfill, O song of our vow.

6

Young maidens, leave your sleep.
Do you not hear the warble
of the early morning birds?
Or the deep sound
of the silvery conch
calling from the temple of Garuda's lord?[167]

The primal cause
slumbers on the serpent
upon the cosmic waters.
He once sucked the poison
from the breast of the demoness.
With a single kick
he shattered the cart
of treacherous Sakata.

The sages and yogis
in whose heart the lord abides
are chanting his holy name.
O maiden, sleep no more.
Arise and join us
for the melodious name of Hari[168]
reverberating
through the air
has entered our souls,
brought us surpassing peace.

Fulfill, O song of our vow.

13

O maiden whose eyes
put the lotus to shame,
Venus has arisen,
Jupiter has gone to slumber;
bird sounds are ringing
through the morning air.
We extol the glorious deeds
of the lord who split open
the beak of the bird,
cut off the many heads
of wicked Ravana.[169]

All young maidens
have gathered at the pavai grounds.[170]
Will you alone
refrain from plunging
into the cool waters?
Will you alone lie abed
on this auspicious day?
Give up your pretence,
come maiden, join us.

Fulfill, O song of our vow.

30

The cowherd maidens of Ayarpati
adorned with bright jewels,
faces radiant like the moon,
worshipped at the feet of Kesava,
of Madhava[171] who churned
the ship-laden ocean.
They received from him
their heart's desire.

This tale was told
by Kaotai of the chief of pattars
of beautiful Putuvai,
who wore a garland
of cool fresh lotuses.

This reward will be theirs
who chant together
faultlessly
this Tamil garland of thirty songs—
the grace of Tirumal,[172]
will be upon them—
that lord of limitless wealth,
of holy countenance and lotus eyes,
whose four great shoulders
rise high as hills.
They will live in joy
for ever more.

Fulfill, O song of our vow.

OMAR KHAYYAM
1048-1123

from **The Rubaiyat**

XII

A BOOK OF VERSES UNDERNEATH THE BOUGH,
A Jug of Wine, a Loaf of Bread—and Thou
Beside me singing in the Wilderness—
Oh, Wilderness were Paradise enow![173]

XIII

Some for the Glories of This World; and some
Sigh for the Prophet's Paradise to come;
Ah, take the Cash, and let the Credit go,
Nor heed the rumble of a distant Drum![174]

XXIV

Ah, make the most of what we yet may spend,
Before we too into the Dust descend;
Dust into Dust, and under Dust to lie
Sans Wine, sans Song, sans Singer, and—sans End!

XXXV

Then to the lip of this poor earthen Urn
I leaned, the Secret of my Life to learn:
And Lip to Lip it murmured—"While you live
Drink!—for, once dead, you never shall return."

LIII

But if in vain, down on the stubborn floor
Of Earth, and up to Heav'n's unopening Door
You gaze To-day, while You are You—how then
To-morrow, You when shall be You no more?

LV

You know, my Friends, with what a brave Carouse
I made a Second Marriage in my house;
Divorced old barren Reason from my Bed
And took the Daughter of the Vine to Spouse.

LVI

For "Is" and "Is-not" though with Rule and Line
And "Up" and "Down" by Logic I define,
Of all that one should care to fathom,
Was never deep in anything but—Wine.

LVIII

And lately, by the Tavern Door agape,
Came shining through the Dusk an Angel Shape
Bearing a Vessel on his Shoulder; and
He bid me taste of it; and 'twas—the Grape!

LIX

The Grape that can with Logic absolute
The Two-and-Seventy jarring Sects confute:
The sovereign Alchemist that in a trice
Life's leaden metal into Gold transmute.

LXI

Why, be this Juice the growth of God, who dare
Blaspheme the twisted tendril as a Snare?
A Blessing, we should use it, should we not?
And if a Curse—why, then, Who set it there?

LXIV

Strange, is it not? That of the myriads who
Before us passed the door of Darkness through,
Not one returns to tell us of the Road,
Which to discover we must travel too.

LXV

The Revelations of Devout and Learned
Who rose before us, and as Prophets burned,
Are all but Stories, which, awoke from Sleep,
They told their comrades, and to Sleep returned.

LXVI

I sent my Soul through the Invisible,
Some letter of that After-life to spell:
And by and by my Soul returned to me,
And answered "I Myself am Heav'n and Hell:"

LXVII

Heav'n but the Vision of fulfilled Desire,
And Hell the Shadow from a Soul on fire,
Cast on the Darkness into which Ourselves,
So late emerged from, shall so soon expire.

LXXIV

Yesterday This Day's Madness did prepare;
To-morrow's Silence, Triumph, or Despair:
Drink! For you know not whence you came, nor why:
Drink! For you know not why you go, nor where.

XCI

Ah, with the Grape my fading Life provide,
And wash the Body whence the Life has died,
And lay me, shrouded in the living Leaf,
By some not unfrequented Garden-side.

XCII

That ev'n my buried Ashes such a snare
Of Vintage shall fling up into the Air
As not a True-believer passing by
But shall be overtaken unaware.

XCIII

Indeed the Idols I have loved so long
Have done my credit in this World much wrong:
Have drowned my Glory in a shallow Cup
And sold my Reputation for a Song.

XCIV

Indeed, indeed, Repentance of before
I swore—but was I sober when I swore?
And then and then came Spring, and Rose-in-hand
My thread-bare Penitence apieces tore.

XCVII

Would but the Desert of the Fountain yield
One glimpse—if dimly, yet indeed, revealed,
To which the fainting Traveler might spring,
As springs the trampled herbage of the field!

XCIX

Ah, Love! Could you and I with Him conspire
To grasp this sorry Scheme of Things entire,
Would not we shatter it to bits—and then
Re-mould it nearer to the Heart's Desire!

C

Yon rising Moon that looks for us again—
How oft hereafter will she wax and wane;
How oft hereafter rising look for us
Through this same Garden—and for one in vain!

CI

And when like her, oh, Saki,[175] you shall pass
Among the Guests Star-scattered on the Grass,
And in your joyous errand reach the spot
Where I made One—turn down an empty Glass!

JETSUN MILAREPA
c. 1052-1135

9

As HAPPY AS A LAYMAN DELIVERED FROM A PIT,
    so is the sage when he has renounced his inheritance.
As happy as a good horse freed from his halter,
    so is the sage when he has transcended partiality.
As happy as a beast dwelling unwounded,
    so is the sage who dwells alone.
As happy as the eagle flying high in the firmament,
    so is the sage who is settled, contemplating.
As happy as the icy wind rushing through the air,
    so is the sage whose path is unhindered.
As happy as the shepherd keeping blessed white sheep,
    so is the sage who keeps the clear void of mind.
As happy as princely Mount Meru in the centre of the universe,
    so is the sage who is immutable.
As happy as the stream of a great river,
    so is the sage who enjoys the stream of thought.
As happy as the corpse in a cemetery,
    so is the sage who forsakes this world's affairs.
As happy as the stone cast into the sea,
    so is the sage who will not return.
As happy as the sun rising in the heavens,
    so is the sage whose light shines for all.
As happy as the leaf plucked from the plane of a tree,
    so is the sage who will not be born again.
This is the song of the sage's twelve happinesses;
    may all of you quicken the faith and practice it.

12

To be resolved to abandon selfishness is joy.
To renounce the love of home is joy.
To be free from the village magistrate is joy.

To make no theft of the common store is joy.
Not to hanker for a householder's estate is joy.
Not to have a reason for covetousness is joy.
To be rich in spiritual wealth is joy.
To ignore the misery of gaining a livelihood is joy.
To have no fear of loss or diminution is joy.
To be unafraid of corruption is joy.
To have assurance deep within the heart is joy.
To be untrammeled by the almsgiver's self-interest is joy.
To be unwearying in help is joy.
To live without hypocrisy is joy.
To walk in the faith in every deed is joy.
To be untired by a fondness for journeying is joy.
To have no fear of sudden death is joy.
To be unafraid of robbery is joy.
To meet furtherance of holiness is joy.
To shun evil deeds is joy.
To be diligent in works of piety is joy.
To have done with the harmful spirit of anger is joy.
To eschew pride and envy is joy.

GONZALO DE BERCEO
1180-1246

The Praise of Spring

I, GONZALO DE BERCEO, IN THE GENTLE SUMMERTIDE,[176]
Wending upon a pilgrimage, came to a meadow's side;
All green was it and beautiful, with flowers far and wide,—
A pleasant spot, I ween,[177] wherein the traveler might abide.

Flowers with the sweetest odors filled all the sunny air,
And not alone refreshed the sense, but stole the mind from every care;
On every side a fountain gushed, whose waters pure and fair,
Ice-cold beneath the summer sun, but warm in winter were.

There on the thick and shadowy trees, amid the foliage green,
Were the fig and the pomegranate,[178] the pear and apple seen;
And other fruits of various kinds, the tufted leaves between,
None were unpleasant to the taste and none decayed, I ween.

The verdure of the meadow green, the odor of the flowers,
The grateful shadows of the trees, tempered with fragrant showers,
Refreshed me in the burning heat of the sultry noontide hours;
Oh, one might live upon the balm and fragrance of those bowers!

Ne'er had I found on earth a spot that had such power to please,
Such shadows from the summer sun, such odors on the breeze;
I threw my mantle on the ground, that I might rest at ease,
And stretched upon the greensward lay in the shadow of the trees.

There soft reclining in the shade, all cares beside me flung,
I heard the soft and mellow notes that through the woodland rung;
Ear never listened to a strain, for instrument or tongue,
So mellow and harmonious as the songs above me sung.

ST. FRANCIS OF ASSISI
1181/82-1226

Canticle of the Sun

(Here begin the praises of the creatures which the blessed Francis made
to the praise and honor of God while he was ill at St. Damian's):

MOST HIGH, OMNIPOTENT, GOOD LORD,[179]
Praise, glory and honor and benediction all, are Thine.
To Thee alone do they belong, most High,
And there is no man fit to mention Thee.
Praise be to Thee, my Lord, with all Thy creatures,
Especially to my worshipful brother sun,
The which lights up the day, and through him dost Thou brightness
    give;
And beautiful is he and radiant with splendor great;
Of Thee, most High, signification gives.
Praised be my Lord, for sister moon and for the stars,
In heaven Thou hast formed them clear and precious and fair.
Praised be my Lord for brother wind
And for the air and clouds and fair and every kind of weather,
By the which Thou givest to Thy creatures nourishment.
Praised be my Lord for sister water,
The which is greatly helpful and humble and precious and pure.
Praised be my Lord for brother fire,
By the which Thou lightest up the dark.
And fair is he and gay and mighty and strong.
Praised be my Lord for our sister, mother earth,
The which sustains and keeps us
And brings forth diverse fruits with grass and flowers bright.
Praised be my Lord for those who for Thy love forgive
And weakness bear and tribulation.
Blessed those who shall in peace endure,
For by Thee, most High, shall they be crowned.
Praised be my Lord for our sister, the bodily death,
From the which no living man can flee.
Woe to them who die in mortal sin;

Blessed those who shall find themselves in Thy most holy will,
For the second death shall do them no ill.
Praise ye and bless ye my Lord, and give Him thanks,
And be subject unto Him with great humility.

RUMI
1207-1273

The Moon-Soul and the Sea

AT MORNING-TIDE A MOON APPEARED IN THE SKY,[180]
And descended from the sky and gazed on me.
Like a falcon which snatches a bird at the time of hunting,
That moon snatched me up and coursed over the sky.
When I looked at myself, I saw myself no more,
Because in that moon my body became by grace even as soul.
When I traveled in soul, I saw naught save the moon,
Till the secret of the Eternal Theophany[181] was revealed.
The nine spheres[182] of heaven were all merged in that moon,
The vessel of my being was completely hidden in the sea.
The sea broke into waves, and again Wisdom rose
And cast abroad a voice; so it happened and thus it befell.
Foamed the sea, and at every foam-fleck
Something took figure and something was bodied forth.
Every foam-fleck of body, which received a sign from that sea,
Melted straightway and turned to spirit in this ocean.

The Finding of the Beloved

I was on that day when the Names were not,
Nor any sign of existence endowed with name,
By me Names and Named were brought to view
On the day when there was not "I" and "We"
For a sign, the tip of the Beloved's curl became a
    center of revelation;
As yet the tip of that curl was not.
Cross and Christians, from end to end,
I surveyed; He was not on the Cross.
I went to the idol-temple, to the ancient pagoda;
No trace was visible there.
I went to the mountains of Heart and Candahar;
I looked; He was not in that hill-and-dale.

I gazed into my own heart;
There I saw Him; He was nowhere else.

Love Sounds the Music of the Spheres

O, soul, if thou, too, would be free,
    Then love the Love that shuts thee in.
'Tis Love that twists every snare;
    'Tis Love that snaps the bond of sin;
Love sounds the Music of the Spheres;
    Love echoes through Earth's harshest din.
The world is God's pure mirror clear,
    To eyes when free from clouds within.
With Love's own eyes the Mirror view,
    And there see God to self akin.[183]

I Saw the Winter Weaving

I saw the winter weaving from flakes a robe of Death;
And the spring found earth in mourning, all naked, lone, and bare.
I heard Time's loom a-whirring that wove the Sun's dim Veil;
I saw a worm a-weaving in Life-threads its own lair.
I saw the Great was smallest, and saw the Smallest Great;
For God had set His likeness on all the things that were.

The Music of Love

Hail to thee, then, O Love, sweet madness!
Thou who heals all our infirmities!
Who art the Physician of our pride and self-conceit!
Who art our Plato and our Galen![184]
Love exalts our earthly bodies to heaven,
And makes the very hills to dance with joy!
O lover, 'twas Love that gave life to Mount Sinai,
When "it quaked, and Moses fell down in a swoon."
Did my Beloved only touch me with His lips,
I, too, like a flute, would burst out into melody.

The Silence of Love

Love is the Astrolabe[185] of God's mysteries.
A lover may hanker after this love or that love,
But at the least he is drawn to the King of Love.
However much we describe and explain Love,
When we fall in love we are ashamed of our words.
Explanation by tongue makes most things clear,
But Love unexplained is better.

The Flame of Love

How long wilt thou dwell on words and superficialities?
A burning heart is what I want; consort with burning!
Kindle in thy heart the flame of Love,
And burn up utterly thoughts and fine expressions.
O Moses! The loves of fair rites are one class,
They whose hearts and souls burn with Love another.

All Religions Are One

In the adorations and benedictions of righteous men
The praises of all the prophets are kneaded together.
All their praises are mingled together into one stream,
All the vessels are emptied into one ewer.[186]
Because He that is praised is, in fact, only One.
Because all praises are directed towards God's Light,
These various forms and figures are borrowed from it.

Through Love

Through Love bitter things become sweet;[187]
Through Love pieces of copper become golden.
Through Love dregs[188] become clear;
Through Love pains become healing.
Through Love the dead is made living;
Through Love the king is made a slave.

This Is Love

This is Love: to fly heavenward;
To rend, every instant, a hundred veils.
The first moment, to renounce life;
The last step, to fare without feet.
To regard this world as invisible,
Not to see what appears to one's self.
"O heart," I said, "may it bless thee
To have entered the circle of lovers,
To look beyond the range of the eye,
To penetrate the windings of the bosom!
When did this breath come to thee, O my soul,
When this throbbing, O my heart?
O bird, speak the language of birds:
I can understand thy hidden meaning."
The soul answered: "I was in the Divine Factory
While the house of water and earth was a-baking.
I was flying away from the earthly workshop
While the workshop was being created.
When I could resist no more, they dragged me
To mold me into shape like a ball."

Thou and I

Happy the moment when we are seated in the palace, thou and I,
With two forms and with two figures but with one soul, thou and I.
The colors of the orchard and the voices of the birds will bestow
    immortality
At the time when we come into the garden, thou and I.
The stars of heaven will come to gaze upon us:
We shall show them the moon herself, thou and I.
Thou and I, individuals no more, shall be mingled in ecstasy,
Joyful and secure from foolish babble, thou and I.
All the bright-plumed birds of heaven will devour their hearts with envy
In the place where we shall laugh in such Fashion, thou and I.
This is the greatest wonder, that thou and I, sitting here in the same
    nook,
Are at this moment in Iraq and Khorasan, thou and I.

Unknowing

What is to be done, O Moslems? For I do not recognize myself.
I am neither Christian nor Jew nor Gabr[189] nor Moslem.
I am not of the East nor of the West nor of the land nor of the sea;
I am not of Nature's mint nor of the circling heavens.
I am not of earth nor of water nor of air nor of fire;
I am not of the empyrean nor of the dust nor of existence nor of entity.
I am not of India nor of China nor of Bulghar nor of Saqsin;
I am not of the kingdom of Iraq nor of the country of Khorasan.
I am not of this world nor of the next nor of Paradise nor of Hell;
I am not of Adam nor of Eve nor of Eden and Rizwan.[190]
My place is the Placeless, my trace is the Traceless;
'Tis neither body nor soul, for I belong to the soul of the Beloved.
I have put duality away, I have seen that the two worlds are one;
One I seek, One I know, One I see, One I call.
He is the First, He is the Last, He is the Outward, He is the Inward;
I know none other than "Ya Hu" and "Ya man Hu."[191]
I am intoxicated with Love's cup, the two worlds have passed out of
    my ken;
I have no business save carouse and revelry.
If once in my life I spent a moment without thee,
From that time and that hour I repent of my life.
If once in this world I win a moment with thee,
I will trample on both worlds, I will dance in triumph forever.
O Shamsi Tabriz,[192] I am so drunken in this world,
That except of drunkenness and revelry I have no tale to tell.

HAFIZ
1315-1390

Ode 7

HEART, HAVE YOU HEARD THE NEWS!
The Spring has come back—have you heard!
With little green shoot and little pink bud, and the little new-hatched
    bird,
And the Rose—yes! yes! The Rose—
Nightingale, have you heard the news!
The Rose has come back and the green and the blue,
And everything is as new as the dew—
New nightingale, new rose.[193]

Wind of the east, flower-footed breeze,
O take my love to the budding trees,
To the cypress take it, and take it, too,
To the tender nurslings of meadows and leas,
To the basil take it, messenger breeze,
And I send it, my love, to you.

So glad am I of the new-found sun,
I believe I could kiss the tavern door;
Why, I could sweep the tavern floor
With the lashes of my eyes!

O April skies!
The winter's done,
O April skies!
The spring's begun;
And honey-humming
Summer's coming
Close behind;
O April skies!
Even the tavern girl is kind.

Hafiz, remember well how short is spring,
And drain the good days deep ere they depart;
Thou nightingale that shall forever sing
Rose of thine own imperishable art!

Brothers, attend
How ye shall spend
This fleeting treasure
Of days that pass:
Fill ye your measure
With present pleasure,
The deep sweet glass,
And love and leisure,
And sunny grass.

Let the pious thunder
Of heaven and hell—
He drinks as well;
Let the proud man rear
His lofty towers—
Have ye no fear;
The little flowers
That grow thereunder
Shall last as long—
Or a little song.

Not our Most High Lord
The Sultan's sword
Can more command,
When he comes to die,
Than you and I
Of simple birth
Can ask of earth—
A little land
In which to lie.

And, even now,
Who more would ask
Than just to bask
The blue sky under:

A little grass,
Wine in the glass,
One's liberty
And Love and wonder:
This, Hafiz, is
Felicity.

Ode 26

Thrice holy night! O hallowed rising moon!
O waiting trees! O stars that burn so bright!
O radiant planet, was it yours the boon?
This is the night of my first wondering look
Into her eyes, the night she came to me
Right out of heaven—like the holy book;
O bright beginning of felicity,
This is the night.

To-night the Mussulman[194] is at his prayers;
Spinning in solemn fury circle-wise,
The dervish[195] chants; for holy church declares
The Koran like a star shot from the skies—
This very night.

I also shall observe the sacred rites:
Bent low before her on adoring knees,
In a strong circle of my faithful love
I'll keep her safe as gold in sanctuaries.
O river singing to the stars above!
O Night of Nights!

So beautiful the face of her I love,
Heaven, like a proud and eager tiring-maid,
Holds up the moon as mirror for her gaze;
And O when all her beauty is arrayed,
She is a being so exceeding bright,
Even the burnished sun, with morn ablaze,
Shows like mere dust beneath her courser's[196] feet—
Yea! All her body is so filled with light.

In her all living brightness is complete,
Bounded in her, as in some blinding sphere;
And to the sun himself, till she appear,
Day is as night.

Ah! Sufi, can you dream I will give up
A love like this—for pious platitude,
Or cease to crush the grape into the cup!
I, Sufi, may be wrong, you may be right—
Hafiz must tread his self-appointed way
And on her red lips find his heavenly food.
If you must talk, O talk some other day—
But not to-night.

Ode 48

No! Saki—take the wine away!
I have no need of it today;
So drunk am I with adoration,
No longer have I any need
Of commonplace intoxication.

How should a man whose eyes may drink
Her beauty, like the Northern Star,
In a delicious meditation,
Remain contented any more
With common wine out of a jar!
No, Saki—take the wine away;
Though it were poured from heaven's brink,
I'd spill it on the tavern floor—
I have no need of it to-day.

Of course, I'll go on getting drunk,
But it will be another way—
A more august inebriation;
And I'm afraid, old Magian monk,[197]
You'll almost have to close your door
When Hafiz buys your wine no more—
That is the worst of reformation.

Ode 330

How my heart aches with happiness to-night—
Here by your shadowy side under the moon!
How strange your face is in the ghostly light—
Under the willows underneath the moon.
O spirit! O child! O unconceived bliss!
For this good night, kind Fates, we give good thanks.
We shall not know again a night like this
Under the willows on the river-banks.

Love, shall I bid the Saki bring the wine?
She waits but yonder underneath the moon;
I have already drunken deep of mine,
Here at these stars—just underneath the moon.
Ah! How it tips the tongue with witty fire,
And makes one's fancy play a thousand pranks!
O! I could sing—yea! Will I to this lyre,
Under the willows on the river-banks.

The fairest jewels of my purest thought
Here will I deck you with under the moon—
Strange deep-sea pearls up many a fathom brought
From my deep heart, far underneath the moon;
And from Earth's center my spirit shall bring to light
Gems without name and number for my bride—
The bride that nature gave me, this fair night,
Under the willows on the river-side.

How sweetly runs the river round yon bend—
O Ruknabad[198] is fair under the moon!
Would that this night of nights might never end,
Or we might die thus underneath the moon!
Too soon shall morning take the stars away,
And all the world be up and open-eyed,
This magic night be turned to common day—
Under the willows on the river-side.

Hafiz must throw him rue upon the fire,
Lest, for this happy night under the moon,
The evil eye of envious desire
Fall on him, singing underneath the moon.

LALLA (LAL DED)
1320-1392

1

WHEN BY REPEATED PRACTICE OF YOGA THE WHOLE EXPANSE OF THE VISIBLE
   universe hath ascended to absorption;
When the qualified universe hath become merged with the ether;
When the ethereal Void itself hath become dissolved, then naught but
   the Weal[199] hath remained.
The true doctrine, O Brahmana,[200] is but this alone.

9

When the sun disappeared, then came the moonlight;
When the moon disappeared, then only mind remained;
When absorbed in the Infinite mind disappeared, then naught
   anywhere was left;
Earth, ether, and sky all took their departure.

47

It is a lake so tiny that in it a mustard seed findeth no room.
Yet from that lake doth every one drink water.
And into it do deer, jackals, rhinoceroses, and sea-elephants
Keep falling, falling, almost before they have time to become born.

58

Whate'er work I did, that was my worship.
Whate'er I uttered with my tongue, that was a mystic formula.
This recognition, and this alone, became one with my body,
That this alone is the essence of the scriptures of the Supreme Shiva.

68

I, Lalla, passed in through the door of the jasmine-garden of my soul.
And there, O Joy! Saw I Shiva seated united with His Shakti.[201]
There became I absorbed in the lake of nectar.
Now, what can existence do unto me?
For, even though alive, I shall in it be dead.

93

The soul is ever new and new; the moon is ever new and new.
So saw I the waste of waters ever new and new.
But since I, Lalla, scoured my body and my mind,
I, Lalla, am ever new and new.

94

My teacher spake to me but one precept.
He said unto me, "from without enter thou inmost part."
That to me became a rule and a precept,
And therefore naked began I to dance.

95

Give the heart to the bellows, like as the blacksmith gives breath to
    the bellows,
And your iron will become gold.
Now it is early morning, seek out your Friend.
A man will not find a shore to the sea, neither is there a bridge over it
Nor any other means of crossing.
Make to yourself wings and fly.
Now it is early morning, seek out your Friend.

KABIR
1440-1518

VI

The moon shines in my body, but my blind eyes cannot see it:
The moon is within me, and so is the sun.
The unstruck drum[202] of Eternity is sounded within me;
    but my deaf ears cannot hear it.
So long as man clamors for the *I* and the *Mine,* his works are as naught:
When all love of the *I* and the *Mine* is dead,
    then the work of the Lord is done.
For work has no other aim than the getting of knowledge:
When that comes, then work is put away.
The flower blooms for the fruit: when the fruit comes, the flower withers.
The musk is in the deer, but it seeks it not within itself:
    it wanders in quest of grass.

IX

O how may I ever express that secret word?
O how can I say He is not like this, and He is like that?
If I say that He is within me, the universe is ashamed:
If I say that He is without me, it is falsehood.
He makes the inner and the outer worlds to be indivisibly one;
The conscious and the unconscious, both are His footstools.
He is neither manifest nor hidden, He is neither revealed nor unrevealed:
There are no words to tell that which He is.

XXIII

The shadows of evening fall thick and deep, and the darkness of
    love envelops the body and the mind.
Open the window to the west, and be lost in the sky of love;
Drink the sweet honey that steeps the petals of the lotus of the heart.
Receive the waves in your body: what splendor is in the region of the
    sea!

Hark! The sounds of conches and bells are rising.
Kabir says: "O brother, behold! The Lord is in this vessel of my body."

XXVI

All things are created by the Om;[203]
The love-form is His body.
He is without form, without quality, without decay:
Seek thou union with Him!
But that formless God takes a thousand forms in the eyes of His
    creatures:
He is pure and indestructible,
His form is infinite and fathomless,
He dances in rapture, and waves of form arise from His dance.
The body and the mind cannot contain themselves,
    when they are touched by His great joy.
He is immersed in all consciousness, all joys, and all sorrows;
He has no beginning and no end;
He holds all within His bliss.

XXXII

Dance, my heart! Dance to-day with joy.
The strains of love fill the days and the nights with music,
    and the world is listening to its melodies:
Mad with joy, life and death dance to the rhythm of this music.
The hills and the sea and the earth dance.
The world of man dances in laughter and tears.
Why put on the robe of the monk, and live aloof from the world in
    lonely pride?
Behold! My heart dances in the delight of a hundred arts; and the
    Creator is well pleased.

XXXIII

Where is the need of words, when love has made drunken the heart?
I have wrapped the diamond in my cloak; why open it again and again?

When its load was light, the pan of the balance went up: now it is full,
    where is the need for weighing?
The swan has taken its flight to the lake beyond the mountains;
    why should it search for the pools and ditches anymore?
Your Lord dwells within you: why need your outward eyes be opened?
Kabir says: "Listen, my brother! My Lord, who ravishes my eyes,
    has united Himself with me."

XLI

O Sadhu![204] The simple union is the best. Since the day when I met
    with my Lord, there has been no end to the sport of our love.
I shut not my eyes, I close not my ears, I do not mortify my body;
I see with eyes open and smile, and behold His beauty everywhere:
I utter His Name, and whatever I see, it reminds me of Him; whatever
    I do: it becomes His worship.
The rising and the setting are one to me; all contradictions are solved.
Wherever I go, I move round Him,
All I achieve is His service:
When I lie down, I lie prostrate at His feet.
He is the only adorable one to me: I have none other.
My tongue has left off impure words, it sings His glory day and night:
Whether I rise or sit down, I can never forget Him;
    for the rhythm of His music beats in my ears.
Kabir says: "My heart is frenzied, and I disclose in my soul what is
    hidden.
I am immersed in that one great bliss which transcends all pleasure
    and pain."

XLIV

The Hidden Banner is planted in the temple of the sky; there the blue
    canopy decked with the moon and set with bright jewels is spread.
There the light of the sun and the moon is shining: still your mind to
    silence before that splendor.
Kabir says: "He who has drunk of this nectar, wanders like one
    who is mad."

XLVII

There is a strange tree, which stands without roots and bears fruits
    without blossoming;
It has no branches and no leaves, it is lotus all over.
Two birds sing there; one is the Guru, and the other the disciple:
The disciple chooses the manifold fruits of life and tastes them,
    and the Guru beholds him in joy.
What Kabir says is hard to understand: "The bird is beyond seeking,
    yet it is most clearly visible.
The Formless is in the midst of all forms. I sing the glory of forms."

XLVIII

I have stilled my restless mind, and my heart is radiant:
    for in Thatness I have seen beyond Thatness.[205]
In company I have seen the Comrade Himself.
Living in bondage, I have set myself free: I have broken away from
    the clutch of all narrowness.
Kabir says: "I have attained the unattainable, and my heart is
    colored with the color of love."

L

The flute of the Infinite is played without ceasing, and its sound is love:
When love renounces all limits, it reaches truth.
How widely the fragrance spreads! It has no end, nothing stands in its
    way.
The form of this melody is bright like a million suns:
    incomparably sounds the vina,[206] the vina of the notes of truth.

LIV

Have you not heard the tune which the Unstruck Music is playing?
In the midst of the chamber the harp of joy is gently and sweetly played;
    and where is the need of going without to hear it?

If you have not drunk of the nectar of that One Love,
    what boots it though you should purge yourself of all stains?
The Kazi[207] is searching the words of the Koran, and instructing others:
    but if his heart be not steeped in that love, what does it avail,
    though he be a teacher of men?
The Yogi dyes his garments with red: but if he knows naught of that
    color of love, what does it avail though his garments be tinted?
Kabir says: "Whether I be in the temple or the balcony,
    in the camp or in the flower garden,
I tell you truly that every moment my Lord is taking His delight in me."

LVIII

Empty the Cup! O be drunken!
Drink the divine nectar of His Name!
Kabir says: "Listen to me, dear Sadhu!
From the sole of the foot to the crown of the
    head this mind is filled with poison."

LXIX

If God be within the mosque, then to whom does this world belong?
If Ram be within the image which you find upon your pilgrimage,
    then who is there to know what happens without?
Hari is in the East: Allah is in the West. Look within your heart,
    for there you will find both Karim and Ram;
All the men and women of the world are His living forms.
Kabir is the child of Allah and of Ram: He is my Guru, He is my Pir.[208]

LXXII

The jewel is lost in the mud, and all are seeking for it;
Some look for it in the east, and some in the west;
    some in the water and some amongst stones.
But the servant Kabir has appraised it at its true value,
    and has wrapped it with care in the end of the mantle of his heart.

LXXVII

O my heart! Let us go to that country where dwells the Beloved,
 the ravisher of my heart!
There Love is filling her pitcher from the well, yet she has no rope
 wherewith to draw water;
There the clouds do not cover the sky, yet the rain falls down
 in gentle showers:
O bodiless one! Do not sit on your doorstep; go forth and bathe
 yourself in that rain!
There it is ever moonlight and never dark; and who speaks of one sun
 only?
That land is illuminate with the rays of a million suns.

LXXXIII

The harp gives forth murmurous music; and the dance goes on
 without hands and feet.
It is played without fingers, it is heard without ears:
 for He is the ear, and He is the listener.
The gate is locked, but within there is fragrance: and there the
 meeting is seen of none.
The wise shall understand it.

XCVII

The Lord is in me, the Lord is in you, as life is in every seed.
O servant! Put false pride away, and seek for Him within you.
A million suns are ablaze with light,
The sea of blue spreads in the sky,
The fever of life is stilled, and all stains are washed away;
 when I sit in the midst of that world.
Hark to the unstruck bells and drums! Take your delight in love!
Rains pour down without water, and the rivers are streams of light.
One Love it is that pervades the whole world, few there are who
 know it fully:
They are blind who hope to see it by the light of reason,
 that reason which is the cause of separation—

The House of Reason is very far away!
How blessed is Kabir, that amidst this great joy he sings within
    his own vessel.
It is the music of the meeting of soul with soul;
It is the music of the forgetting of sorrows;
It is the music that transcends all coming in and all going forth.

C

Hang up the swing of love to-day! Hang the body and the mind
    between the arms of the Beloved, in the ecstasy of love's joy:
Bring the tearful streams of the rainy clouds to your eyes,
    and cover your heart with the shadow of darkness:
Bring your face nearer to His ear, and speak of the deepest longings
    of your heart.
Kabir says: "Listen to me, brother! Bring the vision of the Beloved
    in your heart."

MIRABAI
c.1498-1547

I Shall Dance

I SHALL DANCE BEFORE THE LORD OF MY HEART, AND THRILL HIM WITH MY ABANDON
  and beg His love.
Love will be the ringing anklet round my flying feet, and emotion will be
  the flowing garment round my swaying figure.
I shall scatter to the four winds all restraints born of high birth or social
  position.
I shall go straight into the arms of my beloved Lord.

In the Company of Saints

In the company of saints I have lost all sense of shame.
  It is well known how I have watered with tears the creeper of love.
At last it has flowered and given me fruits of nectar.
  When I came, the Bhaktas[209] knew but the world wept.
Now I have none with me, no attendant, no friends, no relations.
  I churned the curds and took the pure butter, discarding the rest.
Mira is now the servant of dear Giridhar,[210] whatever happens.

The Charm of Thy Face

The charm of thy face has made me captive, my beloved.
When once I saw that face the whole world lost its charm for me and
  my mind remained no longer attached to it.
To go for the pleasures of this world is like trying to hold water in a sieve.
I can now disdain those.
Lucky is Mira; her hopes have come true.
Now am I the most fortunate of all.

122

Oh Beloved

Oh beloved, how can I express myself fully to thee.
I was born with this love for thee; how can I quench it now?
Looking at thy face, oh dear, my love is born anew.
Come now to my cottage, oh Giridhar; the girls will sing sweet songs
    at thy approach and I will dedicate my body and soul to thee.
Mira says, oh beloved of the gopis,[211] I have become a bramacharini;[212]
    and I, thy servant, have taken absolute refuge at thy feet.
Tarry no more.

It Is Raining

It is raining outside and my beloved is with me in my cottage.
Light showers are falling and my cup is full to the brim.
It is a union after age-long separation, and I am afraid of losing my
    beloved any moment.
Says Mira, "My Lord, you have satisfied my great thirst for love and
    have accepted me, oh my husband of former births."

Beloved, I Have Dyed Myself

Beloved, I have dyed myself with the dye of thy love.
The beloved of others live abroad and so they send letters to them,
    but my beloved lives within my heart and with him I am day and
        night.
Dressed in beautiful garments I go out to play with my beloved.
In play I meet him and I hold him to me.
Others get drunk by drinking wine but I get drunk without that.
I drink of the wine of love and intoxicated I go about day and night.
I have lighted the lamp of constant remembrance and my mind is the
    wick which burns.
The oil comes from the unknowable mill and the lamp burns ever
    and ever.
Giridhar is the Lord of Mira and she is the servant of his feet.

JUAN DE LA CRUZ
(St. John of the Cross)
1542-1591

The Dark Night of the Soul

IN A DARK NIGHT,
With anxious love inflamed,
O, happy lot!
Forth unobserved I went,
My house being now at rest.

In darkness and in safety,
By the secret ladder, disguised,
O, happy lot!
In darkness and concealment,
My house being now at rest.

In that happy night,
In secret, seen of none,
Seeing nought myself,
Without other light or guide
Save that which in my heart was burning.

That light guided me
More surely than the noonday sun
To the place where He was waiting for me,
Whom I knew well,
And where none appeared.

O, guiding night;
O, night more lovely than the dawn;
O, night that has united
The lover with His beloved,
And changed her into her love.

On my flowery bosom,
Kept whole for Him alone,

There he reposed and slept;
And I cherished Him, and the waving
Of the cedars fanned Him.

As his hair floated in the breeze
That from the turret blew,
He struck me on the neck
With his gentle hand,
And all sensation left me.

I continued in oblivion lost,
My head was resting on my love;
Lost to all things and myself,
And, amid the lilies forgotten,
Threw all my cares away.

THOMAS CAMPION
1567-1620

Rose-Cheeked Laura

ROSE-CHEEKED LAURA, COME,
Sing thou smoothly with thy beauty's
Silent music, either other
Sweetly gracing.

Lovely forms do flow
From concent[213] divinely framed;
Heav'n is music, and thy beauty's
Birth is heavenly.

These dull notes we sing
Discords need for helps to grace them;
Only beauty purely loving
Knows no discord,

But still moves delight,
Like clear springs renewed by flowing,
Ever perfect, ever in them-
Selves eternal.

There Is a Garden in Her Face

There is a garden in her face
Where roses and white lilies grow;
A heav'nly paradise is that place
Wherein all pleasant fruits do flow.
There cherries grow which none may buy,
Till 'Cherry ripe' themselves do cry.

Those cherries fairly do enclose
Of orient pearl a double row,
Which when her lovely laughter shows,

They look like rose-buds filled with snow;
Yet them nor peer nor prince can buy,
Till 'Cherry ripe' themselves do cry.

Her eyes like angels watch them still,
Her brows like bended bows do stand,
Threat'ning with piercing frowns to kill
All that attempt with eye or hand
Those sacred cherries to come nigh,
Till 'Cherry ripe' themselves do cry.

JOHN DONNE
1572-1631

The Ecstasy

Where, like a pillow on a bed
A pregnant bank swelled up to rest
The violet's reclining head,
Sat we two, one another's best.
Our hands were firmly cemented
With a fast balm, which thence did spring;
Our eye-beams twisted, and did thread
Our eyes upon one double string;
So to engraft our hands, as yet
Was all the means to make us one,
And pictures in our eyes to get
Was all our propagation.
As 'twixt two equal armies fate
Suspends uncertain victory,
Our souls (which to advance their state
Were gone out) hung 'twixt her and me.
And whilst our souls negotiate there,
We like sepulchral[214] statues lay;
All day, the same our postures were,
And we said nothing, all the day.
If any, so by love refined
That he soul's language understood,
And by good love were grown all mind,
Within convenient distance stood,
He (though he knew not which soul spake,
Because both meant, both spake the same)
Might thence a new concoction take
And part far purer than he came.
This ecstasy doth unperplex,[215]
We said, and tell us what we love;
We see by this it was not sex,
We see we saw not what did move;
But as all several souls contain

128

Mixture of things, they know not what,
Love these mixed souls doth mix again
And makes both one, each this and that.
A single violet transplant,
The strength, the color, and the size,
(All which before was poor and scant)
Redoubles still, and multiplies.
When love with one another so
Interinanimates two souls,
That abler soul, which thence doth flow,
Defects of loneliness controls.
We then, who are this new soul, know
Of what we are composed and made,
For th' atomies of which we grow
Are souls. Whom no change can invade.
But oh alas, so long, so far,
Our bodies why do we forbear?
They are ours, though not we; we are
The intelligences, they the spheres.
We owe them thanks, because they thus
Did us, to us, at first convey,
Yielded their senses' force to us,
Nor are dross to us, but allay.
On man heaven's influence works not so,
But that it first imprints the air;
So soul into the soul may flow,
Though it to body first repair.
As our blood labors to beget
Spirits, as like souls as it can,
Because such fingers need to knit
That subtle knot which makes us man,
So must pure lovers' souls descend
T' affections, and to faculties,
Which sense may reach and apprehend,
Else a great prince in prison lies.
To our bodies turn we then, that so
Weak men on love revealed may look;
Love's mysteries in souls do grow,
But yet the body is his book.
And if some lover, such as we,

Have heard this dialogue of one,
Let him still mark us, he shall see
Small change, when we're to body gone.

BEN JONSON
1572-1637

from **Volpone**

Song: To Celia (I)

COME, MY CELIA, LET US PROVE
While we may, the sports of love;
Time will not be ours forever;
He at length our good will sever.
Spend not then his gifts in vain.
Suns that set may rise again;
But if once we lose this light,
'Tis with us perpetual night.
Why should we defer our joys?
Fame and rumor are but toys.
Cannot we delude the eyes
Of a few poor household spies,
Or his easier ears beguile,
So removed by our wile?
'Tis no sin love's fruit to steal;
But the sweet theft to reveal.
To be taken, to be seen,
These have crimes accounted been.

Song: To Celia (II)

Drink to me only with thine eyes,
    And I will pledge with mine;
Or leave a kiss but in the cup
    And I'll not look for wine.
The thirst that from the soul doth rise
    Doth ask a drink divine;
But might I of Jove's nectar sup,
    I would not change for thine.

I sent thee late a rosy wreath,
   Not so much honoring thee
As giving it a hope that there
   It could not withered be;
But thou thereon didst only breathe,
   And sent'st it back to me;
Since when it grows, and smells, I swear,
   Not of itself but thee!

TUKARAM
c. 1577-1650

426

NOUGHT AM I BUT A POOR BLIND MAN
Afoot upon the path which leads to life unbodied.
Behind me lies the life that is not life,
The life of impulse and of self.
Before me lies the life in God,
The life of peace, of full forgetfulness of earthly things,
The life of death to self.
My eyes are set beyond the world,
    On Him.
What here I saw,
I see no longer.
    But Him I see.

672

I have found the sea,
An ocean limitless.
I have opened a treasury unending,
Its jewels blaze with the luster of a thousand thousand suns,
And they blaze here, in my soul.
Of a sudden,
Without an effort of mine own,
I have heard the eternal Secret,
I have learned to know God.
Here in my life hath blossomed
The flower of the perfect union.

2479

My friends are the trees, and the creatures of the wilderness.
The birds by their songs bring me courage of heart:
    In loneliness comes to me richest delight,
I am free from men, with their petty virtues and vices:
    The sky is my canopy,
    The earth is my bed,
    There my spirit finds deepest joy.
All that my body needs is a threadbare cloak,
And a begging bowl.
The breezes of morning and evening,
These are my time-piece.
The praise of Thy name, O my God,
This is the choicest of food.
Much of that food will I forthwith[216] make ready,
And eat of it heartily!
Then will I hold sweet converse
With the Soul of my soul,
I will talk of Myself with Myself.

3204

Thou, Lord, hast lifted from mine eyes
The film of thick darkness.
Now I can see.
And what I see is this—
The whole vast universe aflame with joy in God.
Self conquered, and desire extinguished,
Now all my thought is fixed on Thee,
In love, and trust, and joy.

3297

You ask me why I sing so many songs:
I sing because I love,
Because I love my God, of whom I sing.

Nought else I care for,
Nought else remember.
In life and death,
To all eternity,
Nought, nought shall sever Him and me,
For soul is merged in soul.
Here, here,
In His great love,
Is joy supreme.

3406

True joy is not Beyond,
In some luxurious paradise,
In total loss of self within the Absolute.
True joy is here,
With Him.
Seize on that joy, with eager haste, my soul,
Here, in this world, have all thy need fulfilled,
In Him, by Him.
Pray not for utter merging,
Pray not for paradise,
Know God, take God, love God,
Now.

3734

Night is vanished,
And nevermore shall sleep bemuse me.
My home is built in God,
And there Joy have I everlastingly.
My dwelling-place is fenced around,
Its ground is cleared of idle, foolish "I" and "mine."
There do I live with Thee,
My Friend, my God,
No severance shall part us, for a moment.

ROBERT HERRICK
1591-1674

The Vine

I DREAMED THIS MORTAL PART OF MINE
Was Metamorphosed to a Vine;
Which crawling one and every way,
Enthralled my dainty Lucia.
Methought, her long small legs & thighs
I with my Tendrils did surprise;
Her Belly, Buttocks, and her Waist
By my soft Nerv'lits were embraced:
About her head I writhing hung,
And with rich clusters (hid among
The leaves) her temples I behung:
So that my Lucia seemed to me
Young Bacchus ravished by his tree.
My curls about her neck did crawl,
And arms and hands they did enthrall:
So that she could not freely stir,
(All parts there made one prisoner.)
But when I crept with leaves to hide
Those parts, which maids keep unespied,
Such fleeting pleasures there I took,
That with the fancy I awoke;
And found (Ah me!) this flesh of mine
More like a Stock, than like a Vine.

To the Virgins, to Make Much of Time

Gather ye rosebuds while ye may,
    Old time is still a-flying;
And the same flower that smiles today
    Tomorrow will be dying.
The glorious lamp of heaven the sun,
    The higher he's a-getting,

The sooner will his race be run,
    And nearer he's to setting.
That age is best which is the first,
    When youth and blood are warmer;
But being spent, the worse, and worst
    Times still succeed the former.
Then be not coy, but use your time,
    And, while ye may, go marry;
For, having lost but once your prime,
    You may forever tarry.

Cherry-Ripe

Cherry-Ripe, Ripe, Ripe, I cry,
Full and fair ones; come and buy:
If so be, you ask me where
They do grow? I answer, There,
Where my Julia's lips do smile;
There's the Land, or Cherry-Isle:
Whose Plantations fully show
All the year, where Cherries grow.

Upon Julia's Clothes

Whenas in silks my Julia goes,
Then, then, methinks, how sweetly flows
The liquefaction of her clothes!
Next, when I cast mine eyes and see
That brave vibration each way free,
—O how that glittering taketh me!

Her Legs

Fain would I kiss my Julia's dainty leg,
Which is as white and hairless as an egg.

To Dianeme

Show me thy feet; show me thy legs, thy thighs;
Show me those fleshly principalities;
Show me that hill (where smiling love doth sit)
Having a living fountain under it.
Show me thy waist; then let me therewithal,
By the ascension of thy lawn, see all.

Upon the Nipples of Julia's Breast

Have ye beheld (with much delight)
A red rose peeping through a white?
Or else a cherry, double graced,
Within a lily centre placed?
Or ever marked the pretty beam
A strawberry shows half-drowned in cream?
Or seen rich rubies blushing through
A pure smooth pearl and orient too?
So like to this, nay all the rest,
Is each neat nipplet of her breast.

ANNE BRADSTREET
1612-1672

To My Dear and Loving Husband

IF EVER TWO WERE ONE, THEN SURELY WE.
If ever man were loved by wife, then thee;
If ever wife was happy in a man,
Compare with me ye women if you can.

I prize thy love more than whole Mines of Gold,
Or all the riches that the East doth hold.
My love is such that Rivers cannot quench,
Nor ought but love from thee, give recompense.

Thy love is such I can no way repay,
The heavens reward thee manifold I pray.
Then while we live, in love let's so persevere,
That when we live no more, we may live ever.

Before the Birth of One of Her Children

All things within this fading world hath end,
Adversity doth still our joys attend;
No ties so strong, no friends so dear and sweet,
But with death's parting blow is sure to meet.
The sentence past is most irrevocable,
A common thing, yet oh, inevitable.
How soon, my Dear, death may my steps attend.
How soon't may be thy lot to lose thy friend,
We both are ignorant, yet love bids me
These farewell lines to recommend to thee,
That when that knot's untied that made us one,
I may seem thine, who in effect am none.
And if I see not half my days that's due,
What nature would, God grant to yours and you;
The many faults that well you know

I have let be interred in my oblivious grave;
If any worth or virtue were in me,
Let that live freshly in thy memory
And when thou feel'st no grief, as I no harms,
Yet love thy dead, who long lay in thine arms.
And when thy loss shall be repaid with gains
Look to my little babes, my dear remains.
And if thou love thyself, or loved'st me,
These O protect from step-dame's injury.
And if chance to thine eyes shall bring this verse,
With some sad sighs honor my absent hearse;
And kiss this paper for thy love's dear sake,
Who with salt tears this last farewell did take.

RICHARD CRASHAW
c. 1613-1649

The Flaming Heart
Upon the book and picture of the seraphical Saint Teresa,
(as she is usually expressed with a Seraphim beside her)

O HEART, THE EQUAL POISE OF LOVE'S BOTH PARTS,
Big alike with wounds and darts,
Live in these conquering leaves; live all the same,
And walk through all tongues one triumphant flame;
Live here, great heart, and love and die and kill,
And bleed and wound, and yield and conquer still.
Let this immortal life, where'er it comes,
Walk in a crowd of loves and martyrdoms;
Let mystic deaths wait on't, and wise souls be
The love-slain witnesses of this life of thee.
O sweet incendiary! show here thy art,
Upon this carcass of a hard cold heart,
Let all thy scattered shafts of light, that play
Among the leaves of thy large books of day,
Combined against this breast, at once break in
And take away from me my self and sin;
This gracious robbery shall thy bounty be,
And my best fortunes such fair spoils of me.
O thou undaunted daughter of desires!
By all thy dow'r of lights and fires,
By all the eagle in thee, all the dove,
By all thy lives and deaths of love,
By thy large draughts of intellectual day,
And by thy thirsts of love more large than they,
By all thy brim-filled bowls of fierce desire,
By thy last morning's draught of liquid fire,
By the full kingdom of that final kiss
That seized thy parting soul and sealed thee his,
By all the heav'ns thou hast in him,
Fair sister of the seraphim!
By all of him we have in thee,

Leave nothing of my self in me:
Let me so read thy life that I
Unto all life of mine may die.

ANDREW MARVELL
1621-1678

On a Drop of Dew

SEE HOW THE ORIENT DEW[217]
Shed from the bosom of the Morn
Into the blowing roses,
Yet careless of its mansion new,
For the clear region where 'twas born,
Round in itself encloses:
And in its little globe's extent
Frames, as it can, its native element.
How it the purple flow'r does slight,
Scarce touching where it lies,
But gazing back upon the skies,
Shines with a mournful light,
Like its own tear,
Because so long divided from the sphere.
Restless it rolls, and unsecure,
Trembling, lest it grow impure,
Till the warm sun pity its pain
And to the skies exhale it back again.
So the soul, that drop, that ray,
Of the clear fountain of eternal day,
Could it within the humane flow'r be seen
Rememb'ring still its former height,
Shuns the sweet leaves and blossoms green,
And, recollecting its own light,
Does, in its pure and circling thoughts, express
The greater heaven in a heaven less.
In how coy a figure wound,
Every way it turns away:
So the world-excluding round
Yet receiving in the day.
Dark beneath, but bright above,
Here disdaining, there in love.
How loose and easy hence to go,
How girt and ready to ascend,

143

Moving but on a point below,
It all about does upwards bend.
Such did the manna's sacred dew distil,
White and entire, though congealed and chill,
Congealed on Earth: but does, dissolving, run
Into the glories of th' almighty sun.

The Garden

1

How vainly men themselves amaze
To win the palm, the oak, or bays,[218]
And their incessant labors see
Crowned from some single herb or tree,
Whose short and narrow-vergèd shade
Does prudently their toils upbraid,
While all the flow'rs and trees do close
To weave the garlands of repose.

2

Fair Quiet, have I found thee here,
And Innocence, thy sister dear!
Mistaken long, I sought you then
In busy companies of men.
Your sacred plants, if here below,
Only among the plants will grow.
Society is all but rude,
To this delicious solitude.

3

No white nor red was ever seen
So am'rous as this lovely green.
Fond lovers, cruel as their flame,
Cut in these trees their mistress' name.

Little, alas, they know, or heed,
How far these beauties hers exceed!
Fair trees! wheresoe'er your barks I wound,
No name shall but your own be found.

4

When we have run our passion's heat,
Love hither makes his best retreat.
The gods, that mortal beauty chase,
Still in a tree did end their race.
Apollo hunted Daphne so,
Only that she might laurel grow.
And Pan did after Syrinx speed,
Not as a nymph, but for a reed.

5

What wondrous life is this I lead!
Ripe apples drop about my head;
The luscious clusters of the vine
Upon my mouth do crush their wine;
The nectarine and curious peach,
Into my hands themselves do reach;
Stumbling on melons, as I pass,
Ensnared with flowers, I fall on grass.

6

Meanwhile the mind, from pleasure less,
Withdraws into its happiness:
The mind, that ocean where each kind
Does straight its own resemblance find,
Yet it creates, transcending these,
Far other worlds, and other seas,
Annihilating all that's made
To a green thought in a green shade.

7

Here at the fountain's sliding foot,
Or at some fruit-tree's mossy root,
Casting the body's vest aside,
My soul into the boughs does glide:
There like a bird it sits, and sings,
Then whets, and combs its silver wings;
And, till prepared for longer flight,
Waves in its plumes the various light.

8

Such was that happy garden-state,
While man there walked without a mate:
After a place so pure and sweet,
What other help could yet be meet!
But 'twas beyond a mortal's share
To wander solitary there:
Two paradises 'twere in one
To live in Paradise alone.

9

How well the skillful gard'ner drew
Of flowers and herbs this dial new,
Where from above the milder sun
Does through a fragrant zodiac run;
And, as it works, th' industrious bee
Computes its time as well as we.
How could such sweet and wholesome hours
Be reckoned but with herbs and flowers!

HENRY VAUGHAN
1621-1695

Peace

My soul, there is a country
    Far beyond the stars,
Where stands a winged sentry
    All skilful in the wars.

There above the noise and danger,
    Sweet Peace sits crowned with smiles,
And One born in a manger
    Commands the beauteous files.

He is thy gracious Friend,
    And—O my Soul awake!—
Did in pure love descend
    To die here for thy sake.

If thou canst get but thither,
    There grows the flower of Peace,
The Rose that cannot wither,
    Thy fortress and thy ease.

Leave then thy foolish ranges,
    For none can thee secure
But One, who never changes,
    Thy God, thy life, thy cure.

The Morning Watch

O joys! infinite sweetness! with what flowers
And shoots of glory, my soul breaks and buds!
      All the long hours
      Of night and rest,
      Through the still shrouds

Of sleep, and clouds,
This dew fell on my breast;
O how it bloods,
And spirits all my earth! hark! in what rings,
And hymning circulations the quick world
Awakes, and sings!
The rising winds,
And falling springs,
Birds, beasts, all things
Adore Him in their kinds.
Thus all is hurled
In sacred hymns and order; the great chime
And symphony of Nature. Prayer is
The world in tune,
A spirit-voice,
And vocal joys,
Whose echo is heaven's bliss.
O let me climb
When I lie down! The pious soul by night
Is like a clouded star, whose beams, though said
To shed their light
Under some cloud,
Yet are above,
And shine and move
Beyond that misty shroud.
So in my bed,
That curtained grave, though sleep, like ashes, hide
My lamp and life, both shall in thee abide.

The Night
John 3.2

Through that pure virgin-shrine,
That sacred veil drawn o'er thy glorious noon
That men might look and live as glow worms shine,
And face the moon,
Wise Nicodemus saw such light
As made him know his God by night.

Most blest believer he!
Who in that land of darkness and blind eyes
Thy long expected healing wings could see,
When thou didst rise,
And what can never more be done,
Did at mid-night speak with the Sun!

O who will tell me, where
He found thee at that dead and silent hour?
What hallowed solitary ground did bear
So rare a flower,
Within whose sacred leaves did lie
The fullness of the Deity?

No mercy-seat of gold,
No dead and dusty Cherub, nor carved stone,
But his own living works did my Lord hold
And lodge alone;
Where trees and herbs did watch and peep
And wonder, while the Jews did sleep.

Dear night! This world's defeat;
The stop to busy fools; care's check and curb;
The day of Spirits; my soul's calm retreat
Which none disturb!
Christ's progress, and his prayer time;
The hours to which high Heaven doth chime;

God's silent, searching flight:
When my Lord's head is filled with dew, and all
His locks are wet with the clear drops of night;
His still, soft call;
His knocking time; the soul's dumb watch,
When Spirits their Fair Kindred catch.

Were all my loud, evil days
Calm and unhaunted as is thy dark Tent,
Whose peace but by some Angel's wing or voice
Is seldom rent;

Then I in Heaven all the long year
Would keep, and never wander here.

But living where the Sun
Doth all things wake, and where all mix and tire
Themselves and others, I consent and run
To every mire,
And by this world's ill-guiding light,
Err more than I can do by night.

There is in God (some say)
A deep but dazzling darkness, as men here
Say it is late and dusky, because they
See not all clear.
O for that night, where I in Him
Might live invisible and dim!

The Revival

Unfold! Unfold! Take in His light,
Who makes thy cares more short than night.
The joys which with His day-star rise
He deals to all but drowsy eyes;
And, what the men of this world miss
Some drops and dews of future bliss.

Hark! how His winds have changed their note!
And with warm whispers call thee out;
The frosts are past, the storms are gone,
And backward life at last comes on.
The lofty groves in express joys
Reply unto the turtle's voice;
And here in dust and dirt, O here
The lilies of His love appear!

THOMAS TRAHERNE
1637-1674

Wonder

How like an angel came I down!
How bright are all things here!
When first among His works I did appear
O how their Glory me did crown!
The world resembled his Eternity,
In which my soul did walk;
And ev'ry thing that I did see
Did with me talk.

The skies in their magnificence,
The lively, lovely air;
Oh how divine, how soft, how sweet, how fair!
The stars did entertain my sense,
And all the works of God, so bright and pure,
So rich and great did seem,
As if they ever must endure
In my esteem.

A native health and innocence
Within my bones did grow,
And while my God did all His Glories show,
I felt a vigor in my sense
That was all Spirit. I within did flow
With seas of life, like wine;
I nothing in the world did know
But 'twas divine.

Harsh ragged objects were concealed,
Oppressions, tears and cries,
Sins, griefs, complaints, dissensions, weeping eyes
Were hid, and only things revealed
Which heav'nly Spirits, and the Angels prize.
The state of Innocence

And bliss, not trades and poverties,
Did fill my sense.

The streets were paved with golden stones,
The boys and girls were mine,
Oh how did all their lovely faces shine!
The sons of men were holy ones,
In joy and beauty they appeared to me,
And everything which here I found,
While like an angel I did see,
Adorned the ground.

Rich diamond and pearl and gold
In ev'ry place was seen;
Rare splendors, yellow, blue, red, white and green,
Mine eyes did everywhere behold.
Great Wonders clothed with glory did appear,
Amazement was my bliss,
That and my wealth was ev'ry where;
No joy to this!

Cursed and devised proprieties,
With envy, avarice
And fraud, those fiends that spoil even Paradise,
Flew from the splendor of mine eyes,
And so did hedges, ditches, limits, bounds,
I dreamed not aught of those,
But wandered over all men's grounds,
And found repose.

Proprieties themselves were mine,
And hedges ornaments;
Walls, boxes, coffers, and their rich contents
Did not divide my joys, but all combine.
Clothes, ribbons, jewels, laces, I esteemed
My joys by others worn:
For me they all to wear them seemed
When I was born.

An Hymn upon St. Bartholomew's Day

What powerful Spirit lives within![219]
What active Angel doth inhabit here!
What heavenly light inspires my skin,
Which doth so like a Deity appear!
A living Temple of all ages, I
Within me see
A Temple of Eternity!
All Kingdoms I descry
In me.

An inward Omnipresence here
Mysteriously like His within me stands,
Whose knowledge is a Sacred Sphere
That in itself at once includes all lands.
There is some Angel that within me can
Both talk and move,
And walk and fly and see and love,
A man on earth, a man
Above.

Dull walls of clay my Spirit leaves,
And in a foreign Kingdom doth appear,
This great Apostle it receives,
Admires His works and sees them, standing here,
Within myself from East to West I move
As if I were
At once a Cherubim[220] and Sphere,
Or was at once above
And here.

The Soul's a messenger whereby
Within our inward Temple we may be
Even like the very Deity
In all the parts of His Eternity.
O live within and leave unwieldy dross!
Flesh is but clay!
O fly my Soul and haste away
To Jesus' Throne or Cross!
Obey!

Innocence

But that which most I wonder at, which most
I did esteem my bliss, which most I boast,
And ever shall enjoy, is that within
I felt no stain, nor spot of sin.

No darkness then did overshade,
But all within was pure and bright,
No guilt did crush, nor fear invade
But all my soul was full of light.

A joyful sense and purity
Is all I can remember;
The very night to me was bright,
'Twas Summer in December.

A serious meditation did employ
My soul within, which taken up with joy
Did seem no outward thing to note, but fly
All objects that do feed the eye,

While it those very objects did
Admire, and prize, and praise, and love,
Which in their glory most are hid,
Which presence only doth remove.

Their constant daily presence I
Rejoicing at, did see,
And that which takes them from the eye
Of others, offered them to me.

No inward inclination did I feel
To avarice or pride; my soul did kneel
In admiration all the day. No lust, nor strife,
Polluted then my infant life.

No fraud nor anger in me moved,
No malice, jealousy, or spite;

All that I saw I truly loved:
Contentment only and delight

Were in my soul. O Heav'n! what bliss
Did I enjoy and feel!
What powerful delight did this
Inspire! for this I daily kneel.

Whether it be that Nature is so pure,
And custom only vicious; or that sure
God did by miracle the guilt remove,
And make my soul to feel his Love

So early: or that 'twas one day,
Wherein this happiness I found,
Whose strength and brightness so do ray,
That still it seems me to surround;

Whate're it is, it is a light
So endless unto me
That I a world of true delight
Did then and to this day do see.

That prospect was the gate of Heav'n, that day
The ancient Light of Eden did convey
Into my soul: I was an Adam there
A little Adam in a sphere

Of joys! O there my ravished sense
Was entertained in Paradise,
And had a sight of Innocence
Which was beyond all bound and price.

An antepast[221] of Heaven sure!
I on the Earth did reign;
Within, without me, all was pure:
I must become a child again.

Love

O nectar! O delicious stream!
O ravishing and only pleasure! Where
    Shall such another theme
Inspire my tongue with joys or please mine ear!
    Abridgement of delights!
    And Queen of sights!
O mine of rarities! O Kingdom wide!
O more! O cause of all! O glorious Bride!
    O God! O Bride of God! O King!
    O soul and crown of everything!

    Did not I covet to behold
Some endless monarch, that did always live
    In palaces of gold,
Willing all kingdoms, realms, and crowns to give
    Unto my soul! Whose love
    A spring might prove
Of endless glories, honors, friendships, pleasures,
Joys, praises, beauties and celestial treasures!
    Lo, now I see there's such a King.
    The fountain-head of everything!

    Did my ambition ever dream
Of such a Lord, of such a love! Did I
    Expect so sweet a stream
As this at any time! Could any eye
    Believe it? Why all power
    Is used here;
Joys down from Heaven on my head do shower,
And Jove beyond the fiction doth appear
    Once more in golden rain to come
    To Danae's[222] pleasing fruitful womb.

    His Ganymede![223] His life! His joy!
Or He comes down to me, or takes me up
    That I might be His boy,
And fill, and taste, and give, and drink the cup.
    But those (tho' great) are all
    Too short and small,

Too weak and feeble pictures to express
The true mysterious depths of Blessedness.
    I am His image, and His friend,
    His son, bride, glory, temple, end.

The Rapture

    Sweet Infancy!
O Fire of heaven! O sacred Light
    How fair and bright,
    How great am I,
Whom all the world doth magnify!

    O Heavenly Joy!
O great and sacred blessedness
    Which I possess!
    So great a joy
Who did into my arms convey?

    From God above
Being sent, the Heavens me enflame:
    To praise his Name
    The stars to move!
The burning sun doth show His love.

    O how divine
Am I! To all this sacred wealth,
    This life and health,
    Who raised? Who mine
Did make the same? What hand divine?

JOSEPH ADDISON
1672-1719

Ode

THE SPACIOUS FIRMAMENT ON HIGH,
With all the blue ethereal sky,
And spangled heav'ns, a shining frame,
Their great original proclaim:
Th' unwearied Sun, from day to day,
Does his Creator's power display,
And publishes to every land
The work of an Almighty Hand.

Soon as the evening shades prevail,
The Moon takes up the wondrous tale,
And nightly to the list'ning Earth
Repeats the story of her birth:
Whilst all the stars that round her burn,
And all the planets, in their turn,
Confirm the tidings as they roll,
And spread the truth from pole to pole.

What though, in solemn silence, all
Move round the dark terrestrial ball?
What though nor real voice nor sound
Amid their radiant orbs be found?
In Reason's ear they all rejoice,
And utter forth a glorious voice,
Forever singing, as they shine,
"The Hand that made us is Divine."

JOHN BYROM
1692-1753

A Hymn for Christmas Day

CHRISTIANS, AWAKE! SALUTE THE HAPPY MORN,
Whereon the savior of the world was born;
Rise, to adore the mystery of love,
Which hosts of angels chanted from above:
With them the joyful tidings first begun
Of God incarnate, and the Virgin's son:
Then to the watchful shepherds it was told,
Who heard the angelic herald's voice—"Behold!
I bring good tidings of a savior's birth
To you, and all the nations of the earth;
This day hath God fulfilled his promised word;
This day is born a savior, Christ, the Lord:
In David's city, shepherds, ye shall find
The long foretold redeemer of mankind;
Wrapped up in swaddling clothes, the babe divine
Lies in a manger; this shall be your sign."
He spoke, and straightway the celestial choir,
In hymns of joy, unknown before, conspire;
The praises of redeeming love they sung,
And heaven's whole orb with halleluhjahs rung:
God's highest glory was their anthem still;
Peace upon earth, and mutual good-will.
To Bethlehem straight the enlightened shepherds ran,
To see the wonder God had wrought for man;
And found, with Joseph and the blessed maid,
Her son, the savior, in a manger laid.
Amazed, the wondrous story they proclaim;
The first apostles of this infant fame:
While Mary keeps, and ponders in her heart,
The heavenly vision, which the swains impart;
They to their flocks, still praising God, return,
And their glad hearts within their bosoms burn.
     Let us, like these good shepherds then, employ

159

Our grateful voices to proclaim the joy:
Like Mary, let us ponder in our mind
God's wondrous love in saving lost mankind;
Artless, and watchful, as these favored swains,
While virgin meekness in the heart remains:
Trace we the babe, who has retrieved our loss,
From his poor manger to his bitter cross;
Treading his steps, assisted by his grace,
Till man's first heavenly state again takes place:
Then may we hope, the angelic thrones among,
To sing, redeemed, a glad triumphal song;
He that was born, upon this joyful day,
Around us all, his glory shall display;
Saved by his love, incessant we shall sing
Of angels, and of angel-men, the King.

CHARLES WESLEY
1707-1788

Arise, My Soul, on Wings Sublime

ARISE, MY SOUL, ON WINGS SUBLIME,
Above the vanities of time;
Let faith now pierce the veil, and see
The glories of eternity.

Born by a new, celestial birth,
Why should I grovel here on earth?
Why grasp at vain and fleeting toys,
So near to heaven's eternal joys?

Shall aught beguile me on the road,
The narrow road that leads to God?
Or can I love this earth so well,
As not to long with God to dwell?

To dwell with God, to taste his love,
Is the full heaven enjoyed above:
The glorious expectation now
Is heavenly bliss begun below.

CHRISTOPHER SMART
1722-1771

Mirth

IF YOU ARE MERRY SING AWAY,
    And touch the organs sweet;
This is the Lord's triumphant day,
Ye children in the gall'ries gay,
    Shout from each goodly seat.

It shall be May to-morrow's morn,
    A field then let us run,
And deck us in the blooming thorn,
Soon as the cock begins to warn,
    And long before the sun.

I give the praise to Christ alone,
    My pinks[224] already show;
And my streaked roses fully blown,
The sweetness of the Lord make known,
    And to his glory grow.

Ye little prattlers that repair
    For cowslips[225] in the mead,
Of those exulting colts beware,
But blithe security is there,
    Where skipping lambkins feed.

With white and crimson laughs the sky,
    With birds the hedgerows[226] ring;
To give the praise to God most High,
And all the sulky fiends defy,
    Is a most joyful thing.

WILLIAM COWPER
1731-1800

Walking With God

OH! FOR A CLOSER WALK WITH GOD,
A calm and heavenly frame;
A light to shine upon the road
That leads me to the Lamb!

Where is the blessedness I knew
When first I saw the Lord?
Where is the soul-refreshing view
Of Jesus and his word?

What peaceful hours I once enjoy'd!
How sweet their memory still!
But they have left an aching void,
The world can never fill.

Return, O holy Dove, return!
Sweet the messenger of rest!
I hate the sins that made thee mourn
And drove thee from my breast.

The dearest idol I have known,
Whate'er that idol be,
Help me to tear it from thy throne,
And worship only thee.

So shall my walk be close with God,
Calm and serene my frame;
So purer light shall mark the road
That leads me to the Lamb.

Joy and Peace in Believing

Sometimes a light surprises
The Christian while he sings;
It is the Lord who rises
With healing on His wings;
When comforts are declining,
He grants the soul again
A season of clear shining,
To cheer it after rain.

In holy contemplation
We sweetly then pursue
The theme of God's salvation,
And find it ever new;
Set free from present sorrow,
We cheerfully can say,
E'en let the unknown to-morrow
Bring with it what it may!

It can bring with it nothing,
But He will bear us through;
Who gives the lilies clothing,
Will clothe His people too;
Beneath the spreading heavens
No creature but is fed;
And He who feeds the ravens
Will give His children bread.

Though vine nor fig tree neither
Their wonted fruit shall bear,
Though all the field should wither,
Nor flocks nor herds be there:
Yet God the same abiding,
His praise shall tune my voice;
For, while in Him confiding,
I cannot but rejoice.

The Happy Change

How blessed Thy creature is, O God,
When with a single eye,
He views the luster of Thy Word,
The dayspring from on high!

Through all the storms that veil the skies
And frown on earthly things,
The Sun of Righteousness he eyes,
With healing on His wings.

Struck by that light, the human heart,
A barren soil no more,
Sends the sweet smell of grace abroad,
Where serpents lurked before.

The soul, a dreary province once
Of Satan's dark domain,
Feels a new empire formed within,
And owns a heavenly reign.

The glorious orb whose golden beams
The fruitful year control,
Since first obedient to Thy Word,
He started from the goal,

Has cheered the nations with the joys
His orient rays impart;
But, Jesus, 'tis Thy light alone
Can shine upon the heart.

The Hidden Life

To tell the Savior all my wants,
How pleasing is the task!
Nor less to praise Him when He grants
Beyond what I can ask.

My laboring spirit vainly seeks
To tell but half the joy,
With how much tenderness He speaks,
And helps me to reply.

Nor were it wise, nor should I choose,
Such secrets to declare;
Like precious wines their taste they lose,
Exposed to open air.

But this with boldness I proclaim,
Nor care if thousands hear,
Sweet is the ointment of His name,
Not life is half so dear.

And can you frown, my former friends,
Who knew what once I was,
And blame the song that thus commends
The Man who bore the cross?

Trust me, I draw the likeness true,
And not as fancy paints;
Such honor may He give to you,
For such have all His saints.

GOETHE
1749-1832

The Park

HOW BEAUTIFUL! A GARDEN FAIR AS HEAVEN,
Flowers of all hues, and smiling in the sun,
Where all was waste and wilderness before.
Well do ye imitate, ye gods of earth,
The great Creator. Rock, lake, and glade,
Bird, fishes, and untamed beasts are here.
Your work were all an Eden, but for this—
Here is no man unconscious of a pang,
No perfect Sabbath of unbroken rest.

Perfect Bliss

All the divine perfections, which, while
Nature in thrift doled out 'mongst many a fair,
　　She showered with open hand, thou peerless one on thee!
And she that was so wondrously endowed,
To whom a throng of noble knees were bowed,
　　Gave all—Love's perfect gift—her glorious self—to me!

Sacred Ground

A place to mark the Graces, when they come
Down from Olympus, still and secretly,
To join the Oreads[227] in their festival,
Beneath the light of the benignant moon.
There lies the poet, watching them unseen,
The whilst they chant the sweetest songs of heaven,
Or, floating o'er the sward[228] without a sound,
Lead on the mystic wonder of the dance.
All that is great in heaven, or fair on earth,
Unveils its glories to the dreamer's eye,

And all he tells the Muses.[229] They again,
Knowing the Gods are jealous of their own,
Teach him, through all the passion of his verse,
To utter these high secrets reverently.

It Is Good

In paradise while moonbeams played,
Jehovah found, in slumber deep,
Adam fast sunk; He gently laid
Eve near him—she, too, fell asleep.
There lay they now, on earth's fair shrine,
God's two most beauteous thoughts divine—
When this He saw, He cried: 'Tis good!
And scarce could move from where He stood.

No wonder, that our joy's complete
While eye and eye responsive meet,
When this blest thought of rapture moves us—
That we're with Him who truly loves us,
And if He cries—Good, let it be!
'Tis so for both, it seems to me.
Thou'rt clasped within these arms of mine,
Dearest of all God's thoughts divine!

The Reunion

Can it be! Of stars the star,
Do I press thee to my heart?
In the night of distance far,
What deep gulf, what bitter smart!
Yes, 'tis thou, indeed at last,
Of my joys the partner dear!
Mindful, though, of sorrows past,
I the present needs must fear.

When the still unfashioned earth
Lay on God's eternal breast,

He ordained its hour of birth,
With creative joy possessed.
Then a heavy sigh arose,
When He spoke the sentence:—"Be!"
And the All, with mighty throes,
Burst into reality.

And when thus was born the light,
Darkness near it feared to stay,
And the elements with might
Fled on every side away;
Each on some far-distant trace,
Each with visions wild employed,
Numb, in boundless realms of space,
Harmony and feeling-void.

Dumb was all, all still and dead,
For the first time, God alone!
Then He formed the morning-red,
Which soon made its kindness known:
It unraveled from the waste
Bright and glowing harmony,
And once more with love was graced
What contended formerly.

And with earnest, noble strife,
Each its own peculiar sought;
Back to full, unbounded life,
Sight and feeling soon were brought.
Wherefore, if 'tis done, explore
How? Why give the manner, name?
Allah need create no more,
We his world ourselves can frame.

So, with morning pinions brought,
To thy mouth was I impelled;
Stamped with thousand seals by night,
Star-clear is the bond fast held.
Paragons on earth are we
Both of grief and joy sublime,

And a second sentence:—"Be!"
Parts us not a second time.

To Luna

Sister of the earliest light,[230]
Type of loveliness in sorrow,
Silver mists thy radiance borrow,
Even as they cross thy sight.
When thou comest to the sky,
In their dusky hollows waken,
Spirits that are sad, forsaken,
Birds that shun the day, and I.

Looking downward far and wide,
Hidden things thou dost discover.
Luna! Help a hapless lover,
Lift him kindly to thy side!
Aided by thy friendly beams,
Let him through the lattice peeping,
Look into the room where, sleeping,
Lies the maiden of his dreams.

Ah, I see her! Now I gaze,
Bending in a trance Elysian,
And I strain my inmost vision,
And I gather all thy rays.
Bright and brighter yet I see
Charms no envious robes encumber;
And she draws me to her slumber
As Endymion[231] once drew thee.

PHILIP FRENEAU
1752-1832

Song of Thyrsis

THE TURTLE ON YON WITHERED BOUGH,[232]
That lately mourned her murdered mate,[233]
Has found another comrade now—
Such changes all await!
Again her drooping plume is drest,
Again she's willing to be blest
And takes her lover to her nest.

If nature has decreed it so
With all above, and all below,
Let us like them forget our woe,
And not be killed with sorrow.
If I should quit your arms tonight
And chance to die before 'twas light,
I would advise you—and you might—
Love again to-morrow.

On the Ruins of a Country Inn

Where now these mingled ruins lie
A temple once to Bacchus rose,
Beneath whose roof, aspiring high,
Full many a guest forgot his woes.

No more this dome, by tempests torn,
Affords a social safe retreat;
But ravens here, with eye forlorn,
And clustering bats henceforth will meet.

The Priestess of this ruined shrine,
Unable to survive the stroke,
Presents no more the ruddy wine,—
Her glasses gone, her china broke.

171

The friendly Host, whose social hand
Accosted strangers at the door,
Has left at length his wonted stand,
And greets the weary guest no more.

Old creeping Time, that brings decay,
Might yet have spared these moldering walls,
Alike beneath whose potent sway
A temple or a tavern falls.

Is this the place where mirth and joy,
Coy nymphs, and sprightly lads were found?
Indeed! No more the nymphs are coy,
No more the flowing bowls go round.

Is this the place where festive song
Deceived the wintry hours away?
No more the swains the tune prolong,
No more the maidens join the lay.

Is this the place where Nancy slept
In downy beds of blue and green?
Dame Nature here no vigils kept,
No cold unfeeling guards were seen.

'T is gone!—and Nancy tempts no more;
Deep, unrelenting silence reigns;
Of all that pleased, that charmed before,
The tottering chimney scarce remains.

Ye tyrant winds, whose ruffian blast
Through doors and windows blew too strong,
And all the roof to ruin cast,—
The roof that sheltered us so long,—

Your wrath appeased, I pray be kind
If Mopsus[234] should the dome renew,
That we again may quaff his wine,
Again collect our jovial crew.

WILLIAM BLAKE
1757-1827

Eternity

HE WHO BINDS TO HIMSELF A JOY
Does the winged life destroy:
But he who kisses the joy as it flies
Lives in eternity's sun rise.

To the Evening Star

Thou fair-haired angel of the evening,
Now, whilst the sun rests on the mountains, light
Thy bright torch of love; thy radiant crown
Put on, and smile upon our evening bed!
Smile on our loves, and while thou drawest the
Blue curtains of the sky, scatter thy silver dew
On every flower that shuts its sweet eyes
In timely sleep. Let thy west wing sleep on
The lake; speak silence with thy glimmering eyes,
And wash the dusk with silver. Soon, full soon,
Dost thou withdraw; then the wolf rages wide,
And the lion glares through the dun forest.
The fleeces of our flocks are covered with
Thy sacred dew; protect with them with thine influence.

To Spring

O thou with dewy locks, who lookest down
Thro' the clear windows of the morning, turn
Thine angel eyes upon our western isle,
Which in full choir hails thy approach, O Spring!

The hills tell each other, and the listening
Valleys hear; all our longing eyes are turned

Up to thy bright pavilions: issue forth,
And let thy holy feet visit our clime.

Come o'er the eastern hills, and let our winds
Kiss thy perfumed garments; let us taste
Thy morn and evening breath; scatter thy pearls
Upon our love-sick land that mourns for thee.

O deck her forth with thy fair fingers; pour
Thy soft kisses on her bosom; and put
Thy golden crown upon her languished head,
Whose modest tresses were bound up for thee.

To Summer

O thou who passest thro' our valleys in
Thy strength, curb thy fierce steeds, allay the heat
That flames from their large nostrils! Thou, O Summer,
Oft pitched'st here thy golden tent, and oft
Beneath our oaks hast slept, while we beheld
With joy thy ruddy limbs and flourishing hair.

Beneath our thickest shades we oft have heard
Thy voice, when noon upon his fervid car
Rode o'er the deep of heaven; beside our springs
Sit down, and in our mossy valleys, on
Some bank beside a river clear, throw thy
Silk draperies off, and rush into the stream:
Our valleys love the Summer in his pride.

Our bards are famed who strike the silver wire:
Our youth are bolder than the southern swains:
Our maidens fairer in the sprightly dance:
We lack not songs, nor instruments of joy,
Nor echoes sweet, nor waters clear as heaven,
Nor laurel wreaths against the sultry heat.

I Love the Jocund Dance

I love the jocund dance,
The softly breathing song,

Where innocent eyes do glance,
And where lisps the maiden's tongue.

I love the laughing vale,
I love the echoing hills,
Where mirth does never fail,
And the jolly swain laughs his fill.

I love the pleasant cot,
I love the innocent bow'r,
Where white and brown is our lot,
Or fruit in the midday hour.

I love the oaken seat,
Beneath the oaken tree,
Where all the old villagers meet,
And laugh our sports to see.

I love our neighbors all,
But Kitty, I better love thee;
And love them I ever shall;
But thou art all to me.

Infant Joy
from **Songs of Innocence**

'I have no name:
I am but two days old.'
What shall I call thee?
'I happy am,
Joy is my name.'
Sweet joy befall thee!

Pretty joy!
Sweet joy, but two days old.
Sweet joy I call thee:
Thou dost smile,
I sing the while,
Sweet joy befall thee!

The Echoing Green
from **Songs of Innocence**

The Sun does arise,
And make happy the skies.
The merry bells ring
To welcome the Spring.
The skylark and thrush,
The birds of the bush,
Sing louder around
To the bells' cheerful sound.
While our sports shall be seen
On the Echoing Green.

Old John with white hair,
Does laugh away care,
Sitting under the oak,
Among the old folk.
They laugh at our play,
And soon they all say:
"Such, such were the joys.
When we all, girls & boys,
In our youth-time were seen,
On the echoing green."

Till the little ones weary
No more can be merry
The sun does descend,
And our sports have an end:
Round the laps of their mothers,
Many sisters and brothers,
Like birds in their nest,

Are ready for rest;
And sport no more seen,
On the darkening Green.

A Cradle Song
from **Songs of Innocence**

Sweet dreams, form a shade
O'er my lovely infant's head;
Sweet dreams of pleasant streams
By happy, silent, moony beams.

Sweet Sleep, with soft down
Weave thy brows an infant crown.
Sweet Sleep, Angel mild,
Hover o'er my happy child.

Sweet smiles, in the night
Hover over my delight;
Sweet smiles, mother's smiles,
All the livelong night beguiles.

Sweet moans, dovelike sighs,
Chase not slumber from thy eyes.
Sweet moans, sweeter smiles,
All the dovelike moans beguiles.

Sleep, sleep, happy child,
All creation slept and smiled;
Sleep, sleep, happy sleep,
While o'er thee thy mother weep.

Sweet babe, in thy face
Holy image I can trace.
Sweet babe, once like thee,
Thy Maker lay and wept for me,

Wept for me, for thee, for all,
When He was an infant small.

Thou His image ever see,
Heavenly face that smiles on thee

Smiles on thee, on me, on all;
Who became an infant small.
Infant smiles are His own smiles;
Heaven and earth to peace beguiles.

Spring
from **Songs of Innocence**

Sound the flute!
Now it's mute.
Birds delight
Day and night;
Nightingale
In the dale,
Lark in sky,
Merrily,
Merrily, merrily, to welcome in the year.

Little boy,
Full of joy;
Little girl,
Sweet and small;
Cock does crow,
So do you;
Merry voice,
Infant noise,
Merrily, merrily, to welcome in the year.

Little lamb,
Here I am;
Come and lick
My white neck;
Let me pull
Your soft wool;
Let me kiss
Your soft face;
Merrily, merrily, we welcome in the year.

The School Boy
from **Songs of Experience**

I love to rise in a summer morn,
When the birds sing on every tree;
The distant huntsman winds his horn,
And the skylark sings with me:
O what sweet company!

But to go to school in a summer morn,—
O it drives all joy away!
Under a cruel eye outworn,
The little ones spend the day
In sighing and dismay.

Ah then at times I drooping sit,
And spend many an anxious hour;
Nor in my book can I take delight,
Nor sit in learning's bower,
Worn through with the dreary shower.

How can the bird that is born for joy
Sit in a cage and sing?
How can a child, when fears annoy,
But droop his tender wing,
And forget his youthful spring?

O father and mother, if buds are nipped,
And blossoms blown away;
And if the tender plants are stripped
Of their joy in the springing day,
By sorrow and care's dismay,—

How shall the summer arise in joy,
Or the summer fruits appear?
Or how shall we gather what griefs destroy,
Or bless the mellowing year,
When the blasts of winter appear?

FRIEDRICH VON SCHILLER
1759-1805

Phantasy—to Laura

NAME, MY LAURA, NAME THE WHIRL-COMPELLING
Bodies to unite in one blest whole—
Name, my Laura, name the wondrous magic
By which Soul rejoins its kindred Soul!

See! It teaches yonder roving Planets
Round the sun to fly in endless race;
And as children play around their mother,
Checkered circles round the orb to trace.

Every rolling star, by thirst tormented,
Drinks with joy its bright and golden rain—
Drinks refreshment from its fiery chalice,
As the limbs are nourished by the brain.

'Tis through Love that atom pairs with atom,
In a harmony eternal, sure;
And 'tis Love that links the spheres together—
Through her only, systems can endure.

Were she but effaced from Nature's clockwork,
Into dust would fly the mighty world;
O'er thy systems thou wouldst weep, great Newton,
When with giant force to Chaos hurled!

Blot the Goddess from the Spirit Order,
It would sink in death, and ne'er arise.
Were Love absent, spring would glad us never;
Were Love absent, none their God would prize!

What is that, which, when my Laura kisses,
Dyes my cheek with flames of purple hue,
Bids my bosom bound with swifter motion,
Like a fever wild my veins runs through?

Ev'ry nerve from out its barriers rises,
O'er its banks the blood begins to flow;
Body seeks to join itself to Body,
Spirits kindle in one blissful glow.

Powerful as in the dead creations
That eternal impulses obey,
O'er the web Arachnine-like[235] of Nature,—
Living Nature,—Love exerts her sway.

Laura, see how Joyousness embraces
E'en the overflow of sorrows wild!
How e'en rigid desperation kindles
On the loving breast of Hope so mild.

Sisterly and blissful raptures softens
Gloomy Melancholy's fearful night,
And, delivered of its golden Children,
Lo, the eye pours forth its radiance bright!

Does not awful Sympathy rule over
E'en the realms that Evil calls its own?
For 'tis Hell our crimes are ever wooing,
While they bear a grudge 'gainst Heaven alone!

Shame, Repentance, pair Eumenides-like,[236]
Weave round sin their fearful serpent-coils:
While around the eagle-wings of Greatness
Treach'rous danger winds its dreaded toils.

Ruin oft with Pride is wont to trifle,
Envy upon Fortune loves to cling;
On her brother, Death, with arms extended,
Lust, his sister, oft is wont to spring.

On the wings of Love the Future hastens
In the arms of ages past to lie;
And Saturnus, as he onwards speeds him,
Long hath sought his bride—Eternity!

Soon Saturnus will his bride discover,—
So the mighty Oracle hath said;
Blazing Worlds will turn to marriage torches
When Eternity with Time shall wed!

Then a fairer, far more beauteous morning,
Laura, on our Love shall also shine,
Long as their blest bridal-night enduring:—
So rejoice thee, Laura—Laura mine!

Rapture—to Laura

From earth I seem to wing my flight,
And sun myself in Heaven's pure light,
When thy sweet gaze meets mine
I dream I quaff ethereal dew,
When mine own form I mirrored view
In those blue eyes divine!

Blest notes from Paradise afar,
Or strains from some benignant star
Enchant my ravished ear;
My Muse feels then the shepherd's hour
When silv'ry tones of magic power
Escape those lips so dear!

Young Loves around thee fan their wings—
Behind, the maddened fir-tree springs,
As when by Orpheus fired;
The poles whirl round with swifter motion,
When in the dance, like waves o'er Ocean,
Thy footsteps float untired!

Thy look, if it but beam with love,
Could make the lifeless marble move,
And hearts in rocks enshrine;
My visions to reality
Will turn, if, Laura, in thine eye
I read—that thou art mine!

The Secret

She sought to breathe one word, but vainly—
Too many listeners were nigh;
And yet my timid glance read plainly
The language of her speaking eye.

Thy silent glades my footstep presses,
Thou fair and leaf-embosomed grove!
Conceal within thy green recesses
From mortal eye our sacred love!

Afar with strange discordant noises,
The busy day is echoing;
And, 'mid the hollow hum of voices,
I hear the heavy hammer ring.
'Tis thus that man, with toil ne'er-ending,
Extorts from Heaven his daily bread;
Yet oft unseen the Gods are sending
The gifts of fortune on his head!

Oh, let mankind discover never
How true love fills with bliss our hearts!
They would but crush our joy forever,
For joy to them no glow imparts.
Thou ne'er wilt from the world obtain it—
'Tis never captured save as prey;
Thou needs must strain each nerve to gain it,
E'er envy dark asserts her sway.

The hours of night and stillness loving,
It comes upon us silently—
Away with hasty footsteps moving
Soon as it sees a treach'rous eye.

Thou gentle stream, soft circlets weaving,
A wat'ry barrier cast around,
And, with thy waves in anger heaving,
Guard from each foe this holy ground!

Dithyramb

Believe me, together
The bright gods come ever,
Still as of old;
Scarce see I Bacchus, the giver of joy,
Than comes up fair Eros, the laugh-loving boy,
And Phoebus,[237] the stately, behold!

They come near and nearer,
The heavenly ones all—
The gods with their presence
Fill earth as their hall!

Say, how shall I welcome,
Human and earthborn,
Sons of the sky?
Pour out to me—pour the full life that ye live!
What to ye, O ye gods! can the mortal one give?

The joys can dwell only
In Jupiter's palace—
Brimmed bright with your nectar,
Oh, reach me the chalice!

"Hebe,[238] the chalice
Fill full to the brim!
Steep his eyes—steep his eyes in the bath of the dew,
Let him dream, while the Styx is concealed from his view,
That the life of the gods is for him!"

It murmurs, it sparkles,
The fount of delight;
The bosom grows tranquil—
The eye becomes bright.

WILLIAM WORDSWORTH
1770-1850

Lines Written in Early Spring

I HEARD A THOUSAND BLENDED NOTES,
While in a grove I sate reclined,
In that sweet mood when pleasant thoughts
Bring sad thoughts to the mind.

To her fair works did Nature link
The human soul that through me ran;
And much it grieved my heart to think
What man has made of man.

Through primrose tufts, in that green bower,
The periwinkle trailed its wreaths,
And 'tis my faith that every flower
Enjoys the air it breathes.

The birds around me hopped and played,
Their thoughts I cannot measure:—
But the least motion which they made
It seemed a thrill of pleasure.

The budding twigs spread out their fan,
To catch the breezy air;
And I must think, do all I can,
That there was pleasure there.

If this belief from heaven be sent,
If such be Nature's holy plan,
Have I not reason to lament
What man has made of man?

To My Sister

It is the first mild day of March:
Each minute sweeter than before
The redbreast sings from the tall larch
That stands beside our door.

There is a blessing in the air,
Which seems a sense of joy to yield
To the bare trees, and mountains bare,
And grass in the green field.

My sister! ('tis a wish of mine)
Now that our morning meal is done,
Make haste, your morning task resign;
Come forth and feel the sun.

Edward will come with you;—and, pray,
Put on with speed your woodland dress;
And bring no book: for this one day
We'll give to idleness.

No joyless forms shall regulate
Our living calendar:
We from to-day, my Friend, will date
The opening of the year.

Love, now a universal birth,
From heart to heart is stealing,
From earth to man, from man to earth:
—It is the hour of feeling.

One moment now may give us more
Than years of toiling reason:
Our minds shall drink at every pore
The spirit of the season.

Some silent laws our hearts will make,
Which they shall long obey:
We for the year to come may take
Our temper from to-day.

And from the blessed power that rolls
About, below, above,
We'll frame the measure of our souls:
They shall be tuned to love.

Then come, my Sister! Come, I pray,
With speed put on your woodland dress;
And bring no book: for this one day
We'll give to idleness.

Expostulation and Reply

"Why, William, on that old grey stone,[239]
Thus for the length of half a day,
Why, William, sit you thus alone,
And dream your time away?

"Where are your books?—that light bequeathed
To Beings else forlorn and blind!
Up! Up! and drink the spirit breathed
From dead men to their kind.

"You look round on your Mother Earth,
As if she for no purpose bore you;
As if you were her first-born birth,
And none had lived before you!"

One morning thus, by Esthwaite lake,
When life was sweet, I knew not why,
To me my good friend Matthew spake,
And thus I made reply.

"The eye—it cannot choose but see;
We cannot bid the ear be still;
Our bodies feel, where'er they be,
Against or with our will.

"Nor less I deem that there are Powers
Which of themselves our minds impress;

That we can feed this mind of ours
In a wise passiveness.

"Think you, 'mid all this mighty sum
Of things for ever speaking,
That nothing of itself will come,
But we must still be seeking?

"—Then ask not wherefore, here, alone,
Conversing as I may,
I sit upon this old grey stone,
And dream my time away."

The Tables Turned
An Evening Scene on
the Same Subject

Up! Up! my Friend, and quit your books;
Or surely you'll grow double:
Up! Up! my Friend, and clear your looks;
Why all this toil and trouble?

The sun above the mountain's head,
A freshening lustre mellow
Through all the long green fields has spread,
His first sweet evening yellow.

Books! 'tis a dull and endless strife:
Come, hear the woodland linnet,
How sweet his music! on my life,
There's more of wisdom in it.

And hark! how blithe the throstle sings!
He, too, is no mean preacher:
Come forth into the light of things,
Let Nature be your teacher.

She has a world of ready wealth,
Our minds and hearts to bless—

Spontaneous wisdom breathed by health,
Truth breathed by cheerfulness.

One impulse from a vernal wood
May teach you more of man,
Of moral evil and of good,
Than all the sages can.

Sweet is the lore which Nature brings;
Our meddling intellect
Mis-shapes the beauteous forms of things:—
We murder to dissect.

Enough of Science and of Art;
Close up those barren leaves;
Come forth, and bring with you a heart
That watches and receives.

To a Butterfly (1)

Stay near me—do not take thy flight!
A little longer stay in sight!
Much converse do I find in thee,
Historian of my infancy!
Float near me; do not yet depart!
Dead times revive in thee:
Thou bring'st, gay creature as thou art!
A solemn image to my heart,
My father's family!

Oh! Pleasant, pleasant were the days,
The time, when, in our childish plays,
My sister Emmeline and I
Together chased the butterfly!
A very hunter did I rush
Upon the prey:—with leaps and springs
I followed on from brake to bush;
But she, God love her, feared to brush
The dust from off its wings.

A Whirl-Blast from Behind the Hill

A Whirl-Blast from behind the hill
Rushed o'er the wood with startling sound;
Then—all at once the air was still,
And showers of hailstones pattered round.
Where leafless oaks towered high above,
I sat within an undergrove
Of tallest hollies, tall and green;
A fairer bower was never seen.
From year to year the spacious floor
With withered leaves is covered o'er,
And all the year the bower is green.
But see! Where'er the hailstones drop
The withered leaves all skip and hop;
There's not a breeze—no breath of air—
Yet here, and there, and everywhere
Along the floor, beneath the shade
By those embowering hollies made,
The leaves in myriads jump and spring,
As if with pipes and music rare
Some Robin Good-fellow were there,
And all those leaves, in festive glee,
Were dancing to the minstrelsy.

My Heart Leaps up When I Behold

My heart leaps up when I behold
    A rainbow in the sky:
So was it when my life began;
So is it now I am a man;
So be it when I shall grow old,
    Or let me die!
The Child is father of the Man;
And I could wish my days to be
Bound each to each by natural piety.[240]

190

Composed upon Westminster Bridge

Earth has not anything to show more fair:
Dull would he be of soul who could pass by
A sight so touching in its majesty:
This City now doth, like a garment, wear
The beauty of the morning; silent, bare,
Ships, towers, domes, theatres and temples lie
Open unto the fields, and to the sky;
All bright and glittering in the smokeless air.
Never did sun more beautifully steep
In his first splendour, valley, rock, or hill;
Ne'er saw I, never felt, a calm so deep!
The river glideth at his own sweet will:
Dear God! The very houses seem asleep;
And all that mighty heart is lying still!

To a Butterfly (2)

I've watched you now a full half-hour;
Self-poised upon that yellow flower
And, little Butterfly! Indeed
I know not if you sleep or feed.
How motionless!—not frozen seas
More motionless! And then
What joy awaits you, when the breeze
Hath found you out among the trees,
And calls you forth again!
This plot of orchard-ground is ours;
My trees they are, my Sister's flowers;
Here rest your wings when they are weary;
Here lodge as in a sanctuary!
Come often to us, fear no wrong;
Sit near us on the bough!
We'll talk of sunshine and of song,
And summer days, when we were young;
Sweet childish days, that were as long
As twenty days are now.

191

Written in March
While Resting on the Bridge
at the Foot of Brother's Water

The cock is crowing,
The stream is flowing,
The small birds twitter,
The lake doth glitter,
    The green field sleeps in the sun;
The oldest and youngest
Are at work with the strongest;
The cattle are grazing,
Their heads never raising;
    There are forty feeding like one!
Like an army defeated
The snow hath retreated,
And now doth fare ill
On the top of the bare hill;
    The plowboy is whooping—anon—anon:
There's joy in the mountains;
There's life in the fountains;
Small clouds are sailing,
Blue sky prevailing;
    The rain is over and gone!

It Is a Beauteous Evening, Calm and Free

It is a beauteous Evening, calm and free,
The holy time is quiet as a Nun
Breathless with adoration; the broad sun
Is sinking down in its tranquility;
The gentleness of heaven broods o'er the Sea:
Listen! the mighty Being is awake,
And doth with his eternal motion make
A sound like thunder—everlastingly.
Dear Child! dear Girl! That walkest with me here,
If thou appear untouched by solemn thought,
Thy nature is not therefore less divine:
Thou liest in Abraham's bosom all the year,

192

And worship'st at the Temple's inner shrine,
God being with thee when we know it not.

She Was a Phantom of Delight

She[241] was a Phantom of delight
When first she gleamed upon my sight;
A lovely apparition, sent
To be a moment's ornament;
Her eyes as stars of Twilight fair;
Like Twilight's, too, her dusky hair;
But all things else about her drawn
From May-time and the cheerful Dawn;
A dancing Shape, an Image gay,
To haunt, to startle, and waylay.

I saw her upon nearer view,
A Spirit, yet a Woman too!
Her household motions light and free,
And steps of virgin-liberty;
A countenance in which did meet
Sweet records, promises as sweet;
A Creature not too bright or good
For human nature's daily food,
For transient sorrows, simple wiles,
Praise, blame, love, kisses, tears, and smiles.
And now I see with eye serene
The very pulse of the machine;
A Being breathing thoughtful breath,
A Traveler between life and death:
The reason firm, the temperate will,
Endurance, foresight, strength, and skill;
A perfect Woman, nobly planned
To warn, to comfort, and command;
And yet a Spirit still, and bright
With something of angelic light.

I Wandered Lonely As a Cloud

I wandered lonely as a cloud
That floats on high o'er vales and hills,
When all at once I saw a crowd,
A host, of golden daffodils;
Beside the lake, beneath the trees,
Fluttering and dancing in the breeze.

Continuous as the stars that shine
And twinkle on the milky way,
They stretched in never-ending line
Along the margin of a bay:
Ten thousand saw I at a glance,
Tossing their heads in sprightly dance.

The waves beside them danced; but they
Out-did the sparkling waves in glee:
A poet could not but be gay,
In such a jocund company:
I gazed—and gazed—but little thought
What wealth the show to me had brought:

For oft, when on my couch I lie
In vacant or in pensive mood,
They flash upon that inward eye
Which is the bliss of solitude;
And then my heart with pleasure fills,
And dances with the daffodils.

SAMUEL TAYLOR COLERIDGE
1772-1834

The Presence of Love

AND IN LIFE'S NOISIEST HOUR,
    There whispers still the ceaseless Love of Thee,
    The heart's Self-solace and soliloquy.

    You mould my Hopes, you fashion me within;
    And to the leading Love-throb in the Heart
    Through all my Being, through my pulse's beat;
    You lie in all my many Thoughts, like Light,
    Like the fair light of Dawn, or summer Eve
    On rippling Stream, or cloud-reflecting Lake.

    And looking to the Heaven, that bends above you,
    How oft! I bless the Lot that made me love you.

Frost at Midnight

The Frost performs its secret ministry,
    Unhelped by any wind. The owlet's cry
    Came loud—and hark, again! loud as before.
    The inmates of my cottage, all at rest,
    Have left me to that solitude, which suits
    Abstruser musings: save that at my side
    My cradled infant slumbers peacefully.
    'Tis calm indeed! so calm, that it disturbs
    And vexes meditation with its strange
    And extreme silentness. Sea, hill, and wood,
    This populous village! Sea, and hill, and wood,
    With all the numberless goings-on of life,
    Inaudible as dreams! the thin blue flame
    Lies on my low-burnt fire, and quivers not;
    Only that film, which fluttered on the grate,
    Still flutters there, the sole unquiet thing.

Methinks, its motion in this hush of nature
Gives it dim sympathies with me who live,
Making it a companionable form,
Whose puny flaps and freaks the idling Spirit
By its own moods interprets, everywhere
Echo or mirror seeking of itself,
And makes a toy of Thought.

                But O! how oft,
How oft, at school, with most believing mind,
Presageful,[242] have I gazed upon the bars,
To watch that fluttering stranger![243] and as oft
With unclosed lids, already had I dreamt
Of my sweet birth-place, and the old church-tower,
Whose bells, the poor man's only music, rang
From morn to evening, all the hot Fair-day,
So sweetly, that they stirred and haunted me
With a wild pleasure, falling on mine ear
Most like articulate sounds of things to come!
So gazed I, till the soothing things, I dreamt,
Lulled me to sleep, and sleep prolonged my dreams!
And so I brooded all the following morn,
Awed by the stern preceptor's face, mine eye
Fixed with mock study on my swimming book:
Save if the door half opened, and I snatched
A hasty glance, and still my heart leaped up,
For still I hoped to see the stranger's face,
Townsman, or aunt, or sister more beloved,
My play-mate when we both were clothed alike!

Dear Babe, that sleepest cradled by my side,
Whose gentle breathings, heard in this deep calm,
Fill up the interspersed vacancies
And momentary pauses of the thought!
My babe so beautiful! it thrills my heart
With tender gladness, thus to look at thee,
And think that thou shalt learn far other lore,
And in far other scenes! For I was reared
In the great city, pent 'mid cloisters dim,
And saw nought lovely but the sky and stars.

But thou, my babe! shalt wander like a breeze
By lakes and sandy shores, beneath the crags
Of ancient mountain, and beneath the clouds,
Which image in their bulk both lakes and shores
And mountain crags: so shalt thou see and hear
The lovely shapes and sounds intelligible
Of that eternal language, which thy God
Utters, who from eternity doth teach
Himself in all, and all things in himself.
Great universal Teacher! he shall mould
Thy spirit, and by giving make it ask.

    Therefore all seasons shall be sweet to thee,
Whether the summer clothe the general earth
With greenness, or the redbreast sit and sing
Betwixt the tufts of snow on the bare branch
Of mossy apple-tree, while the nigh thatch
Smokes in the sun-thaw; whether the eave-drops fall
Heard only in the trances of the blast,
Or if the secret ministry of frost
Shall hang them up in silent icicles,
Quietly shining to the quiet Moon.

The Eolian Harp

My pensive Sara! Thy soft cheek reclined
    Thus on mine arm, most soothing sweet it is
    To sit beside our cot, our cot o'ergrown
    With white-flowered jasmin, and the broad-leaved myrtle,
    (Meet emblems they of Innocence and Love!)
    And watch the clouds, that late were rich with light,
    Slow saddening round, and mark the star of eve
    Serenely brilliant (such should wisdom be)
    Shine opposite! How exquisite the scents
    Snatched from yon bean-field! and the world so hushed!
    The stilly murmur of the distant Sea
    Tells us of silence.

And that simplest lute,[244]
Placed length-ways in the clasping casement, hark!
How by the desultory breeze caressed,
Like some coy maid half yielding to her lover,
It pours such sweet upbraiding, as must needs
Tempt to repeat the wrong! And now, its strings
Boldlier swept, the long sequacious[245] notes
Over delicious surges sink and rise,
Such a soft floating witchery of sound
As twilight Elfins make, when they at eve
Voyage on gentle gales from Fairy-Land,
Where Melodies round honey-dropping flowers,
Footless and wild, like birds of Paradise,
Nor pause, nor perch, hovering on untamed wing!
O the one Life within us and abroad,
Which meets all motion and becomes its soul,
A light in sound, a sound-like power in light,
Rhythm in all thought, and joyance everywhere—
Methinks, it should have been impossible
Not to love all things in a world so filled;
Where the breeze warbles, and the mute still air
Is Music slumbering on her instrument.

And thus, my love! as on the midway slope
Of yonder hill I stretch my limbs at noon,
Whilst through my half-closed eye-lids I behold
The sunbeams dance, like diamonds, on the main,
And tranquil muse upon tranquility;
Full many a thought uncalled and undetained,
And many idle flitting phantasies,
Traverse my indolent and passive brain,
As wild and various as the random gales
That swell and flutter on this subject lute!

And what if all of animated nature
Be but organic Harps diversely framed,
That tremble into thought, as o'er them sweeps
Plastic and vast, one intellectual breeze,
At once the Soul of each, and God of All?

But thy more serious eye a mild reproof
Darts, O beloved woman! nor such thoughts
Dim and unhallowed dost thou not reject,
And biddest me walk humbly with my God.
Meek daughter in the family of Christ!
Well hast thou said and holily dispraised
These shapings of the unregenerate[246] mind;
Bubbles that glitter as they rise and break
On vain Philosophy's aye-babbling spring.
For never guiltless may I speak of him,
The Incomprehensible! save when with awe
I praise him, and with Faith that inly feels;
Who with his saving mercies healed me,
A sinful and most miserable man,
Wildered and dark, and gave me to possess
Peace, and this cot, and thee, heart-honored Maid!

Love

All thoughts, all passions, all delights,
Whatever stirs this mortal frame,
All are but ministers of Love,
    And feed his sacred flame.
Oft in my waking dreams do I
Live o'er again that happy hour,
When midway on the mount I lay,
    Beside the ruined tower.
The moonshine, stealing o'er the scene
Had blended with the lights of eve;
And she was there, my hope, my joy,
    My own dear Genevieve!
She leant against the arméd man,
The statue of the arméd knight;
She stood and listened to my lay,
    Amid the lingering light.
Few sorrows hath she of her own,
My hope! my joy! my Genevieve!
She loves me best, whene'er I sing
    The songs that make her grieve.

I played a soft and doleful air,
I sang an old and moving story—
An old rude song, that suited well
    That ruin wild and hoary.
She listened with a flitting blush,
With downcast eyes and modest grace;
For well she know, I could not choose
    But gaze upon her face.
I told her of the Knight that wore
Upon his shield a burning brand;
And that for ten long years he wooed
    The Lady of the Land.
I told her how he pined: and ah!
The deep, the low, the pleading tone
With which I sang another's love,
    Interpreted my own.
She listened with a flitting blush,
With downcast eyes, and modest grace;
And she forgave me, that I gazed
    Too fondly on her face!
But when I told the cruel scorn
That crazed that bold and lovely Knight,
And that he crossed the mountain-woods,
    Nor rested day nor night;
That sometimes from the savage den,
And sometimes from the darksome shade,
And sometimes starting up at once
    In green and sunny glade,—
There came and looked him in the face
An angel beautiful and bright;
And that he knew it was a Fiend,
    This miserable Knight!
And that unknowing what he did,
He leaped amid a murderous band,
And saved from outrage worse than death
    The Lady of the Land!
And how she wept, and clasped his knees;
And how she tended him in vain—
And ever strove to expiate
    The scorn that crazed his brain;—

And that she nursed him in a cave;
And how his madness went away,
When on the yellow forest-leaves
    A dying man he lay;—
His dying words—but when I reached
That tenderest strain of all the ditty,
My faultering voice and pausing harp
    Disturbed her soul with pity!
All impulses of soul and sense
Had thrilled my guileless Genevieve;
The music and the doleful tale,
    The rich and balmy eve;
And hopes, and fears that kindle hope,
An undistinguishable throng,
And gentle wishes long subdued,
    Subdued and cherished long!
She wept with pity and delight,
She blushed with love, and virgin-shame;
And like the murmur of a dream,
    I heard her breathe my name.
Her bosom heaved—she stepped aside,
As conscious of my look she stepped—
Then suddenly, with timorous eye
    She fled to me and wept.
She half enclosed me with her arms,
She pressed me with a meek embrace;
And bending back her head, looked up,
    And gazed upon my face.
'Twas partly love, and partly fear,
And partly 'twas a bashful art,
That I might rather feel, than see,
    The swelling of her heart.
I calmed her fears, and she was calm,
And told her love with virgin pride;
And so I won my Genevieve,
    My bright and beauteous Bride.

NOVALIS
(Georg Friedrich Philipp von Hardenberg)
1772 -1801

To the Virgin

A THOUSAND HANDS, DEVOUTLY TENDER,[247]
   Have sought thy beauty to express,
But none, oh Mary, none can render,
   As my soul sees, thy loveliness.

I gaze as earth's confusion fadeth
   Like to a dream, and leaves behind
A heaven of sweetness which pervadeth
   My whole rapt being—heart and mind.

from **Hymn to the Night**

1

Before all the wondrous shows of the widespread space around him, what living, sentient thing loves not the all-joyous light—with its colors, its rays and undulations, its gentle omnipresence in the form of the wakening Day? The giant-world of the unresting constellations inhales it as the innermost soul of life, and floats dancing in its blue flood—the sparkling, ever-tranquil stone, the thoughtful, imbibing plant, and the wild, burning multiform beast inhales it—but more than all, the lordly stranger with the sense-filled eyes, the swaying walk, and the sweetly closed, melodious lips. Like a king over earthly nature, it rouses every force to countless transformations, binds and unbinds innumerable alliances, hangs its heavenly form around every earthly substance.—Its presence alone reveals the marvelous splendor of the kingdoms of the world.

Aside I turn to the holy, unspeakable, mysterious Night. Afar lies the world—sunk in a deep grave—waste and lonely is its place. In the chords of the bosom blows a deep sadness. I am ready to sink away in drops of dew, and mingle with the ashes.—The distances of memory, the wishes of youth, the dreams of childhood, the brief joys and vain hopes of a whole long life, arise in gray garments, like an evening vapor after the sunset. In other regions the light has pitched its joyous tents. What if it should never return to its children, who wait for it with the faith of innocence?

What springs up all at once so sweetly boding in my heart, and stills the soft air of sadness? Dost thou also take a pleasure in us, dark Night? What holdest thou under thy mantle, that with hidden power affects my soul? Precious balm drips from thy hand out of its bundle of poppies. Thou upliftest the heavy-laden wings of the soul. Darkly and inexpressibly are we moved—joy-startled, I see a grave face that, tender and worshipful, inclines toward me, and, amid manifold entangled locks, reveals the youthful loveliness of the Mother. How poor and childish a thing seems to me now the Light—how joyous and welcome the departure of the day—because the Night turns away from thee thy servants, you now strew in the gulfs of space those flashing globes, to proclaim thy omnipotence—thy return—in seasons of thy absence. More heavenly than those glittering stars we hold the eternal eyes which the Night hath opened within us. Farther they see than the palest of those countless hosts—needing no aid from the light, they penetrate the depths of a loving soul—that fills a loftier region with bliss ineffable. Glory to the queen of the world, to the great prophet of the holier worlds, to the guardian of blissful love—she sends thee to me—thou tenderly beloved—the gracious sun of the Night,—now am I awake—for now am I thine and mine—thou hast made me know the Night—made of me a man—consume with spirit-fire my body, that I, turned to finer air, may mingle more closely with thee, and then our bridal night endure forever.

GEORGE GORDON, LORD BYRON
1788-1824

from **Childe Harold's Pilgrimage—Canto III**

XIII

WHERE ROSE THE MOUNTAINS, THERE TO HIM WERE FRIENDS;
Where rolled the ocean, thereon was his home;
Where a blue sky, and glowing clime, extends,
He had the passion and the power to roam;
The desert, forest, cavern, breaker's foam,
Were unto him companionship; they spake
A mutual language, clearer than the tome
Of his land's tongue, which he would oft forsake
For nature's pages glassed by sunbeams on the lake.

LXXII

I live not in myself, but I become
Portion of that around me; and to me,
High mountains are a feeling, but the hum
Of human cities torture: I can see
Nothing to loathe in Nature, save to be
A link reluctant in a fleshly chain,
Classed among creatures, when the soul can flee,
And with the sky, the peak, the heaving plain
Of ocean, or the stars, mingle, and not in vain.

LXXV

Are not the mountains, waves, and skies a part
Of me and of my soul, as I of them?
Is not the love of these deep in my heart
With a pure passion? Should I not contemn
All objects, if compared with these? And stem

A tide of suffering, rather than forego
Such feelings for the hard and worldly phlegm
Of those whose eyes are only turned below,
Gazing upon the ground, with thoughts which dare not glow?

LXXXVIII

Ye stars! Which are the poetry of heaven,
If in your bright leaves we would read the fate
Of men and empires,—'tis to be forgiven,
That in our aspirations to be great,
Our destinies o'erleap their mortal state,
And claim a kindred with you; for ye are
A beauty and a mystery, and create
In us such love and reverence from afar,
That fortune, fame, power, life, have named themselves a star.

LXXXIX

All heaven and earth are still—though not in sleep,
But breathless, as we grow when feeling most;
And silent, as we stand in thoughts too deep:—
All heaven and earth are still: from the high host
Of stars, to the lulled lake and mountain-coast,
All is concentered[248] in a life intense,
Where not a beam, nor air, nor leaf is lost,
But hath a part of being, and a sense
Of that which is of all Creator and defense.

XC

Then stirs the feeling infinite, so felt
In solitude, where we are least alone;
A truth, which through our being then doth melt,
And purifies from self: it is a tone,
The soul and source of music, which makes known
Eternal harmony, and sheds a charm,

Like to the fabled Cytherea's[249] zone,
   Binding all things with beauty;—'twould disarm
The specter Death, had he substantial power to harm.

XCII

   The sky is changed!—and such a change! O night,
   And storm, and darkness, ye are wondrous strong,
   Yet lovely in your strength, as is the light
   Of a dark eye in woman! Far along,
   From peak to peak, the rattling crags among,
   Leaps the live thunder! Not from one lone cloud,
   But every mountain now hath found a tongue;
   And Jura answers, through her misty shroud,
Back to the joyous Alps, who call to her aloud!

XCIII

   And this is in the night:—Most glorious night!
   Thou wert not sent for slumber! Let me be
   A sharer in thy fierce and far delight—
   A portion of the tempest and of thee!
   How the lit lake shines, a phosphoric sea,
   And the big rain comes dancing to the earth!
   And now again 'tis black, and now, the glee
   Of the loud hills shakes with its mountain-mirth,
As if they did rejoice o'er a young earthquake's birth.

CHARLOTTE EATON
1788–1859

Song of Psyyha

I LOVE YOU PASSIONATELY![250]
I love you as I love the sun overhead,
The earth underfoot,
The flowers that spring out of the earth,
The fresh breezes of the sea,
The morning star, gold-fluctuating Venus,
Or calm white steadfast Jupiter.

I love you passionately!
The brawny beautiful arms made for enfolding,
The eyes brown and limpid, brimming over with sweetness.

It is necessary to me that your heart beats,
And that you inhale with conscious pleasure the soft spring air,
That you love light, color, action, and are ambitious,
That you love the beauty of the human face and form,
And portray them both with mastery;
That you grasp that which is not graspable by all,
And know that which is not knowable to all;
That you have eyes—for a purpose,
A heart—for a purpose,
And an inquisitive soul—for a purpose.

CHIPPEWA SONGS
(Native American)

Dream Song

IN THE SKY
I am walking,
A bird
I Accompany.

Love Song

Oh
I am thinking
Oh
I am thinking
I have found my lover
Oh
I think it is so!

JOSEPH von EICHENDORFF
1788-1857

Morning Prayer

O Silence, wondrous and profound![251]
    O'er earth doth solitude still reign;
The woods alone incline their heads,
    As if the Lord walked o'er the plain.

I feel new life within me glow;
    Where now is my distress and care?
Here in the blush of waking morn,
    I blush at yesterday's despair.

To me, a pilgrim, shall the world,
    With all its joy and sorrows, be
But as a bridge that leads, O Lord,
    Across the stream of time to Thee.

And should my song woo worldly gifts,
    The base rewards of vanity—
Dash down my lyre! I'll hold my peace
    Before thee to eternity.

PERCY BYSSHE SHELLEY
1792-1822

Hymn of Pan

FROM THE FORESTS AND HIGHLANDS
We come, we come;
From the river-girt islands,
Where loud waves are dumb
Listening to my sweet pipings.
The wind in the reeds and the rushes,
The bees on the bells of thyme,
The birds on the myrtle-bushes,
The cicale above in the lime,
And the lizards below in the grass,
Were as silent as ever old Tmolus[252] was,
Listening to my sweet pipings.

Liquid Peneus[253] was flowing,
And all dark Temple lay
In Pelion's shadow, outgrowing
The light of the dying day,
Speeded by my sweet pipings.
The Sileni[254] and Sylvans[255] and Fauns,
And the Nymphs of the woods and waves,
To the edge of the moist river-lawns,
And the brink of the dewy caves,
And all that did then attend and follow,
Were silent with love, as you now, Apollo,
With envy of my sweet pipings.

I sang of the dancing stars,
I sang of the dedal[256] earth,
And of Heaven, and the giant wars,
And Love, and Death, and Birth.
And then I changed my pipings,—
Singing how down the vale of Maenalus
I pursued a maiden, and clasped a reed:

Gods and men, we are all deluded thus!
It breaks in our bosom, and then we bleed.
All wept—as I think both ye now would,
If envy or age had not frozen your blood—
At the sorrow of my sweet pipings.

To a Sky-Lark

Hail to thee, blithe Spirit!
Bird thou never wert—
That from Heaven, or near it,
Pourest thy full heart
In profuse strains of unpremeditated art.

Higher still and higher
From the earth thou springest
Like a cloud of fire;
The blue deep thou wingest,
And singing still dost soar, and soaring ever singest.

In the golden lightning
Of the sunken Sun—
O'er which clouds are bright'ning,
Thou dost float and run;
Like an unbodied joy whose race is just begun.

The pale purple even
Melts around thy flight,
Like a star of Heaven
In the broad day-light
Thou art unseen,—but yet I hear thy shrill delight,

Keen as are the arrows
Of that silver sphere,
Whose intense lamp narrows
In the white dawn clear
Until we hardly see—we feel that it is there.

211

All the earth and air
With thy voice is loud,
As, when Night is bare,
From one lonely cloud
The moon rains out her beams—and Heaven is overflowed.

What thou art we know not;
What is most like thee?
From rainbow clouds there flow not
Drops so bright to see
As from thy presence showers a rain of melody.

Like a Poet hidden
In the light of thought,
Singing hymns unbidden,
Till the world is wrought
To sympathy with hopes and fears it heeded not:

Like a high-born maiden
In a palace tower,
Soothing her love-laden
Soul in secret hour,
With music sweet as love—which overflows her bower:

Like a glow-worm golden
In a dell of dew,
Scattering unbeholden
Its aerial hue
Among the flowers and grass which screen it from the view:

Like a rose embowered
In its own green leaves—
By warm winds deflowered—
Till the scent it gives
Makes faint with too much sweet those heavy-winged thieves:

Sound of vernal showers
On the twinkling grass,
Rain-awakened flowers,

All that ever was
Joyous, and clear, and fresh, thy music doth surpass.

Teach us, Sprite or Bird,
What sweet thoughts are thine;
I have never heard
Praise of love or wine
That panted forth a flood of rapture so divine:

Chorus hymeneal
Or triumphal chaunt[257]
Matched with thine, would be all
But an empty vaunt,
A thing wherein we feel there is some hidden want.

What objects are the fountains
Of thy happy strain?
What fields, or waves, or mountains?
What shapes of sky or plain?
What love of thine own kind? what ignorance of pain?

With thy clear keen joyance
Languor cannot be—
Shadow of annoyance
Never came near thee;
Thou lovest—but ne'er knew love's sad satiety.

Waking or asleep,
Thou of death must deem
Things more true and deep
Than we mortals dream,
Or how could thy notes flow in such a crystal stream?

We look before and after,
And pine for what is not—
Our sincerest laughter
With some pain is fraught—
Our sweetest songs are those that tell of saddest thought.

Yet if we could scorn
Hate and pride and fear;
If we were things born
Not to shed a tear,
I know not how thy joy we ever should come near.

Better than all measures
Of delightful sound—
Better than all treasures
That in books are found—
Thy skill to poet were, thou Scorner of the ground!

Teach me half the gladness
That thy brain must know,
Such harmonious madness
From my lips would flow
The world should listen then—as I am listening now.

RALPH WALDO EMERSON
1803-1882

Eros

THE SENSE OF THE WORLD IS SHORT,—
Long and various the report,—
To love and be beloved;
Men and gods have not outlearned it;
And how oft soe'er they've turned it,
'Tis not to be improved.

Give All to Love

Give all to love;
Obey thy heart;
Friends, kindred, days,
Estate, good-fame,
Plans, credit, and the muse,
Nothing refuse.

'T is a brave master;
Let it have scope:
Follow it utterly,
Hope beyond hope:
High and more high,
It dives into noon,
With wing unspent,
Untold intent;
But it is a god,
Knows its own path,
And the outlets of the sky.
It was never for the mean;
It requireth courage stout.
Souls above doubt,
Valor unbending,
It will reward,

They shall return
More than they were,
And ever ascending.

Leave all for love;
Yet, hear me, yet,
One word more thy heart behoved,
One pulse more of firm endeavor,
Keep thee to-day,
To-morrow, forever,
Free as an Arab
Of thy beloved.

Cling with life to the maid;
But when the surprise,
Vague shadow of surmise
Flits across her bosom young,
Of a joy apart from thee,
Free be she, fancy-free;
Nor thou detain her vesture's hem,
Nor the palest rose she flung
From her summer diadem.

Though thou loved her as thyself,
As a self of purer clay,
Though her parting dims the day,
Stealing grace from all alive;
Heartily know,
When half-gods go,
The gods arrive.

To Eva

O Fair and stately maid, whose eye
Was kindled in the upper sky
At the same torch that lighted mine;
For so I must interpret still
Thy sweet dominion o'er my will,
A sympathy divine.

Ah! let me blameless gaze upon
Features that seem in heart my own,
Nor fear those watchful sentinels
Which charm the more their glance forbids,
Chaste glowing underneath their lids
With fire that draws while it repels.

Thine eyes still shined for me, though far
I lonely roved the land or sea,
As I behold yon evening star,
Which yet beholds not me.

This morn I climbed the misty hill,
And roamed the pastures through;
How danced thy form before my path,
Amidst the deep-eyed dew!

When the red bird spread his sable wing,
And showed his side of flame,
When the rose-bud ripened to the rose,
In both I read thy name.

Bacchus

Bring me wine, but wine which never grew
In the belly of the grape,
Or grew on vine whose tap-roots, reaching through
Under the Andes to the Cape,
Suffer no savor of the world to 'scape.

Let its grapes the morn salute
From a nocturnal root,
Which feels the acrid juice
Of Styx and Erebus;[258]
And turns the woe of Night,
By its own craft, to a more rich delight.

We buy ashes for bread;
We buy diluted wine;

Give me of the true,—
Whose ample leaves and tendrils curled
Among the silver hills of heaven
Draw everlasting dew;
Wine of wine,
Blood of the world,
Form of forms and mould of statures,
That I intoxicated,
And by the draught assimilated,
May float at pleasure through all natures;
The bird-language rightly spell,
And that which roses say so well.

Wine that is shed
Like the torrents of the sun
Up the horizon walls,
Or like the Atlantic streams which run
When the South Sea calls.

Water and bread,
Food which needs no transmuting,
Rainbow-flowering, wisdom-fruiting,
Wine which is already man,
Food which teach and reason can.

Wine which music is,—
Music and wine are one,—
That I, drinking this,
Shall hear far Chaos talk with me;
Kings unborn shall walk with me;
And the poor grass shall plot and plan
What it will do when it is man.
Quickened so, will I unlock
Every crypt of every rock.

I thank the joyful juice
For all I know;—
Winds of remembering
Of the ancient being blow,

218

And seeming-solid walls of use
Open and flow.

Pour, Bacchus! the remembering wine;
Retrieve the loss of me and mine!
Vine for vine be antidote,
And the grape requite the lote!
Haste to cure the old despair,—
Reason in nature's lotus drenched,
The memory of ages quenched;
Give them again to shine;
Let wine repair what this undid;
And where the infection slid,
And dazzling memory revive;
Refresh the faded tints,
Recut the aged prints,
And write my old adventures, with the pen
Which, on the first day drew,
Upon the tablets blue,
The dancing Pleiads and the eternal men.

SARAH F. ADAMS
1805-1848

Near, My God, to Thee

NEAR, MY GOD, TO THEE,
Nearer to Thee!
E'en though it be a cross
That raiseth me;
Still, all my song would be,—
Nearer, my God, to Thee,
Nearer to Thee![259]

Though, like a wanderer,
Daylight all gone,
Darkness be over me,
My rest a stone;
Yet in my dreams I'd be
Nearer, my God, to Thee,
Nearer to Thee!

There let the way appear
Steps unto Heaven;
All that thou sendest me
In mercy given;
Angels to beckon me
Nearer, my God, to Thee,
Nearer to Thee!

Then with my waking thoughts,
Bright with thy praise,
Out of my stony griefs
Bethel I'll raise;
So by my woes to be
Nearer, my God, to Thee,
Nearer to Thee!

Sarah F. Adams

Or if on joyful wing,
Cleaving the sky,
Sun, moon, and stars forgot.
Upwards I fly,—
Still, all my song shall be:
Nearer, my God, to Thee,
Nearer to Thee!

ELIZABETH BARRETT BROWNING
1806-1861

from Sonnets from the Portuguese

X

YET, LOVE, MERE LOVE, IS BEAUTIFUL INDEED
And worthy of acceptation. Fire is bright,
Let temple burn, or flax; and equal light
Leaps in the flame from cedar-plank or weed:
And love is fire. And when I say at need
I love thee ... mark! ... *I love thee*—in thy sight
I stand transfigured, glorified aright,
With conscience of the new rays that proceed
Out of my face toward thine. There's nothing low
In love, when love the lowest: meanest creatures
Who love God, God accepts while loving so.
And what I *feel,* across the inferior features
Of what I *am,* doth flash itself, and show
How that great work of Love enhances Nature's.

XXV

A heavy heart, Belovèd, have I borne
From year to year until I saw thy face,
And sorrow after sorrow took the place
Of all those natural joys as lightly worn
As the stringed pearls, each lifted in its turn
By a beating heart at dance-time. Hopes apace
Were changed to long despairs, till God's own grace
Could scarcely lift above the world forlorn
My heavy heart. Then *thou* didst bid me bring
And let it drop adown thy calmly great
Deep being! Fast it sinketh, as a thing
Which its own nature doth precipitate,
Which thine doth close above it, mediating
Betwixt the stars and the unaccomplished fate.

XXIX

I think of thee!—my thoughts do twine and bud
About thee, as wild vines, about a tree,
Put out broad leaves, and soon there's nought to see
Except the straggling green which hides the wood.
Yet, O my palm-tree, be it understood
I will not have my thoughts instead of thee
Who art dearer, better! Rather, instantly
Renew thy presence; as a strong tree should,
Rustle thy boughs and set thy trunk all bare,
And let these bands of greenery which insphere[260] thee
Drop heavily down,—burst, shattered, everywhere!
Because, in this deep joy to see and hear thee
And breathe within thy shadow a new air,
I do not think of thee—I am too near thee.

XLIII

How do I love thee? Let me count the ways.
I love thee to the depth and breadth and height
My soul can reach, when feeling out of sight
For the ends of Being and ideal Grace.
I love thee to the level of everyday's
Most quiet need, by sun and candle-light.
I love thee freely, as men strive for Right;
I love thee purely, as they turn from Praise.
I love thee with a passion put to use
In my old griefs, and with my childhood's faith.
I love thee with a love I seemed to lose
With my lost saints,—I love thee with the breath,
Smiles, tears, of all my life!—and, if God choose,
I shall but love thee better after death.

ANASTASIUS GRÜN
1806-1876

The Bridge

THERE'S A WONDROUS BRIDGE, AND O'ER IT,[261]
    Joyous loves pass to and fro;
There with sweetest balsam breathings,
    Airs of Spring forever blow.

Forth from heart to heart extending,
    Leads the bridge its wondrous way;
Yet alone to Love 'tis open,
    Love, and those who own her sway,

Love alone its part hath builded,
    All its forms of roses plied:
Soul to soul thereon doth wander,
    As the bridegroom to the bride.

Love did form its beauteous arches,
    Finished and adorned the whole:
Love doth stand thereon as keeper,
    Kisses are the bridge's toll.

Sweetest maiden, wouldst thou gladly,
    Such a bridge of wonder see?
Be it so, yet must thou truly,
    Join in building it with me.

Chase the clouds from off thy forehead,
    Let my eyes thy love glance meet,
Join thy lips to mine in kisses,
    And the bridge is all complete.

JOHN GREENLEAF WHITTIER
1807-1892

The Worship of Nature

THE HARP AT NATURE'S ADVENT STRUNG
Has never ceased to play;
The song the stars of morning sung
Has never died away.

And prayer is made, and praise is given,
By all things near and far;
The ocean looketh up to heaven,
And mirrors every star.

Its waves are kneeling on the strand,
As kneels the human knee,
Their white locks bowing to the sand,
The priesthood of the sea!

They pour their glittering treasures forth,
Their gifts of pearl they bring,
And all the listening hills of earth
Take up the song they sing.

The green earth sends its incense up
From many a mountain shrine;
From folded leaf and dewy cup
She pours her sacred wine.

The mists above the morning rills
Rise white as wings of prayer;
The altar-curtains of the hills
Are sunset's purple air.

The winds with hymns of praise are loud,
Or low with sobs of pain,—

The thunder-organ of the cloud,
The dropping tears of rain.

With drooping head and branches crossed
The twilight forest grieves,
Or speaks with tongues of Pentecost
From all its sunlit leaves.

The blue sky is the temple's arch,
Its transept earth and air,
The music of its starry march
The chorus of a prayer.

So Nature keeps the reverent frame
With which her years began,
And all her signs and voices shame
The prayerless heart of man.

PAPAGO SONGS
(Native American)

Dream Song of a Woman

WHERE THE MOUNTAIN CROSSES,
On top of the mountain,
   I do not myself know where.
I wandered where my mind and my heart
   Seemed to be lost.
I wandered away.

Ceremonial Sun Song

In the east is the dwelling of the sun.
On top of this dwelling place
The sun comes up and travels over our heads.
Below we travel.
I raise my right hand to the sun
And then stroke my body
In the ceremonial manner.

Rain Song (1)

Close to the east the great ocean is singing.
The waves are rolling toward me, covered with many clouds.
Even here I catch the sound.
The earth is shaking beneath me and I hear the deep rumbling.

Rain Song (2)

A cloud on top of Evergreen Mountain is singing,
A cloud on top of Evergreen Mountain is standing still,
It is raining and thundering up there,
Under the mountain the corn tassels are shaking,
Under the mountain the horns of the child corn are glistening.

JOHN STUART BLACKIE
1809-1895

All Things Are Full of God

ALL THINGS ARE FULL OF GOD. THUS SPOKE[262]
Wise Thales[263] in the days
When subtle Greece to thought awoke
And soared in lofty ways.
And now what wisdom have we more?
No sage divining-rod
Hath taught than this a deeper lore,
ALL THINGS ARE FULL OF GOD.

The Light that gloweth in the sky
And shimmers in the sea,
That quivers in the painted fly
And gems the pictured lea,
The million hues of Heaven above
And Earth below are one,
And every lightful eye doth love
The primal light, the Sun.

Even so, all vital virtue flows
From life's first fountain, God;
And he who feels, and he who knows,
Doth feel and know from God.
As fishes swim in briny sea,
As fowl do float in air,
From Thy embrace we cannot flee;
We breathe, and Thou art there.

Go, take thy glass, astronomer,
And all the girth survey
Of sphere harmonious linked to sphere,
In endless bright array.
All that far-reaching Science there
Can measure with her rod,

All powers, all laws, are but the fair
Embodied thoughts of God.

Trimurti

Trimurti, Trimurti,[264]
Despise not the name;
Think and know
Before thou blame!

Look upon the face of Nature
In the flush of June;
BRAHMA is the great Creator,
Life is Brahma's boon.
Dost thou hear the zephyr blowing?
That is Brahma's breath,
Vital breath, live virtue showing
'Neath the ribs of death.
Dost thou see the fountain flowing?
That is Brahma's blood,
Lucid blood—the same is glowing
In the purpling bud.
Brahma's Eyes look forth divining
From the welkin's brow,
Full bright eyes—the same are shining
In the sacred cow.
Air, and Fire, and running River,
And the procreant clod,
Are but faces changing ever
Of one changeless God.
When thy wingèd thought ascendeth
Where high thoughts are free,
This is Brahma when he lendeth
Half the God to thee.
Brahma is the great Creator,
Life a mystic drama;
Heaven, and Earth, and living Nature
Are but masks of Brahma.

ALFRED, LORD TENNYSON
1809-1892

from **In Memoriam**

LXXXVI

SWEET AFTER SHOWERS, AMBROSIAL AIR,
That rollest from the gorgeous gloom
Of evening over brake and bloom
And meadow, slowly breathing bare

The round of space, and rapt below
Thro' all the dewy-tasseled wood,
And shadowing down the horned flood
In ripples, fan my brows and blow

The fever from my cheek, and sigh
The full new life that feeds thy breath
Throughout my frame, till Doubt and Death,
Ill brethren, let the fancy fly

From belt to belt of crimson seas
On leagues of odor streaming far,
To where in yonder orient star
A hundred spirits whisper 'Peace.'

St. Agnes' Eve

Deep on the convent-roof the snows
    Are sparkling to the moon:
My breath to heaven like vapor goes:
    May my soul follow soon!
The shadows of the convent-towers
    Slant down the snowy sward,
Still creeping with the creeping hours
    That lead me to my Lord:
Make Thou my spirit pure and clear
    As are the frosty skies,

Or this first snowdrop of the year
    That in my bosom lies.

As these white robes are soiled and dark,
    To yonder shining ground;
As this pale taper's earthly spark,
    To yonder argent round;
So shows my soul before the Lamb,
    My spirit before Thee;
So in mine earthly house I am,
    To that I hope to be.
Break up the heavens, O Lord! and far,
    Thro' all yon starlight keen,
Draw me, thy bride, a glittering star,
    In raiment white and clean.

He lifts me to the golden doors;
    The flashes come and go;
All heaven bursts her starry floors,
    And strows her lights below,
And deepens on and up! the gates
    Roll back and far within
For me the heavenly bridegroom waits,
    To make me pure of sin.
The Sabbaths of Eternity,
    One Sabbath deep and wide—
A light upon the shining sea—
    The Bridegroom with his bride!

Now Sleeps the Crimson Petal

Now sleeps the crimson petal, now the white;
Nor waves the cypress in the palace walk;
Nor winks the gold fin in the porphyry[265] font:
The firefly wakens: waken thou with me.

Now droops the milk-white peacock like a ghost,
And like a ghost she glimmers on to me.

Now lies the Earth all Danaë[266] to the stars,
And all thy heart lies open unto me.

Now slides the silent meteor on, and leaves
A shining furrow, as thy thoughts in me.

Now folds the lily all her sweetness up,
And slips into the bosom of the lake:
So fold thyself, my dearest, thou, and slip
Into my bosom and be lost in me.

CHARLOTTE BRONTË
1816-1855

Life

LIFE, BELIEVE, IS NOT A DREAM
So dark as sages say;
Oft a little morning rain
Foretells a pleasant day.
Sometimes there are clouds of gloom,
But these are transient all;
If the shower will make the roses bloom,
O why lament its fall?
Rapidly, merrily,
Life's sunny hours flit by,
Gratefully, cheerily
Enjoy them as they fly!
What though Death at times steps in,
And calls our Best away?
What though sorrow seems to win,
O'er hope, a heavy sway?
Yet Hope again elastic springs,
Unconquered, though she fell;
Still buoyant are her golden wings,
Still strong to bear us well.
Manfully, fearlessly,
The day of trial bear,
For gloriously, victoriously,
Can courage quell despair!

Passion

Some have won a wild delight,
By daring wilder sorrow;
Could I gain thy love to-night,
I'd hazard death to-morrow.

Could the battle-struggle earn
One kind glance from thine eye,
How this withering heart would burn,
The heady fight to try!

Welcome nights of broken sleep,
And days of carnage cold,
Could I deem that thou wouldst weep
To hear my perils told.

Tell me, if with wandering bands
I roam full far away,
Wilt thou to those distant lands
In spirit ever stray?

Wild, long, a trumpet sounds afar;
Bid me—bid me go
Where Seik[267] and Briton meet in war,
On Indian Sutlej's flow.

Blood has dyed the Sutlej's waves
With scarlet stain, I know;
Indus' borders yawn with graves,
Yet, command me go!

Though rank and high the holocaust
Of nations steams to heaven,
Glad I'd join the death-doomed host,
Were but the mandate given.

Passion's strength should nerve my arm,
Its ardor stir my life,
Till human force to that dread charm
Should yield and sink in wild alarm,
Like trees to tempest-strife.

If, hot from war, I seek thy love,
Darest thou turn aside?
Darest thou then my fire reprove,
By scorn, and maddening pride?

No—my will shall yet control
Thy will, so high and free,
And love shall tame that haughty soul—
Yes—tenderest love for me.

I'll read my triumph in thine eyes,
Behold, and prove the change;
Then leave, perchance, my noble prize,
Once more in arms to range.

I'd die when all the foam is up,
The bright wine sparkling high;
Nor wait till in the exhausted cup
Life's dull dregs only lie.

Then Love thus crowned with sweet reward,
Hope blest with fullness large,
I'd mount the saddle, draw the sword,
And perish in the charge!

EMILY BRONTË
1818-1849

A Little While, A Little While

A LITTLE WHILE, A LITTLE WHILE,
The weary task is put away,
And I can sing and I can smile,
Alike, while I have holiday.

Where wilt thou go, my harassed heart—
What thought, what scene invites thee now
What spot, or near or far apart,
Has rest for thee, my weary brow?

There is a spot, 'mid barren hills,
Where winter howls, and driving rain;
But, if the dreary tempest chills,
There is a light that warms again.

The house is old, the trees are bare,
Moonless above bends twilight's dome;
But what on earth is half so dear—
So longed for—as the hearth of home?

The mute bird sitting on the stone,
The dank moss dripping from the wall,
The thorn-trees gaunt, the walks o'ergrown,
I love them—how I love them all!

Still, as I mused, the naked room,
The alien firelight died away;
And from the midst of cheerless gloom,
I passed to bright, unclouded day.

A little and a lone green lane
That opened on a common wide;

A distant, dreamy, dim blue chain
Of mountains circling every side.

A heaven so clear, an earth so calm,
So sweet, so soft, so hushed an air;
And, deepening still the dream-like charm,
Wild moor-sheep feeding everywhere.

That was the scene, I knew it well;
I knew the turfy pathway's sweep,
That, winding o'er each billowy swell,
Marked out the tracks of wandering sheep.

Could I have lingered but an hour,
It well had paid a week of toil;
But Truth has banished Fancy's power:
Restraint and heavy task recoil.

Even as I stood with raptured eye,
Absorbed in bliss so deep and dear,
My hour of rest had fleeted by,
And back came labor, bondage, care.

A Daydream

On a sunny brae alone I lay
One summer afternoon;
It was the marriage-time of May,
With her young lover, June.

From her mother's heart seemed loath to part
That queen of bridal charms,
But her father smiled on the fairest child
He ever held in his arms.

The trees did wave their plumy crests,
The glad birds caroled clear;
And I, of all the wedding guests,
Was only sullen there!

There was not one, but wished to shun
My aspect void of cheer;
The very gray rocks, looking on,
Asked, "What do you here?"

And I could utter no reply;
In sooth, I did not know
Why I had brought a clouded eye
To greet the general glow.

So, resting on a heathy bank,
I took my heart to me;
And we together sadly sank
Into a reverie.

We thought, "When winter comes again,
Where will these bright things be?
All vanished, like a vision vain,
An unreal mockery!

"The birds that now so blithely sing,
Through deserts, frozen dry,
Poor spectres of the perished spring,
In famished troops will fly.

"And why should we be glad at all?
The leaf is hardly green,
Before a token of its fall
Is on the surface seen!"

Now, whether it were really so,
I never could be sure;
But as in fit of peevish woe,
I stretched me on the moor,

A thousand thousand gleaming fires
Seemed kindling in the air;
A thousand thousand silvery lyres
Resounded far and near:

Methought, the very breath I breathed
Was full of sparks divine,
And all my heather-couch was wreathed
By that celestial shine!

And, while the wide earth echoing rung
To that strange minstrelsy
The little glittering spirits sung,
Or seemed to sing, to me:

"O mortal! mortal! let them die;
Let time and tears destroy,
That we may overflow the sky
With universal joy!

"Let grief distract the sufferer's breast,
And night obscure his way;
They hasten him to endless rest,
And everlasting day.

"To thee the world is like a tomb,
A desert's naked shore;
To us, in unimagined bloom,
It brightens more and more!

"And, could we lift the veil, and give
One brief glimpse to thine eye,
Thou wouldst rejoice for those that live,
Because they live to die."

The music ceased; the noonday dream,
Like dream of night, withdrew;
But Fancy, still, will sometimes deem
Her fond creation true.

The Visionary

Silent is the house: all are laid asleep:
One alone looks out o'er the snow-wreaths deep,
Watching every cloud, dreading every breeze
That whirls the wildering drift, and bends the groaning trees.

Cheerful is the hearth, soft the matted floor;
Not one shivering gust creeps through pane or door;
The little lamp burns straight, its rays shoot strong and far:
I trim it well, to be the wanderer's guiding-star.

Frown, my haughty sire! chide, my angry dame!
Set your slaves to spy; threaten me with shame:
But neither sire nor dame, nor prying serf shall know,
What angel nightly tracks that waste of frozen snow.

What I love shall come like visitant of air,
Safe in secret power from lurking human snare;
What loves me, no word of mine shall e'er betray,
Though for faith unstained my life must forfeit pay.

Burn, then, little lamp; glimmer straight and clear—
Hush! a rustling wing stirs, methinks, the air:
He for whom I wait, thus ever comes to me;
Strange Power! I trust thy might; trust thou my constancy.

APACHE SONGS
(Native American)

Songs of the Masked Dancers

I

WHEN THE EARTH WAS MADE;[268]
When the sky was made;
When my songs were first heard;
The holy mountain was standing toward me with life.
At the center of the sky, the holy boy walks four ways with life.
Just mine, my mountain became; standing toward me with life.
Gan[269] children became; standing toward me with life.
When the sun goes down to the earth,
Where Mescal Mountain lies with its head toward the sunrise,
Black spruce became; standing up with me.

II

Right at the center of the sky the holy boy with life walks in four
    directions.
Lightening with life in four colors comes down four times.
The place which is called black spot with life;
The place which is called blue spot with life;
The place which is called yellow spot with life;
The place which is called white spot with life;
They have heard about me,
The black Gans dance in four places.
The sun starts down toward the earth.

III

The living sky black-spotted;
The living sky blue-spotted;
The living sky yellow-spotted;

The living sky white-spotted;
The young spruce as girls stood up for their dance in the way of life.
When my songs first were, they made my songs with words of jet.
Earth when it was made,
Sky when it was made,
Earth to that end,
Sky to that end,
Black Gan, black thunder, when they came toward each other,
The various bad things that used to be vanished.
The bad wishes which were in the world vanished.
The lightning of black thunder struck four times for them.
It struck four times for me.

IV

When first my songs became,
When the sky was made,
When the earth was made,
The breath of the Gans on me made only of down;
When they heard about my life;
Where they got their life;
When they heard about me;
It stands.

V

The day broke with slender rain.
The place which is called "lightning's water stands,"
The place which is called "where the dawn strikes,"
Four places where it is called "it dawns with life,"
I land there.
The sky boys, I go among them.
He came to me with long life.
When he talked over my body with the longest life,
The voice of thunder spoke well four times.
Holy sky boy spoke to me four times.
When he talked to me my breath became.

Song of the Gotal Ceremony

The black turkey gobbler, under the east, the middle of his trail;[270]
    toward us it is about to dawn.
The black turkey gobbler, the tips of his beautiful tail;
    above us the dawn whitens.
The black turkey gobbler, the tips of his beautiful tail;
    above us the dawn becomes yellow.
The sunbeams stream forward, dawn boys,
    with shimmering shoes of yellow.
On top of the sunbeams that stream toward us they are dancing.
At the east the rainbow moves forward, dawn maidens,
    with shimmering shoes and shirts of yellow dance over us.
Beautifully over us it is dawning.

Above us among the mountains, the herbs are becoming green.
Above us on top of the mountain the herbs are becoming yellow.

Above us among the mountains, with shoes of yellow
I go around the fruits and the herbs that shimmer.
Above us among the mountains, the shimmering fruits with shoes
    and shirts of yellow are bent toward him.
On the beautiful mountains above it is daylight.

WALT WHITMAN
1819-1892

Beginning My Studies

BEGINNING MY STUDIES THE FIRST STEP PLEASED ME SO MUCH,
The mere fact consciousness, these forms, the power of motion,
The least insect or animal, the senses, eyesight, love,
The first step I say awed me and pleased me so much,
I have hardly gone and hardly wished to go any farther,
But stop and loiter all the time to sing it in ecstatic songs.

from **Song of Myself**

5

I believe in you my soul, the other I am must not abase itself to you,
And you must not be abased to the other.
Loaf with me on the grass, loose the stop from your throat,
Not words, not music or rhyme I want, not custom or lecture,
    not even the best,
Only the lull I like, the hum of your valvéd voice.
I mind how once we lay such a transparent summer morning,
How you settled your head athwart my hips and gently turned
    over upon me,
And parted the shirt from my bosom-bone, and plunged your
    tongue to my bare-stript heart,
And reached till you felt my beard, and reached till you held my feet.
Swiftly arose and spread around me the peace and knowledge that
    pass all the argument of the earth,
And I know that the hand of God is the promise of my own,
And I know that the spirit of God is the brother of my own,
And that all the men ever born are also my brothers,
    and the women my sisters and lovers,
And that a kelson[271] of the creation is love,
And limitless are leaves stiff or drooping in the fields,
And brown ants in the little wells beneath them,

And mossy scabs of the worm fence, heaped stones, elder,
　　mullein and poke-weed.

50

There is that in me—I do not know what it is—but I know it is in me.
Wrenched and sweaty—calm and cool then my body becomes,
I sleep—I sleep long.
I do not know it—it is without name—it is a word unsaid,
It is not in any dictionary, utterance, symbol.
Something it swings on more than the earth I swing on,
To it the creation is the friend whose embracing awakes me.
Perhaps I might tell more. Outlines! I plead for my brothers and sisters.
Do you see O my brothers and sisters?
It is not chaos or death—it is form, union, plan—it is eternal life—
　　it is Happiness.

from I Sing the Body Electric

1

I sing the body electric,
The armies of those I love engirth me and I engirth[272] them,
They will not let me off till I go with them, respond to them,
And discorrupt them, and charge them full with the charge of the soul.
Was it doubted that those who corrupt their own bodies conceal
　　themselves?
And if those who defile the living are as bad as they who defile the dead?
And if the body does not do fully as much as the soul?
And if the body were not the soul, what is the soul?

5

This is the female form,
A divine nimbus exhales from it from head to foot,
It attracts with fierce undeniable attraction,
I am drawn by its breath as if I were no more than a helpless vapor,
　　all falls aside but myself and it,

245

Books, art, religion, time, the visible and solid earth, and what
    was expected of heaven or feared of hell, are now consumed,
Mad filaments, ungovernable shoots play out of it, the response
    likewise ungovernable,
Hair, bosom, hips, bend of legs, negligent falling hands all
    diffused, mine too diffused,
Ebb stung by the flow and flow stung by the ebb, love-flesh swelling
    and deliciously aching,
Limitless limpid jets of love hot and enormous, quivering jelly of
    love, white-blow and delirious juice,
Bridegroom night of love working surely and softly into the prostrate
    dawn,
Undulating into the willing and yielding day,
Lost in the cleave of the clasping and sweet-fleshed day.
This the nucleus—after the child is born of woman, man is born of
    woman,
This the bath of birth, this the merge of small and large, and the
    outlet again.
Be not ashamed women, your privilege encloses the rest, and is the
    exit of the rest,
You are the gates of the body, and you are the gates of the soul.
The female contains all qualities and tempers them,
She is in her place and moves with perfect balance,
She is all things duly veiled, she is both passive and active,
She is to conceive daughters as well as sons, and sons as well as
    daughters.
As I see my soul reflected in Nature,
As I see through a mist, One with inexpressible completeness,
    sanity, beauty,
See the bent head and arms folded over the breast, the Female I see.

6

The male is not less the soul nor more, he too is in his place,
He too is all qualities, he is action and power,
The flush of the known universe is in him,
Scorn becomes him well, and appetite and defiance become him well,
The wildest largest passions, bliss that is utmost, sorrow that is
    utmost become him well, pride is for him,

The full-spread pride of man is calming and excellent to the soul,
Knowledge becomes him, he likes it always, he brings everything to
    the test of himself,
Whatever the survey, whatever the sea and the sail he strikes
    soundings at last only here,
(Where else does he strike soundings except here?)
The man's body is sacred and the woman's body is sacred,
No matter who it is, it is sacred—is it the meanest one in the
    laborers' gang?
Is it one of the dull-faced immigrants just landed on the wharf?
Each belongs here or anywhere just as much as the well-off, just as
    much as you,
Each has his or her place in the procession.

(All is a procession,
The universe is a procession with measured and perfect motion.)

Do you know so much yourself that you call the meanest ignorant?
Do you suppose you have a right to a good sight, and he or she has
    no right to a sight?
Do you think matter has cohered together from its diffuse float, and
    the soil is on the surface, and water runs and vegetation sprouts,
For you only, and not for him and her?

When I Heard the Learned Astronomer

When I heard the learned astronomer,
When the proofs, the figures, were ranged in columns before me,
When I was shown the charts and diagrams, to add, divide,
    and measure them,
When I sitting heard the astronomer where he lectured with much
    applause in the lecture-room,
How soon unaccountable I became tired and sick,
Till rising and gliding out I wandered off by myself,
In the mystical moist night-air, and from time to time,
Looked up in perfect silence at the stars.

Miracles

Why, who makes much of a miracle?
As to me I know of nothing else but miracles,
Whether I walk the streets of Manhattan,
Or dart my sight over the roofs of houses toward the sky,
Or wade with naked feet along the beach just in the edge of the water,
Or stand under trees in the woods,
Or talk by day with any one I love, or sleep in the bed at night with
    any one I love,
Or sit at table at dinner with the rest,
Or look at strangers opposite me riding in the car,
Or watch honey-bees busy around the hive of a summer forenoon,
Or animals feeding in the fields,
Or birds, or the wonderfulness of insects in the air,
Or the wonderfulness of the sundown, or of stars shining so quiet
    and bright,
Or the exquisite delicate thin curve of the new moon in spring;
These with the rest, one and all, are to me miracles,
The whole referring, yet each distinct and in its place.

To me every hour of the light and dark is a miracle,
Every cubic inch of space is a miracle,
Every square yard of the surface of the earth is spread with the same,
Every foot of the interior swarms with the same.

To me the sea is a continual miracle,
The fishes that swim—the rocks—the motion of the waves—
    the ships with men in them,
What stranger miracles are there?

Sparkles from the Wheel

Where the city's ceaseless crowd moves on the livelong day,
Withdrawn I join a group of children watching, I pause aside with them.

By the curb toward the edge of the flagging,
A knife-grinder works at his wheel sharpening a great knife,
Bending over he carefully holds it to the stone, by foot and knee,

With measured tread he turns rapidly, as he presses with light but
    firm hand,
Forth issue then in copious golden jets,
Sparkles from the wheel.

The scene and all its belongings, how they seize and affect me,
The sad sharp-chinned old man with worn clothes and broad
    shoulder-band of leather,
Myself effusing and fluid, a phantom curiously floating, now here
    absorbed and arrested,
The group, (an unminded point set in a vast surrounding,)
The attentive, quiet children, the loud, proud, restive base of the streets,
The low hoarse purr of the whirling stone, the light-pressed blade,
Diffusing, dropping, sideways-darting, in tiny showers of gold,
Sparkles from the wheel.

Song at Sunset

Splendor of ended day floating and filling me,
Hour prophetic, hour resuming the past,
Inflating my throat, you divine average,
You earth and life till the last ray gleams I sing.
Open mouth of my soul uttering gladness,
Eyes of my soul seeing perfection,
Natural life of me faithfully praising things,
Corroborating forever the triumph of things.

Illustrious every one!
Illustrious what we name space, sphere of unnumbered spirits,
Illustrious the mystery of motion in all beings, even the tiniest insect,
Illustrious the attribute of speech, the senses, the body,
Illustrious the passing light—illustrious the pale reflection on
    the new moon in the western sky,
Illustrious whatever I see or hear or touch, to the last.

Good in all,
In the satisfaction and aplomb of animals,
In the annual return of the seasons,
In the hilarity of youth,

In the strength and flush of manhood,
In the grandeur and exquisiteness of old age,
In the superb vistas of death.

Wonderful to depart!
Wonderful to be here!
The heart, to jet the all-alike and innocent blood!
To breathe the air, how delicious!
To speak—to walk—to seize something by the hand!
To prepare for sleep, for bed, to look on my rose-colored flesh!
To be conscious of my body, so satisfied, so large!
To be this incredible God I am!
To have gone forth among other Gods, these men and women I love.

Wonderful how I celebrate you and myself!
How my thoughts play subtly at the spectacles around!
How the clouds pass silently overhead!
How the earth darts on and on! and how the sun, moon, stars,
    dart on and on!
How the water sports and sings! (surely it is alive!)
How the trees rise and stand up, with strong trunks, with branches
    and leaves!
(Surely there is something more in each of the trees, some living soul.)

O amazement of things—even the least particle!
O spirituality of things!
O strain musical flowing through ages and continents, now reaching
    me and America!
I take your strong chords, intersperse them, and cheerfully pass
    them forward.
I too carol the sun, ushered or at noon, or as now, setting,
I too throb to the brain and beauty of the earth and of all the
    growths of the earth,
I too have felt the resistless call of myself.

As I steamed down the Mississippi,
As I wandered over the prairies,
As I have lived, as I have looked through my windows my eyes,
As I went forth in the morning, as I beheld the light breaking in the east,
As I bathed on the beach of the Eastern Sea, and again on the beach

of the Western Sea,
As I roamed the streets of inland Chicago, whatever streets I have
  roamed,
Or cities or silent woods, or even amid the sights of war,
Wherever I have been I have charged myself with contentment and
  triumph.

I sing to the last the equalities modern or old,
I sing the endless finalés of things,
I say Nature continues, glory continues,
I praise with electric voice,
For I do not see one imperfection in the universe,
And I do not see one cause or result lamentable at last in the universe.

O setting sun! though the time has come,
I still warble under you, if none else does, unmitigated adoration.

Joy, Shipmate, Joy!

Joy, shipmate, joy!
(Pleased to my soul at death I cry,)
Our life is closed, our life begins,
The long, long anchorage we leave,
The ship is clear at last, she leaps!
She swiftly courses from the shore,
Joy, shipmate, joy.

ANNE BRONTË
1820-1849

In a Wood on a Windy Day

MY SOUL IS AWAKENED, MY SPIRIT IS SOARING
And carried aloft on the wings of the breeze;
For above and around me the wild wind is roaring,
Arousing to rapture the earth and the seas.

The long withered grass in the sunshine is glancing,
The bare trees are tossing their branches on high;
The dead leaves beneath them are merrily dancing,
The white clouds are scudding across the blue sky.

I wish I could see how the ocean is lashing
The foam of its billows to whirlwinds of spray;
I wish I could see how its proud waves are dashing,
And hear the wild roar of their thunder to-day!

The Student's Serenade

I have slept upon my couch,
But my spirit did not rest,
For the labors of the day
Yet my weary soul oppressed;

And before my dreaming eyes
Still the learned volumes lay,
And I could not close their leaves,
And I could not turn away.

But I oped my eyes at last,
And I heard a muffled sound;
'Twas the night-breeze, come to say
That the snow was on the ground.

Then I knew that there was rest
On the mountain's bosom free;
So I left my fevered couch,
And I flew to waken thee!

I have flown to waken thee—
For, if thou wilt not arise,
Then my soul can drink no peace
From these holy moonlight skies.

And this waste of virgin snow
To my sight will not be fair,
Unless thou wilt smiling come,
Love, to wander with me there.

Then, awake! Maria, wake!
For, if thou couldst only know
How the quiet moonlight sleeps
On this wilderness of snow,

And the groves of ancient trees,
In their snowy garb arrayed,
Till they stretch into the gloom
Of the distant valley's shade;

I know thou wouldst rejoice
To inhale this bracing air;
Thou wouldst break thy sweetest sleep
To behold a scene so fair.

O'er these wintry wilds, alone,
Thou wouldst joy to wander free;
And it will not please thee less,
Though that bliss be shared with me.

Home

How brightly glistening in the sun
The woodland ivy plays!
While yonder beeches from their barks
Reflect his silver rays.

That sun surveys a lovely scene
From softly smiling skies;
And wildly through unnumbered trees
The wind of winter sighs:

Now loud, it thunders o'er my head,
And now in distance dies.
But give me back my barren hills
Where colder breezes rise;

Where scarce the scattered, stunted trees
Can yield an answering swell,
But where a wilderness of heath
Returns the sound as well.

For yonder garden, fair and wide,
With groves of evergreen,
Long winding walks, and borders trim,
And velvet lawns between;

Restore to me that little spot,
With gray walls compassed round,
Where knotted grass neglected lies,
And weeds usurp the ground.

Though all around this mansion high
Invites the foot to roam,
And though its halls are fair within—
Oh, give me back my home!

CHARLES BAUDELAIRE
1821-1867

Correspondences

In Nature's temple living pillars rise,
And words are murmured none have understood,
And man must wander through a tangled wood
Of symbols watching him with friendly eyes.

As long-drawn echoes heard far-off and dim
Mingle to one deep sound and fade away;
Vast as the night and brilliant as the day,
Colour and sound and perfume speak to him.

Some perfumes are as fragrant as a child,
Sweet as the sound of hautboys,[273] meadow-green;
Others, corrupted, rich, exultant, wild,

Have all the expansion of things infinite:
As amber, incense, musk, and benzoin,
Which sing the sense's and the soul's delight.

Exotic Perfume

When with closed eyes in autumn's eves of gold
I breathe the burning odors of your breast,
Before my eyes the hills of happy rest
Bathed in the sun's monotonous fires, unfold.

Islands of Lethe where exotic boughs
Bend with their burden of strange fruit bowed down,
Where men are upright, maids have never grown
Unkind, but bear a light upon their brows.

Led by that perfume to these lands of ease,
I see a port where many ships have flown
With sails outwearied of the wandering seas;

While the faint odors from green tamarisks blown,
Float to my soul and in my senses throng,
And mingle vaguely with the sailor's song.

Music

Music doth uplift me like a sea
Towards my planet pale,
Then through dark fogs or heaven's infinity
I lift my wandering sail.

With breast advanced, drinking the winds that flee,
And through the cordage wail,
I mount the hurrying waves night hides from me
Beneath her somber veil.

I feel the tremblings of all passions known
To ships before the breeze;
Cradled by gentle winds, or tempest-blown

I pass the abysmal seas
That are, when calm, the mirror level and fair
Of my despair!

MATTHEW ARNOLD
1822-1888

The Buried Life

LIGHT FLOWS OUR WAR OF MOCKING WORDS, AND YET,
Behold, with tears mine eyes are wet!
I feel a nameless sadness o'er me roll.
Yes, yes, we know that we can jest,
We know, we know that we can smile!
But there's a something in this breast,
To which thy light words bring no rest,
And thy gay smiles no anodyne.
Give me thy hand, and hush awhile,
And turn those limpid eyes on mine,
And let me read there, love! thy inmost soul.

Alas! is even love too weak
To unlock the heart, and let it speak?
Are even lovers powerless to reveal
To one another what indeed they feel?
I knew the mass of men concealed
Their thoughts, for fear that if revealed
They would by other men be met
With blank indifference, or with blame reproved;
I knew they lived and moved
Tricked in disguises, alien to the rest
Of men, and alien to themselves—and yet
The same heart beats in every human breast!

But we, my love!—doth a like spell benumb
Our hearts, our voices?—must we too be dumb?

Ah! well for us, if even we,
Even for a moment, can get free
Our heart, and have our lips unchained;
For that which seals them hath been deep-ordained!

Fate, which foresaw
How frivolous a baby man would be—
By what distractions he would be possessed,
How he would pour himself in every strife,
And well-nigh change his own identity—
That it might keep from his capricious play
His genuine self, and force him to obey
Even in his own despite his being's law,
Bade through the deep recesses of our breast
The unregarded river of our life
Pursue with indiscernible flow its way;
And that we should not see
The buried stream, and seem to be
Eddying at large in blind uncertainty,
Though driving on with it eternally.

But often, in the world's most crowded streets,
But often, in the din of strife,
There rises an unspeakable desire
After the knowledge of our buried life;
A thirst to spend our fire and restless force
In tracking out our true, original course;
A longing to inquire
Into the mystery of this heart which beats
So wild, so deep in us—to know
Whence our lives come and where they go.
And many a man in his own breast then delves,
But deep enough, alas! none ever mines.
And we have been on many thousand lines,
And we have shown, on each, spirit and power;
But hardly have we, for one little hour,
Been on our own line, have we been ourselves—
Hardly had skill to utter one of all
The nameless feelings that course through our breast,
But they course on forever unexpressed.
And long we try in vain to speak and act
Our hidden self, and what we say and do
Is eloquent, is well—but 'tis not true!
And then we will no more be racked
With inward striving, and demand

Of all the thousand nothings of the hour
Their stupefying power;
Ah yes, and they benumb us at our call!
Yet still, from time to time, vague and forlorn,
From the soul's subterranean depth upborne
As from an infinitely distant land,
Come airs, and floating echoes, and convey
A melancholy into all our day.

Only—but this is rare—
When a belovéd hand is laid in ours,
When, jaded with the rush and glare
Of the interminable hours,
Our eyes can in another's eyes read clear,
When our world-deafened ear
Is by the tones of a loved voice caressed—
A bolt is shot back somewhere in our breast,
And a lost pulse of feeling stirs again.
The eye sinks inward, and the heart lies plain,
And what we mean, we say, and what we would, we know.
A man becomes aware of his life's flow,
And hears its winding murmur; and he sees
The meadows where it glides, the sun, the breeze.

And there arrives a lull in the hot race
Wherein he doth for ever chase
That flying and elusive shadow, rest.
An air of coolness plays upon his face,
And an unwonted calm pervades his breast.
And then he thinks he knows
The hills where his life rose,
And the sea where it goes.

Lines Written in Kensington Gardens

In this lone, open glade I lie,
Screened by deep boughs on either hand;
And at its end, to stay the eye,
Those black-crowned, red-boled[274] pine-trees stand!

Birds here make song, each bird has his,
Across the girdling city's hum.
How green under the boughs it is!
How thick the tremulous sheep-cries come!

Sometimes a child will cross the glade
To take his nurse his broken toy;
Sometimes a thrush flit overhead
Deep in her unknown day's employ.

Here at my feet what wonders pass,
What endless, active life is here!
What blowing daisies, fragrant grass!
An air-stirred forest, fresh and clear.

Scarce fresher is the mountain-sod
Where the tired angler lies, stretched out,
And, eased of basket and of rod,
Counts his day's spoil, the spotted trout.

In the huge world, which roars hard by,
Be others happy if they can!
But in my helpless cradle I
Was breathed on by the rural Pan.

I, on men's impious uproar hurled,
Think often, as I hear them rave,
That peace has left the upper world
And now keeps only in the grave.

Yet here is peace forever new!
When I who watch them am away,
Still all things in this glade go through
The changes of their quiet day.

Then to their happy rest they pass!
The flowers upclose, the birds are fed,
The night comes down upon the grass,
The child sleeps warmly in his bed.

Calm soul of all things! make it mine
To feel, amid the city's jar,
That there abides a peace of thine,
Man did not make, and cannot mar.

The will to neither strive nor cry,
The power to feel with others give!
Calm, calm me more! nor let me die
Before I have begun to live.

AUGUSTA THEODOSIA DRANE
1823-1894

What the Soul Desires

THERE IS A RAPTURE THAT MY SOUL DESIRES,
There is a something that I cannot name;
I know not after what my soul aspires,
Nor guess from whence the restless longing came;
But ever from my childhood have I felt it,
In all things beautiful and all things gay,
And ever has its gentle, unseen presence
Fallen, like a shadow-cloud, across my way.

It is the melody of all sweet music,
In all fair forms it is the hidden grace;
In all I love, a something that escapes me,
Flies my pursuit, and ever veils its face.
I see it in the woodland's summer beauty,
I hear it in the breathing of the air;
I stretch my hands to feel for it, and grasp it,
But ah! too well I know, it is not there.

In sunset-hours, when all the earth is golden,
And rosy clouds are hastening to the west,
I catch a waving gleam, and then 'tis vanished,
And the old longing once more fills my breast.
It is not pain, although the fire consumes me,
Bound up with memories of my happiest years;
It steals into my deepest joys—O mystery!
It mingles, too, with all my saddest tears.

Once, only once, there rose the heavy curtain,
The clouds rolled back, and for too brief a space
I drank in joy as from a living fountain,
And seemed to gaze upon it, face to face:
But of that day and hour who shall venture
With lips untouched by seraph's fire to tell?

I saw Thee, O my Life! I heard, I touched Thee,—
Then o'er my soul once more the darkness fell.

The darkness fell, and all the glory vanished;
I strove to call it back, but all in vain:
O rapture! to have seen it for a moment!
O anguish! that it never came again!
That lightning-flash of joy that seemed eternal,
Was it indeed but wandering fancy's dream?
Ah, surely no! that day the heavens opened,
And on my soul there fell a golden gleam.

O Thou, my Life, give me what then Thou gavest!
No angel vision do I ask to see,
I seek no ecstasy of mystic rapture,
Naught, naught, my Lord, my Life, but only Thee!
That golden gleam hath purged my sight, revealing,
In the fair ray reflected from above,
Thyself, beyond all sight, beyond all feeling,
The hidden Beauty, and the hidden Love.

As the hart panteth for the water-brooks,
And seeks the shades whence cooling fountains burst;
Even so for Thee, O Lord, my spirit fainteth,
Thyself alone hath power to quench its thirst.
Give me what then Thou gavest, for I seek it
No longer in Thy creatures, as of old,
I strive no more to grasp the empty shadow,
The secret of my life is found and told!

PUEBLO SONGS
(Native American)

Song of the Sky Loom

O OUR MOTHER OF THE EARTH, O OUR FATHER OF THE SKY,[275]
Your children are we, and with tired backs
We bring you the gifts you love.
Then weave for us a garment of brightness;
May the warp be the white light of morning,
May the weft be the red light of evening,
May the fringes be the falling rain,
May the border be the standing rainbow.
Thus weave for us a garment of brightness,
That we may walk fittingly where birds sings,
That we may walk fittingly where grass is green,
O our Mother the Earth, O our Father the Sky.

Song of the Departing Spirit

I

All the white-cloud eagles,
Lift me up with your wings and take me to Shipap.[276]
And also you other eagles,
Come and lift me up with your wings, way up high,
All over the world; no one can see the place where you are taking me.
Way down in the southwest where our fathers and mothers have gone,
Put me there with your wings.

II

Thanks to Mother Earth, the whole world, and Mother Eagle.
Bless my people.
I am the spirit.

I am leaving for my own place where I shall be happy all my life.
I shall remember you people all the time.
I thank you all.

COVENTRY KERSEY DIGHTON PATMORE
1823-1896

Life of Life

WHAT'S THAT, WHICH, ERE I SPAKE, WAS GONE!
So joyful and intense a spark
That, whilst o'erhead the wonder shone,
The day, before but dull, grew dark?
I do not know, but this I know,
That, had the splendor lived a year,
The truth that I some heavenly show
Did see, could not be now more clear.
This know I too: might mortal breath
Express the passion then inspired,
Evil would die a natural death,
And nothing transient be desired;
And error from the soul would pass,
And leave the senses pure and strong
As sunbeams. But the best, alas,
Has neither memory nor tongue!

DANTE GABRIEL ROSSETTI
1828-1882

Nuptial Sleep

AT LENGTH THEIR LONG KISS SEVERED, WITH SWEET SMART:
   And as the last slow sudden drops are shed
   From sparkling eaves when all the storm has fled,
So singly flagged the pulses of each heart.
Their bosoms sundered, with the opening start
   Of married flowers to either side outspread
   From the knit stem; yet still their mouths, burnt red,
Fawned on each other where they lay apart.

Sleep sank them lower than the tide of dreams,
   And their dreams watched them sink, and slid away.
Slowly their souls swam up again, through gleams
   Of watered light and dull drowned waifs of day;
Till from some wonder of new woods and streams
   He woke, and wondered more: for there she lay.

Silent Noon

Your hands lie open in the long fresh grass,—
   The finger-points look through like rosy blooms:
   Your eyes smile peace. The pasture gleams and glooms
'Neath billowing skies that scatter and amass.
All round our nest, far as the eye can pass,
   Are golden kingcup-fields with silver edge
   Where the cow-parsley skirts the hawthorn hedge.
'Tis visible silence, still as the hourglass.

Deep in the sun-searched growths the dragon-fly
Hangs like a blue thread loosened from the sky:—
   So this winged hour is dropt to us from above.
Oh! clasp we to our hearts, for deathless dower,
This close-companioned inarticulate hour
   When twofold silence was the song of love.

The Sea-Limits

Consider the sea's listless chime:
    Time's self it is, made audible,—
    The murmur of the earth's own shell.
Secret continuance sublime
    Is the sea's end: our sight may pass
    No furlong farther. Since time was,
This sound hath told the lapse of time.

No quiet, which is death's,—it hath
    The mournfulness of ancient life,
    Enduring always at dull strife.
As the world's heart of rest and wrath,
    Its painful pulse is in the sands.
    Last utterly, the whole sky stands,
Grey and not known, along its path.

Listen alone beside the sea,
    Listen alone among the woods;
    Those voices of twin solitudes
Shall have one sound alike to thee:
    Hark where the murmurs of thronged men
    Surge and sink back and surge again,—
Still the one voice of wave and tree.

Gather a shell from the strown beach
    And listen at its lips: they sigh
    The same desire and mystery,
The echo of the whole sea's speech
    And all mankind is thus at heart
    Not anything but what thou art:
And Earth, Sea, Man, are all in each.

VICTOR RYDBERG
1828-1895

Heaven's Blue

WONDERFUL
Unfathomed clearness,
O Heavenly azure,
That, smiling,
Descends to me,
Lifting my soul
To cool spaces
And holy serenity!
Enchanting Nirvana,
Where, bathed in purity,
I exhale myself
In the infinite,
And reborn
In the next breath,
Baptized in longing,
Sink back
To the dust of Earth.

EMILY DICKINSON
1830-1886

76

EXULTATION IS THE GOING
Of an inland soul to sea,—
Past the houses, past the headlands,
Into deep Eternity!

Bred as we, among the mountains,
Can the sailor understand
The divine intoxication
Of the first league out from land?

157

Musicians wrestle everywhere:
All day, among the crowded air
I hear the silver strife;
And—walking—long before the morn—
Such transport breaks upon the town
I think it that "new life!"

If is not Bird, it has no nest;
Nor band, in brass and scarlet, drest
Nor Tamborine, nor Man;
It is not Hymn from pulpit read,—
The morning stars the treble led
On time's first afternoon!

Some say it is "the spheres" at play!²⁷⁷
Some say that bright majority
Of vanished dames and Men!
Some think it service in the place
Where we, with late, celestial face,
Please God, shall Ascertain!

172

'T is so much joy! 'T is so much joy!
If I should fail, what poverty!
And yet, as poor as I
Have ventured all upon a throw;
Have gained! Yes! Hesitated so
This side the Victory!

Life is but life, and death, but death!
Bliss is but bliss, and breath but breath!
And if, indeed, I fail,
At least to know the worst is sweet!
Defeat means nothing but defeat,
No drearier, can befall!

And if I gain—oh, gun at sea,
Oh, bells that in the steeples be,
At first repeat it slow!
For heaven is a different thing
Conjectured, and waked sudden in,
And might o'erwhelm me so.

214

I taste a liquor never brewed,
From tankards scooped in pearl;
Not all the vats upon the Rhine
Yield such an alcohol!

Inebriate of air am I,
And debauchee of dew,
Reeling, through endless summer days,
From inns of molten blue.

When the landlord turn the drunken bee
Out of the foxglove's door,
When butterflies renounce their drams,[278]
I shall but drink the more!

Till seraphs swing their snowy hats,
And saints to windows run,
To see the little tippler
Leaning against the sun!

249

Wild Nights! Wild Nights!
Were I with thee,
Wild nights should be
Our luxury!

Futile the winds
To a heart in port,—
Done with the compass,
Done with the chart.

Rowing in Eden!
Ah! the sea!
Might I but moor
To-night in thee!

365

Dare you see a soul at the white heat?
Then crouch within the door.
Red is the fire's common tint;
But when the vivid ore
Has vanquished flame's conditions,
It quivers from the Forge
Without a color but the light
Of unanointed blaze.
Least village has its blacksmith
Whose anvil's even ring
Stands symbol for the finer forge
That soundless tugs within,
Refining these impatient ores
With hammer and with blaze,

Until the designated light
Repudiate the Forge.

632

The brain is wider than the sky,
For, put them side by side,
The one the other will include
With ease, and you beside.

The brain is deeper than the sea,
For, hold them, Blue to Blue,
The one the other will absorb,
As sponges, buckets do.

The brain is just the weight of God,
For, heft[279] them, pound for pound,
And they will differ, if they do,
As syllable from sound.

1118

Exhilaration is the Breeze
That lifts us from the ground
And leaves us in another place
Whose statement is not found;

Returns us not, but after time
We soberly descend,
A little newer for the term
Upon enchanted ground.

CHRISTINA ROSSETTI
1830-1894

A Birthday

MY HEART IS LIKE A SINGING BIRD
   Whose nest is in a watered shoot;
My heart is like an apple-tree
   Whose boughs are bent with thickset fruit;
My heart is like a rainbow shell
   That paddles in a halcyon sea;
My heart is gladder than all these
   Because my love is come to me.

Raise me a dais of silk and down;
   Hang it with vair[280] and purple dyes;
Carve it in doves, and pomegranates,
   And peacocks with a hundred eyes;
Work it in gold and silver grapes,
   In leaves, and silver fleurs-de-lys;[281]
Because the birthday of my life
   Is come, my love is come to me.

LOUISA MAY ALCOTT
1832-1888

The Mother Moon

THE MOON UPON THE WIDE SEA
Placidly looks down,
Smiling with her mild face,
Though the ocean frown.
Clouds may dim her brightness,
But soon they pass away,
And she shines out, unaltered,
O'er the little waves at play.
So 'mid the storm or sunshine,
Wherever she may go,
Led on by her hidden power
The wild sea must plow.

As the tranquil evening moon
Looks on that restless sea,
So a mother's gentle face,
Little child, is watching thee.
Then banish every tempest,
Chase all your clouds away,
That smoothly and brightly
Your quiet heart may play.
Let cheerful looks and actions
Like shining ripples flow,
Following the mother's voice,
Singing as they go.

The Fairy Song

The moonlight fades from flower and tree,
And the stars dim one by one;
The tale is told, the song is sung,
And the Fairy feast is done.

The night-wind rocks the sleeping flowers,
And sings to them, soft and low.
The early birds erelong will wake:
'Tis time for the Elves to go.

O'er the sleeping earth we silently pass,
Unseen by mortal eye,
And send sweet dreams, as we lightly float
Through the quiet moonlit sky;—
For the stars' soft eyes alone may see,
And the flowers alone may know,
The feasts we hold, the tales we tell:
So 'tis time for the Elves to go.

From bird, and blossom, and bee,
We learn the lessons they teach;
And seek, by kindly deeds, to win
A loving friend in each.
And though unseen on earth we dwell,
Sweet voices whisper low,
And gentle hearts most joyously greet
The Elves where'er they go.

When next we meet in the Fairy dell,
May the silver moon's soft light
Shine then on faces gay as now,
And Elfin hearts as light.
Now spread each wing, for the eastern sky
With sunlight soon will glow.
The morning star shall light us home:
Farewell! for the Elves must go.

ALFRED COMYN LYALL
1835-1911

Siva

Mora Janua Vitae

I AM THE GOD[282] OF THE SENSUOUS FIRE[283]
That moulds all Nature in forms divine;
The symbols of death and of man's desire,
The springs of change in the world, are mine;
The organs of birth and the circlet of bones,
And the light loves carved on the temple stones.

I am the lord of delights and pain,
Of the pest that killeth, of fruitful joys;
I rule the currents of heart and vein;
A touch gives passion, a look destroys;
In the heat and cold of my lightest breath
Is the might incarnate of Lust and Death.

If a thousand altars stream with blood
Of the victims slain by the chanting priest,
Is a great God lured by the savory food?
I reck[284] not of worship, or song, or feast;
But that millions perish, each hour that flies,
Is the mystic sign of my sacrifice.

Ye may plead and pray for the millions born;
They come like dew on the morning grass;
Your vows and vigils I hold in scorn,
The soul stays never, the stages pass;
All life is the play of the power that stirs
In the dance of my wanton worshippers.

And the strong swift river my shrine below
It runs, like man, its unending course
To the boundless sea from eternal snow;

Mine is the Fountain—and mine the Force
That spurs all nature to ceaseless strife;
And my image is Death at the gates of Life.

In many a legend and many a shape,
In the solemn grove and the crowded street,
I am the Slayer, whom none escape;
I am Death trod under a fair girl's feet;
I govern the tides of the sentient sea
That ebbs and flows to eternity.

And the sum of the thought and the knowledge of man
Is the secret tale that my emblems tell;
Do ye seek God's purpose, or trace his plan?
Ye may read your doom in my parable:
For the circle of life in its flower and its fall
Is the writing that runs on my temple wall.

O Race that labours, and seeks, and strives,
With thy Faith, thy wisdom, thy hopes and fears,
Where now is the Future of myriad lives?
Where now is the Creed of a thousand years?
Far as the Western spirit may range,
It finds but the travail of endless change;

For the earth is fashioned by countless suns,
And planets wander, and stars are lost,
As the rolling flood of existence runs
From light to shadow, from fire to frost.
Your search is ended, ye hold the keys
Of my inmost ancient mysteries.

Now that your hands have lifted the veil,
And the crowd may know what my symbols mean,
Will not the faces of men turn pale
At the sentence heard, and the vision seen
Of strife and sleep, of the soul's brief hour,
And the careless tread of unyielding Power?

Though the world repent of its cruel youth,
And in age grow soft, and its hard law bend,
Ye may spare or slaughter; by rage or ruth
All forms speed on to the far still end;
For the gods who have mercy, who save or bless,
Are the visions of man in his hopelessness.

Let my temples fall, they are dark with age,
Let my idols break, they have stood their day;
On their deep hewn stones the primeval sage
Has figured the spells that endure alway;
My presence may vanish from river and grove,
But I rule for ever in Death and Love.

THOMAS BAILEY ALDRICH
1836-1906

Song from the Persian

AH, SAD ARE THEY WHO KNOW NOT LOVE,
But, far from passion's tears and smiles,
Drift down a moonless sea, beyond
The silvery coasts of fairy isles.

And sadder they whose longing lips
Kiss empty air, and never touch
The dear warm mouth of those they love—
Waiting, wasting, suffering much.

But clear as amber, fine as musk,
Is life to those who, pilgrim-wise,
Move hand in hand from dawn to dusk,
Each morning nearer Paradise.

Oh, not for them shall angels pray!
They stand in everlasting light,
They walk in Allah's smile by day,
And slumber in his heart by night.

EDWARD DOWDEN
1843-1913

The Secret of the Universe: An Ode
(By a Spinning Dervish)

I SPIN, I SPIN, AROUND, AROUND,
And close my eyes,
And let the bile arise
From the sacred region of the soul's Profound;
Then gaze upon the world; how strange! how new!
The earth and heaven are one,
The horizon-line is gone,
The sky how green! the land how fair and blue!
Perplexing items fade from my large view,
And thought which vexed me with its false and true
Is swallowed up in Intuition; this,
This is the sole true mode
Of reaching God,
And gaining the universal synthesis
Which makes All—One; while fools with peering eyes
Dissect, divide, and vainly analyze.
So round, and round, and round again!
How the whole globe swells within my brain,
The stars inside my lids appear,
The murmur of the spheres I hear
Throbbing and beating in each ear;
Right in my navel I can feel
The centre of the world's great wheel.   ·
Ah peace divine, bliss dear and deep,
No stay, no stop,
Like any top
Whirling with swiftest speed, I sleep.
O ye devout ones round me coming,
Listen! I think that I am humming;
No utterance of the servile mind
With poor chop-logic rules agreeing
Here shall ye find,

But inarticulate burr of man's unsundered[285] being.
Ah, could we but devise some plan,
Some patent jack by which a man
Might hold himself ever in harmony
With the great Whole, and spin perpetually,
As all things spin
Without, within,
As Time spins off into Eternity,
And Space into the inane Immensity,
And the Finite into God's Infinity,
Spin, spin, spin, spin.

The Initiation

Under the flaming wings of cherubim
I moved toward that high altar. O, the hour!
And the light waxed intenser, and the dim
Low edges of the hills and the grey sea
Were caught and captured by the present Power,
My sureties and my witnesses to be.

Then the light drew me in. Ah, perfect pain!
Ah, infinite moment of accomplishment!
Thou terror of pure joy, with neither wane
Nor waxing, but long silence and sharp air
As womb-forsaking babes breathe. Hush! the event
Let him who wrought Love's marvelous things declare.

Shall I who feared not joy, fear grief at all?
I on whose mouth Life laid his sudden lips
Tremble at Death's weak kiss, and not recall
That sundering from the flesh, the flight from time,
The judgments stern, the clear apocalypse,
The lightnings, and the Presences sublime.

How came I back to earth? I know not how,
Nor what hands led me, nor what words were said.
Now all things are made mine,—joy, sorrow; now
I know my purpose deep, and can refrain;

I walk among the living, not the dead;
My sight is purged; I love and pity men.

EDWARD CARPENTER
1844-1929

Love's Vision

AT NIGHT IN EACH OTHER'S ARMS,[286]
Content, overjoyed, resting deep deep down in the darkness,
Lo! the heavens opened and He appeared—
Whom no mortal eye may see,
Whom no eye clouded with Care,
Whom none who seeks after this or that, whom none who has not
    escaped from self.

There—in the region of Equality, in the world of Freedom no
    longer limited,
Standing as a lofty peak in heaven above the clouds,
From below hidden, yet to all who pass into that region most clearly
    visible—
He the Eternal appeared.

INNUIT SONGS

Song of Joy

AJAJA—AJA—JAJA,
The lands around my dwelling[287]
Are more beautiful
From the day
When it is given me to see
Faces I have never seen before.
All is more beautiful,
All is more beautiful,
And life is thankfulness.
The guests of mine
Make my house grand,
Ajaja—aja—jaja.

Utitiaq's Song

Aja, I am joyful; this is good![288]
Aja, there is nothing but ice around me, that is good!
Aja, I am joyful; this is good!
My country is nothing but slush, that is good!
Aja, I am joyful; this is good!
Aja, when, indeed, will this end? This is good!
I am tired of watching and waking, this is good!

GERARD MANLEY HOPKINS
1844-1889

God's Grandeur

THE WORLD IS CHARGED WITH THE GRANDEUR OF GOD.
It will flame out, like shining from shook foil;
It gathers to a greatness, like the ooze of oil
Crushed. Why do men then now not reck[289] his rod?[290]
Generations have trod, have trod, have trod;
   And all is seared with trade; bleared,[291] smeared with toil;
   And wears man's smudge and shares man's smell: the soil
Is bare now, nor can foot feel, being shod.

And for all this, nature is never spent;
   There lives the dearest freshness deep down things;
And though the last lights off the black West went
   Oh, morning, at the brown brink eastward, springs—
Because the Holy Ghost over the bent
   World broods with warm breast and with ah! bright wings.

Pied Beauty

Glory be to God for dappled[292] things—
   For skies of couple-color as a brinded[293] cow;
     For rose-moles all in stipple[294] upon trout that swim;
Fresh-firecoal chestnut-falls; finches' wings;
   Landscape plotted and pieced—fold, fallow, and plough;[295]
   And all trades, their gear and tackle and trim.

All things counter, original, spare, strange;
   Whatever is fickle, freckled (who knows how?)
     With swift, slow; sweet, sour; adazzle, dim;
He fathers-forth whose beauty is past change:
       Praise him.

As Kingfishers Catch Fire

As kingfishers catch fire, dragonflies draw flame;
  As tumbled over rim in roundy wells
  Stones ring; like each tucked string tells, each hung bell's
Bow swung finds tongue to fling out broad its name;
Each mortal thing does one thing and the same:
  Deals out that being indoors each one dwells;
  Selves[296]—goes itself; *myself* it speaks and spells,
Crying *What I do is me: for that I came.*

I say more: the just man justices;
  Keeps grace: that keeps all his goings graces;
Acts in God's eye what in God's eye he is—
  Christ—for Christ plays in ten thousand places,
Lovely in limbs, and lovely in eyes not his
  To the Father through the features of men's faces.

The Caged Skylark

As a dare-gale skylark scanted[297] in a dull cage
  Man's mounting spirit in his bone-house, mean house, dwells—
  That bird beyond the remembering his free fells;
This in drudgery, day-laboring-out life's age.

Though aloft on turf or perch or poor low stage,
  Both sing sometimes the sweetest, sweetest spells,
  Yet both droop deadly sometimes in their cells
Or wring their barriers in bursts of fear or rage.

Not that the sweet-fowl, song-fowl, needs no rest—
Why, hear him, hear him babble and drop down to his nest,
  But his own nest, wild nest, no prison.

Man's spirit will be flesh-bound when found at best,
But uncumbered: meadow-down is not distressed
  For a rainbow footing it nor he for his bones risen.

The Windhover:
To Christ Our Lord

I caught this morning morning's minion, king-
   dom of daylight's dauphin, dapple-dawn-drawn Falcon, in his riding
   Of the rolling level underneath him steady air, and striding
High there, how he rung upon the rein of a wimpling[298] wing
In his ecstasy! then off, off forth on swing,
   As a skate's heel sweeps smooth on a bow-bend: the hurl and gliding
   Rebuffed the big wind. My heart in hiding
Stirred for a bird,—the achieve of, the mastery of the thing!

Brute beauty and valor and act, oh, air, pride, plume, here
   Buckle! and the fire that breaks from thee then, a billion
Times told lovelier, more dangerous, O my chevalier!

No wonder of it: sheer plod makes plough down sillion[299]
Shine, and blue-bleak embers, ah my dear,
   Fall, gall themselves, and gash gold-vermillion.

The Starlight Night

Look at the stars! look, look up at the skies!
   O look at all the fire-folk sitting in the air!
   The bright boroughs, the circle-citadels there!
Down in dim woods the diamond delves! the elves'-eyes!
The grey lawns cold where gold, where quickgold lies!
   Wind-beat whitebeam! airy abeles[300] set on a flare!
   Flake-doves sent floating forth at a farmyard scare!—
Ah well! it is all a purchase, all is a prize.

Buy then! bid then!—What?—Prayer, patience, aims, vows.
Look, look: a May-mess, like on orchard boughs!
   Look! March-bloom, like on mealed-with-yellow sallows![301]
These are indeed the barn; withindoors house
The shocks. This piece-bright paling shuts the spouse
   Christ home, Christ and his mother and all his hallows.

Spring

Nothing is so beautiful as Spring—
    When weeds, in wheels, shoot long and lovely and lush;
    Thrush's eggs look little low heavens, and thrush
Through the echoing timber does so rinse and wring
The ear, it strikes like lightnings to hear him sing;
    The glassy peartree leaves and blooms, they brush
    The descending blue; that blue is all in a rush
With richness; the racing lambs too have fair their fling.

What is all this juice and all this joy?
    A strain of the earth's sweet being in the beginning
In Eden garden.—Have, get, before it cloy,
    Before it cloud, Christ, lord, and sour with sinning,
Innocent mind and Mayday in girl and boy,
    Most, O maid's child, thy choice and worthy the winning.

Hurrahing in Harvest

Summer ends now; now, barbarous in beauty, the stooks[302] rise
    Around; up above, what wind-walks! what lovely behavior
    Of silk-sack clouds! has wilder, willful-wavier
Meal-drift molded ever and melted across skies?

I walk, I lift up, I lift up heart, eyes,
    Down all that glory in the heavens to glean our Savior;
    And, eyes, heart, what looks, what lips yet gave you a
Rapturous love's greeting of realer, of rounder replies?

And the azurous hung hills are his world-wielding shoulder
    Majestic—as a stallion stalwart, very-violet-sweet!—
These things, these things were here and but the beholder
    Wanting; which two when they once meet,
The heart rears wings bold and bolder
    And hurls for him, O half hurls earth for him off under his feet.

JOHN BANNISTER TABB
1845-1909

Communion

ONCE WHEN MY HEART WAS PASSION-FREE[303]
  To learn of things divine,
The soul of nature suddenly
  Outpoured itself in mine.

I held the secrets of the deep,
  And of the heavens above;
I knew the harmonies of sleep,
  The mysteries of love.

And for a moment's interval
  The earth, the sky, the sea—
My soul encompassed, each and all,
  As now they compass me.

To one in all, to all in one—
  Since Love the work began—
Life's ever widening circles run,
  Revealing God and man.

FRANCIS SALTUS
1846-1889

To ...

SLEEP AND DREAM, LISSOME[304] MAID, WHILE IN RAPTURE[305]
I caress thy grand poem of flesh;
While I toy with each rich purple mesh
Or gnarled tresses: when striving to capture
All the hot biting odors from lips—
Half apart with the sweetness that slips
From thy dimpled white smilings, sleep-fresh.

'Tis the perfect round curve of thy shoulder,
And thy sleek supple flanks I admire,
For thy moonish-white skin doth inspire
My hot, vexed, restless gaze to pierce bolder;
For thou sleepest, and red is thy dream
With the Naphla of lust, and its gleam
From the snows of thy breasts hurl its fire.

Nay, awake not, nor turn, till I press thee,
For thy sleep is consoling as Night.
And thy calm dreams shall taste the fire-night
Of Love's blendings, as mad, I caress thee,
And thy white form with red kisses mark—
Till thine eyes wake from lethargies dark—
To the glamors and splendors of light.

Then from dream-bliss to Life-bliss arisen,
Thine hot tears, my hot tears will dispute,
Then thy low pant sounds softer than lute
To my ear; and thy bare arms imprison—
A no longer wild phantom of sighs,
For thou closest thy large blurred eyes,
And liest wond'ring, nude, pallid, and mute!

Let my kisses then follow incessant,
O'er thy lips, o'er thy soft cheek of fur:
Let them moisten, as sultry they err
The black shade of thy silk brow's crescent—
While I breathe the mysterious air,
From thy chaos of undulate hair,
Vague and dreamy as memories of myrrh.

CHRISTINA CATHERINE FRASER-TYTLER
1848-1927

In Summer Fields

SOMETIMES, AS IN THE SUMMER FIELDS[306]
I walk abroad, there comes to me
So strange a sense of mystery,
My heart stands still, my feet must stay,
I am in such strange company.

I look on high—the vasty deep
Of blue outreaches all my mind;
And yet I think beyond to find
Something more vast—and at my feet
The little bryony is twined.

Clouds sailing as to God go by,
Earth, sun, and stars are rushing on;
And faster than swift time, more strong
Than rushing of the worlds, I feel
A something Is, of name unknown.

And turning suddenly away,
Grown sick and dizzy with the sense
Of power, and mine own impotence,
I see the gentle cattle feed
In dumb unthinking innocence.

The great Unknown above; below,
The cawing rooks, the milking-shed;
God's awful silence overhead;
Below, the muddy pool, the path
The thirsty herds of cattle tread.

Sometimes, as in the summer fields
I walk abroad, there comes to me
So wild a sense of mystery,

My senses reel, my reason fails,
I am in such strange company.

Yet somewhere, dimly, I can feel
The wild confusion dwells in me,
And I, in no strange company,
Am the lost link 'twixt Him and these,
And touch Him through the mystery.

EDMUND GOSSE
1849-1928

The Tide of Love

LOVE, FLOODING ALL THE CREEKS OF MY DRY SOUL,
From which the warm tide ebbed when I was born,
Following the moon of destiny, doth roll
His slow rich wave along the shore forlorn,
To make the ocean—God—and me, one whole.

So, shuddering in its ecstasy, it lies,
And, freed from mire and tangle of the ebb,
Reflects the waxing and the waning skies,
And bears upon its panting breast the web
Of night and her innumerable eyes.

Nor can conceive at all that it was blind,
But trembling with the sharp approach of love,
That, strenuous, moves without one breath of wind,
Gasps, as the wakening maid, on whom the Dove
With folded wings of deity declined.

She in the virgin sweetness of her dream
Thought nothing strange to find her vision true;
And I thus bathed in living rapture deem
No moveless drought my channel ever knew,
But rustled always with the murmuring stream.

Old and New

I. B.C.

Come, Hesper, and ye Gods of mountain waters,
Come, nymphs and Dryads,
Come, silken choir of soft Pierian daughters,[307]
And girls of lakes and seas,

Evoë![308] and evoë Io! crying,
  Fill all the earth and air;
Evoë! till the quivering words, replying,
  Shout back the echo there!

All day in soundless swoon or heavy slumber,
  We lay among the flowers,
But now the stars break forth in countless number
  To watch the dewy hours;
And now Iacchus,[309] beautiful and glowing,
  Adown the hill-side comes,
Mid tabrets shaken high, and trumpets blowing,
  And resonance of drums.

The leopard-skin is round his smooth white shoulders,
  The vine-branch round his hair,
Those eyes that rouse desire in maid-beholders
  Are glittering, glowworm-fair;
Crowned king of all the provinces of pleasure,
  Lord of a wide domain,
He comes, and brings delight that knows no measure,
  A full Saturnian reign.

Take me, too, Maenads,[310] to your fox-skin chorus,
  Rose-lipped like volute-shells,
For I would follow where your host canorous
  Roars down the forest-dells;
The sacred frenzy rends my throat and bosom!
  I shout, and whirl where He,
Our Vine-God, tosses like some pale blood-blossom
  Swept on a stormy sea.

Around his car, with streaming hair, and frantic,
  The Maenads and wild gods
And shaggy fauns and wood-girls corybantic
  Toss high the ivy-rods;
Brown limbs with white limbs madly intertwining
  Whirl in a fiery dance,
Till, when at length Orion is declining,
  We glide into a trance.

The satyr's heart is faintly, faintly beating,
    The choir of nymphs is mute;
Iacchus up the western slope is fleeting,
    Uncheered by horn or flute;
Hushed, hushed are all the shouting and the singing,
    The frenzy, the delight,
Since out into the cold grey air upspringing,
    The morning-star shines bright.

II. A.D.

Not with a choir of angels without number,
    And noise of lutes and lyres,
But gently, with the woven veil of slumber
    Across Thine awful fires,
We yearn to watch Thy face, serene and tender,
    Melt, smiling, calm and sweet,
Where round the print of thorns, in thornlike splendor,
    Transcendent glories meet.

We have no hopes if Thou art close beside us,
    And no profane despairs,
Since all we need is Thy great hand to guide us,
    Thy heart to take our cares;
For us is no to-day, to-night, to-morrow,
    No past time nor to be,
We have no joy but Thee, there is no sorrow,
    No life to live but Thee.

The cross, like pilgrim-warriors, we follow,
    Led by our eastern star;
The wild crane greets us, and the wandering swallow
    Bound southward for Shinar;[311]
All night that single star shines bright above us;
    We go with weary feet,
But in the end we know are they who love us,
    Whose pure embrace is sweet.

Most sweet of all, when dark the way and moonless,
  To feel a touch, a breath,
And know our weary spirits are not tuneless,
  Our unseen goal not Death;
To know that Thou, in all Thy old sweet fashion,
  Art near us to sustain!
We praise Thee, Lord, by all Thy tears and passion,
  By all Thy cross and pain!

For when this night of toil and tears is over,
  Across the hills of spice,
Thyself wilt meet us, glowing like a lover
  Before Love's Paradise;
There are the saints, with palms and hymns and roses,
  And better still than all,
The long, long day of bliss that never closes,
  Thy marriage festival!

NEGRO SPIRITUALS

Swing Low Sweet Chariot

LEAD: SWING LOW, SWEET CHARIOT[312]
   Chorus: Coming for to carry me home
Lead: Swing low, sweet chariot
   Chorus: Coming for to carry me home
Lead: If you get there before I do
   Chorus: Coming for to carry me home
Lead: Tell all my friends, I'm coming too
   Chorus: Coming for to carry me home[313]

All God's Chillun Got Wings

I got a robe, you got a robe
All o' God's chillun got a robe
When I get to heab'n I'm goin' to put on my robe
I'm goin' to shout all ovah God's Heab'n
Heab'n, Heab'n
Ev'rybody talkin' 'bout heab'n ain't goin' dere
Heab'n, Heab'n
I'm goin' to shout all ovah God's Heab'n

I got-a wings, you got-a wings
All o' God's chillun got-a wings
When I get to heab'n I'm goin' to put on my wings
I'm goin' to fly all ovah God's Heab'n
Heab'n, Heab'n
Ev'rybody talkin' 'bout heab'n ain't goin' dere
Heab'n, Heab'n
I'm goin' to fly all ovah God's Heab'n

I got a harp, you got a harp
All o' God's chillun got a harp
When I get to heab'n I'm goin' to take up my harp
I'm goin' to play all ovah God's Heab'n

Heab'n, Heab'n
Ev'rybody talkin' 'bout heab'n ain't goin' dere
Heab'n, Heab'n
I'm goin' to play all ovah God's Heab'n

I got shoes, you got shoes
All o' God's chillun got shoes
When I get to heab'n I'm goin' to put on my shoes
I'm goin' to walk all ovah God's Heab'n
Heab'n, Heab'n
Ev'rybody talkin' 'bout heab'n ain't goin' dere
Heab'n, Heab'n
I'm goin' to walk all ovah God's Heab'n

I've Got Peace Like a River

I've got peace like a river in my soul
I've got a river in my soul
I've got joy like a fountain in my soul
I've got a fountain in my soul

WILLIAM JAMES DAWSON
1854-1928

Inspirations

SOMETIMES, I KNOW NOT WHY, NOR HOW, NOR WHENCE,[314]
    A change comes over me, and then the task
    Of common life slips from me. Would you ask
What power is this which bids the world go hence?
    Who knows? I only feel a faint perfume
Steal through the rooms of life; a saddened sense
Of something lost; a music as of brooks
That babble to the sea; pathetic looks
    Of closing eyes that in a darkened room
    Once dwelt on mine: I feel the general doom
Creep nearer, and with God I stand alone.
    O mystic sense of sudden quickening!
Hope's lark-song rings, or life's deep undertone
    Wails through my heart—and then I needs must sing.

JANE BARLOW
1857-1917

Beyond All Shores and Seas

LIES YET A WELL OF WONDER
All shores and seas beyond,
Where shines that dimness under,
More deep than in a dream,
Full many a diamond
With elfin gleam,

Glows up the glimmering water
Full many a ruby's fire:
If ever an earth-born daughter
Their wizard light behold,
She may no more desire
Our gems and gold.

Nay, some in sooth, who only
A dream thereon did gaze,
Thenceforth fare wandering lonely,
And seek with sorrow vain
The glory of such rays
To find again.

Oft, oft, high-heavenward turning
The quivering stars have conned,
Or watched the wide west burning
Nor shall their hearts appease,
Whose hope lies hid beyond
All shores and seas.

AGNES MARY FRANCES DUCLAUX
1857-1944

The Idea

BENEATH THIS WORLD OF STARS AND FLOWERS
That rolls in visible deity,
I dream another world is ours
And is the soul of all we see.

It hath no form, it hath no spirit;
It is perchance the Eternal Mind;
Beyond the sense that we inherit
I feel it dim and undefined.

How far below the depth of being,
How wide beyond the starry bound
It rolls unconscious and unseeing,
And is as Number or as Sound.

And through the vast fantastic visions
Of all this actual universe,
It moves unswerved by our decisions,
And is the play that we rehearse.

BLISS CARMAN
1861-1929

Earth Voices

I

I HEARD THE SPRING WIND WHISPER
Above the brushwood fire,
"The world is made forever
Of transport and desire.

"I am the breath of being,
The primal urge of things;
I am the whirl of star dust,
I am the lift of wings.

"I am the splendid impulse
That comes before the thought,
The joy and exaltation
Wherein the life is caught.

"Across the sleeping furrows
I call the buried seed,
And blade and bud and blossom
Awaken at my need.

"Within the dying ashes
I blow the sacred spark,
And make the hearts of lovers
To leap against the dark."

II

I heard the spring light whisper
Above the dancing stream,

"The world is made forever
In likeness of a dream.

"I am the law of planets,
I am the guide of man;
The evening and the morning
Are fashioned to my plan.

"I tint the dawn with crimson,
I tinge the sea with blue;
My track is in the desert,
My trail is in the dew.

"I paint the hills with color,
And in my magic dome
I light the star of evening
To steer the traveler home.

"Within the house of being,
I feed the lamp of truth
With tales of ancient wisdom
And prophecies of youth."

III

I heard the spring rain murmur
Above the roadside flower,
"The world is made forever
In melody and power.

"I keep the rhythmic measure
That marks the steps of time,
And all my toil is fashioned
To symmetry and rhyme.

"I plow the untilled upland,
I ripe the seeding grass,
And fill the leafy forest
With music as I pass.

"I hew the raw, rough granite
To loveliness of line,
And when my work is finished,
Behold, it is divine!

"I am the master-builder
In whom the ages trust.
I lift the lost perfection
To blossom from the dust."

IV

Then Earth to them made answer,
As with a slow refrain
Born of the blended voices
Of wind and sun and rain,
"This is the law of being
That links the threefold chain:
The life we give to beauty
Returns to us again."

Moment Musicale

The round moon hangs above the rim
Of silent and blue shadowed trees,
And all the earth is vague and dim
In its blue veil of mysteries.

On such a night one must believe
The Golden Age returns again
With lyric beauty, to retrieve
The world from dreariness and pain.

And down the wooded aisles, behold
What dancers through the dusk appear!
Piping their raptures as of old,
They bring immortal freedom near.

A moment on the brink of night
They tread their transport in the dew,
And to the rhythm of their delight,
Behold, all things are made anew!

RABINDRANATH TAGORE
1861-1941

from **Gitanjali**

2

WHEN THOU COMMANDEST ME TO SING IT SEEMS THAT MY HEART WOULD BREAK WITH pride; and I look to thy face, and tears come to my eyes. All that is harsh and dissonant in my life melts into one sweet harmony—and my adoration spreads wings like a glad bird on its flight across the sea. I know thou takest pleasure in my singing. I know that only as a singer I come before thy presence. I touch by the edge of the far-spreading wing of my song thy feet which I could never aspire to reach. Drunk with the joy of singing I forget myself and call thee friend who art my lord.

11

Leave this chanting and singing and telling of beads! Whom dost thou worship in this lonely dark corner of a temple with doors all shut? Open thine eyes and see thy God is not before thee! He is there where the tiller is tilling the hard ground and where the pathmaker is breaking stones. He is with them in sun and in shower, and his garment is covered with dust. Put off thy holy mantle and even like him come down on the dusty soil! Deliverance? Where is this deliverance to be found? Our master himself has joyfully taken upon him the bonds of creation; he is bound with us all forever. Come out of thy meditations and leave aside thy flowers and incense! What harm is there if thy clothes become tattered and stained? Meet him and stand by him in toil and in sweat of thy brow.

45

Have you not heard his silent steps? He comes, comes, ever comes. Every moment and every age, every day and every night he comes, comes, ever comes. Many a song have I sung in many a mood of mind, but all their notes have always proclaimed, "He comes, comes, ever comes." In the fragrant days of sunny April through the forest path he comes, comes, ever comes. In the rainy gloom of July nights on the thundering chariot of clouds he comes, comes, ever comes. In sorrow after sorrow it is his steps that press upon my heart, and it is the golden touch of his feet that makes my joy to shine.

58

Let all the strains of joy mingle in my last song—the joy that makes the earth flow over in the riotous excess of the grass, the joy that sets the twin brothers, life and death, dancing over the wide world, the joy that sweeps in with the tempest, shaking and waking all life with laughter, the joy that sits still with its tears on the open red lotus of pain, and the joy that throws everything it has upon the dust, and knows not a word.

60

On the seashore of endless worlds children meet. The infinite sky is motionless overhead and the restless water is boisterous. On the seashore of endless worlds the children meet with shouts and dances. They build their houses with sand and they play with empty shells. With withered leaves they weave their boats and smilingly float them on the vast deep. Children have their play on the seashore of worlds. They know not how to swim, they know not how to cast nets. Pearl fishers dive for pearls, merchants sail in their ships, while children gather pebbles and scatter them again. They seek not for hidden treasures, they know not how to cast nets. The sea surges up with laughter and pale gleams the smile of the sea beach. Death-dealing waves sing meaningless ballads to the children, even like a mother while rocking her baby's cradle. The sea plays with children, and pale gleams the smile of the sea beach. On the seashore of endless worlds children meet. Tempest roams in the pathless sky, ships get wrecked in the trackless water, death is abroad and children play. On the seashore of endless worlds is the great meeting of children.

61

The sleep that flits on baby's eyes—does anybody know from where it comes? Yes, there is a rumor that it has its dwelling there, in the fairy village among shadows of the forest dimly lit with glow-worms, there hang two timid buds of enchantment. From there it comes to kiss baby's eyes. The smile that flickers on baby's lips when he sleeps—does anybody know where it was born? Yes, there is a rumor that a young pale beam of a crescent moon touched the edge of a vanishing autumn cloud, and there the smile was first born in the dream of a dew-washed morning—the smile that flickers on baby's lips when he sleeps. The sweet, soft freshness that blooms on baby's limbs—does anybody know where it was hidden so long? Yes, when the mother was a young girl it lay pervading her heart in tender and silent mystery of love—the sweet, soft freshness that has bloomed on baby's limbs.

69

The same stream of life that runs through my veins night and day runs through the world and dances in rhythmic measures. It is the same life that shoots in joy through the dust of the earth in numberless blades of grass and breaks into tumultuous waves of leaves and flowers. It is the same life that is rocked in the ocean-cradle of birth and of death, in ebb and in flow. I feel my limbs are made glorious by the touch of this world of life. And my pride is from the life-throb of ages dancing in my blood this moment.

73

Deliverance is not for me in renunciation. I feel the embrace of freedom in a thousand bonds of delight. Thou ever pourest for me the fresh draught of thy wine of various colors and fragrance, filling this earthen vessel to the brim. My world will light its hundred different lamps with thy flame and place them before the altar of thy temple. No, I will never shut the doors of my senses. The delights of sight and hearing and touch will bear thy delight. Yes, all my illusions will burn into illumination of joy, and all my desires ripen into fruits of love.

80

I am like a remnant of a cloud of autumn uselessly roaming in the sky, O my sun ever-glorious! Thy touch has not yet melted my vapor, making me one with thy light, and thus I count months and years separated from thee. If this be thy wish and if this be thy play, then take this fleeting emptiness of mine, paint it with colors, gild it with gold, float it on the wanton wind and spread it in varied wonders. And again when it shall be thy wish to end this play at night, I shall melt and vanish away in the dark, or it may be in a smile of the white morning, in a coolness of purity transparent.

100

I dive down into the depth of the ocean of forms, hoping to gain the perfect pearl of the formless. No more sailing from harbor to harbor with this my weather-beaten boat. The days are long passed when my sport was to be tossed on waves. And now I am eager to die into the deathless. Into the audience hall by the fathomless abyss where swells up the music of toneless strings I shall take this harp of my life. I shall tune it to the notes of forever, and when it has sobbed out its last utterance, lay down my silent harp at the feet of the silent.

DUNCAN CAMPBELL SCOTT
1862-1947

Ecstasy

THE SHORE-LARK SOARS TO HIS TOPMOST FLIGHT,
Sings at the height where morning springs,
What though his voice be lost in the light,
The light comes dropping from his wings.

Mount, my soul, and sing at the height
Of thy clear flight in the light and the air,
Heard or unheard in the night in the light
Sing there! Sing there!

TETON SIOUX SONGS
(Native American)

Two Dream Songs of Siyaka

I

AT NIGHT MAY I ROAM
Against the winds may I roam
At night may I roam
When the owl is hooting
May I roam.

At dawn may I roam
Against the winds may I roam
At dawn may I roam
When the crow is calling
May I roam.

II

Where the wind is blowing
The wind is roaring
I stand.

Westward the wind is blowing
The wind is roaring—
I stand.

Opening Prayer of the Sun Dance

Grandfather!
A voice I am going to send,
Hear me!
All over the universe
A voice I am going to send,

313

Hear me,
Grandfather!
I will live!
I have said it.

Prayer Spoken during the Sun Dance

Wakan'tanka[315]
When I pray to him
Hears me.
Whatever is good he
Grants me.

Song of a Man who Received a Vision

Friends, behold!
Sacred I have been made.
Friends, behold!
In a sacred manner
I have been influenced
At the gathering of the clouds.
Sacred I have been made,
Friends, behold!
Sacred I have been made.

ARTHUR SYMONDS
1865-1945

The Turning Dervish

STARS IN THE HEAVENS TURN,
I worship like a star,
And in its footsteps learn
Where peace and wisdom are.

Man crawls as a worm crawls;
Till dust with dust he lies,
A crooked line he scrawls
Between the earth and skies.

Yet God, having ordained
The course of star and sun,
No creature hath constrained
A meaner course to run.

I, by his lesson taught,
Imaging his design,
Have diligently wrought
Motion to be divine.

I turn until my sense,
Dizzied with waves of air,
Spins to a point intense,
And spires and centers there.

There, motionless in speed,
I drink that flaming peace,
Which in the heavens doth feed
The stars with bright increase.

Some spirit in me doth move
Through ways of light untrod,
Till, with excessive love,
I drown, and am in God.

RUBEN DARIO
1867-1916

Primaveral

NOW IS COME THE MONTH OF ROSES![316]
To the woods my verse has flown
Gathering fragrance and honey
From the blossoms newly blown.
Beloved, come to the forest,
The woodland shall be our shrine
Scented with the holy perfume
Of the laurel and the vine.
From tree-top to tree-top flitting
The birds greet you with sweet lay,
Finding joyance in your beauty
Fairer than the birth of day;
And the haughty oaks and hemlocks
Bend their leafy branches green
Forming rustling, regal arches
For the passage of a queen.
All is perfume, song and radiance;
Flowers open and birds sing:
O Beloved, 'tis the season
Of the Spring!

Flowing from a haunted cavern
Is a crystal fountain where
Naiads nude and flower-breasted
Bathe and play and freight the air
With the joyance of their laughter
And the gladness of the wave
When they stoop over the fountain
And their tresses 'gin to lave.[317]
And they know the hymns of Eros
That in lovely Grecian tongue
Pan one day made in the forest
In the glorious age of song.

Sweetest, of that glorious hymnal
I shall choose the fairest phrase
To enrich with ancient music
The full cadence of my lays.
Sweet as sweetest Grecian honey
Will my song be when I sing,
O Beloved, in the season
Of the Spring![318]

RICHARD LE GALLIENNE
1866-1947

May Is Building Her House

MAY IS BUILDING HER HOUSE. WITH APPLE BLOOMS[319]
  She is roofing over the glimmering rooms;
Of the oak and the beech hath she builded its beams,
  And, spinning all day at her secret looms,
With arras of leaves each wind-swayed wall
She pictureth over, and peopleth it all
    With echoes and dreams,
    And singing of streams.

May is building her house. Of petal and blade,
Of the roots of the oak, is the flooring made,
  With a carpet of mosses and lichen and clover,
  Each small miracle over and over,
And tender, traveling green things strayed.

Her windows, the morning and evening star,
And her rustling doorways, ever ajar
    With the coming and going
    Of fair things blowing,
The thresholds of the four winds are.

May is building her house. From the dust of things
She is making the songs and the flowers and the wings;
  From October's tossed and trodden gold
  She is making the young year out of the old;
  Yea: out of winter's flying sleet
  She is making all the summer sweet,
  And the brown leaves spurned of November's feet
She is changing back again to spring's.

Richard Le Gallienne

The Second Crucifixion

Loud mockers in the roaring street
   Say Christ is crucified again:
Twice pierced His gospel-bearing feet,
   Twice broken His great heart in vain.

I hear, and to myself I smile,
For Christ talks with me all the while.

No angel now to roll the stone
   From off His unawaking sleep,
In vain shall Mary watch alone,
   In vain the soldiers vigil keep.

Yet while they deem my Lord is dead
My eyes are on His shining head.

Ah! never more shall Mary hear
   That voice exceeding sweet and low
Within the garden calling clear:
   Her Lord is gone, and she must go.

Yet all the while my Lord I meet
In every London lane and street.

Poor Lazarus shall wait in vain,
   And Bartimaeus[320] still go blind;
The healing hem shall ne'er again
   Be touched by suffering humankind.

Yet all the while I see them rest,
The poor and outcast, on His breast.

No more unto the stubborn heart
   With gentle knocking shall He plead,
No more the mystic pity start,
   For Christ twice dead is dead indeed.

So in the street I hear men say,
Yet Christ is with me all the day.

Julia's Clothes

Ah, when at night my lady sweet
Loosens the honeyed linen from her thigh,
Girdle and smock and all the warm things lie
Fall'n in a snowdrift round her feet;
Or like the foam that kissed the toes
Of Venus, nailed with pearl,
When from the sea she rose,
The wondrous golden girl.
Then, bending low, I take the sweet cloud up,
Stained through with sweets from arm and breast and thigh,
And, like a greedy gloating butterfly,
Upon the hoarded fragrance sup and sup.
Yea, as I feast upon my lady's clothes,
I dream I am a bee, and they a rose.

GEORGE WILLIAM RUSSELL
1867-1935

Star Teachers

EVEN AS A BIRD SPRAYS MANY-COLORED FIRES,
The plumes of paradise, the dying light
Rays through the fevered air in misty spires
That vanish in the height.

These myriad eyes that look on me are mine;
Wandering beneath them I have found again
The ancient ample moment, the divine,
The God-root within men.

For this, for this the lights innumerable
As symbols shine that we the true light win:
For every star and every deep they fill
Are stars and deeps within.

Unity

One thing in all things have I seen:
One thought has haunted earth and air:
Clangor and silence both have been
Its palace chambers. Everywhere

I saw the mystic vision flow
And live in men and woods and streams,
Until I could no longer know
The stream of life from my own dreams.

Sometimes it rose like fire in me
Within the depths of my own mind,
And spreading to infinity,
It took the voices of the wind:

It scrawled the human mystery—
Dim heraldry—on light and air;
Wavering along the starry sea
I saw the flying vision there.

Each fire that in God's temple lit
Burns fierce before the inner shrine,
Dimmed as my fire grew near to it
And darkened at the light of mine.

At last, at last, the meaning caught—
The spirit wears its diadem;[321]
It shakes its wondrous plumes of thought
And trails the stars along with them.

WILLA CATHER
1873-1947

The Hawthorn Tree

ACROSS THE SHIMMERING MEADOWS—
Ah, when he came to me!
In the spring-time,
In the night-time,
In the starlight,
Beneath the hawthorn tree.

Up from the misty marsh-land—
Ah, when he climbed to me!
To my white bower,
To my sweet rest,
To my warm breast,
Beneath the hawthorn tree.

Ask of me what the birds sang,
High in the hawthorn tree;
What the breeze tells,
What the rose smells,
What the stars shine—
Not what he said to me!

RAINER MARIA RILKE
1875-1926

Presaging

I AM LIKE A FLAG UNFURLED IN SPACE,[322]
I sense the oncoming winds and must bend with them,
While the things beneath are not yet stirring,
While the doors close gently and there is silence in the chimneys
And the windows do not yet tremble and the dust is still heavy—
Then I feel the storm and am vibrant like the sea
And expand and withdraw into myself
And thrust forth and am alone in the great storm.

Moonlight Night

South-German night! The ripe moon hangs above
Weaving enchantment o'er the shadowy lea.
From the old tower the hours fall heavily
Into the dark as though into the sea—
A rustle, a call of night-watch in the grove,
Then for a while void silence fills the air;
And then a violin (from God knows where)
Awakes and slowly sings: Oh Love … Oh Love …

Love Song

When my soul touches yours a great chord sings!
How shall I tune it then to other things?
O! That some spot in darkness can be found
That does not vibrate whene'er your depth sound.
But everything that touches you and me
Welds us as played strings sound one melody.
Where is the instrument whence the sounds flow?
And who's[323] the master-hand that holds the bow?
O! Sweet song—

The Book of Pilgrimage

In the deep nights I dig for you, O Treasure!
To seek you over the wide world I roam,
For all abundance is but meager measure
Of your bright beauty which is yet to come.

Over the road to you the leaves are blowing,
Few follow it, the way is long and steep.
You dwell in solitude—Oh, does your glowing
Heart in some far off valley lie asleep?

My bloody hands, with digging bruised, I've lifted,
Spread like a tree I stretch them in the air
To find you before day to night has drifted;
I reach out into space to seek you there ...

Then, as though with a swift impatient gesture,
Flashing from distant stars on sweeping wing,
You come, and over earth a magic vesture
Steals gently as the rain falls in the spring.

SAROJINI NAIDU
1879-1949

Ecstasy

COVER MINE EYES, O MY LOVE!
Mine eyes that are weary of bliss
As of light that is poignant and strong
O silence my lips with a kiss,
My lips that are weary of song!

Shelter my soul, O my love!
My soul is bent low with the pain
And the burden of love, like the grace
Of a flower that is smitten with rain:
O shelter my soul from thy face!

Indian Dancers

Eyes ravished with rapture, celestially panting, what passionate bosoms
    aflaming with fire,
Drink deep of the hush of the hyacinth heavens that glimmer around
    them in fountains of light;
O wild and entrancing the strain of keen music that cleaveth the stars
    like a wail of desire,
And beautiful dancers with houri-like[324] faces bewitch the voluptuous
    watches of night.

The scents of red roses and sandalwood flutter and die in the maze of
    their gem-tangled hair,
And smiles are entwining like magical serpents the poppies of lips that
    are opiate-sweet;
Their glittering garments of purple are burning like tremulous dawns in
    the quivering air,
And exquisite, subtle and slow are the tinkle and tread of their
    rhythmical, slumber-soft feet.

Now silent, now singing and swaying and swinging, like blossoms that
    bend to the breezes or showers,
Now wantonly winding, they flash, now they falter, and, lingering,
    languish in radiant choir;
Their jewel-girt arms and warm, wavering, lily-long fingers enchant
    through melodious hours,
Eyes ravished with rapture, celestially panting, what passionate bosoms
    aflaming with fire!

In Salutation to the Eternal Peace

Men say the world is full of fear and hate,
And all life's ripening harvest-fields await
The restless sickle of relentless fate.

But I, sweet Soul, rejoice that I was born,
When from the climbing terraces of corn
I watch the golden orioles of Thy morn.

What care I for the world's desire and pride,
Who know the silver wings that gleam and glide,
The homing pigeons of Thine eventide?

What care I for the world's loud weariness,
Who dream in twilight granaries Thou dost bless
With delicate sheaves of mellow silences?

Say, shall I heed dull presages of doom,
Or dread the rumored loneliness and gloom,
The mute and mythic terror of the tomb?

For my glad heart is drunk and drenched with Thee,
O inmost wine of living ecstasy!
O intimate essence of eternity!

SARA TEASDALE
1884-1933

Joy

I AM WILD, I WILL SING TO THE TREES,
    I will sing to the stars in the sky,
I love, I am loved, he is mine,
    Now at last I can die!

I am sandaled with wind and with flame,
    I have heart-fire and singing to give,
I can tread on the grass or the stars,
    Now at last I can live!

The Lamp

If I can bear your love like a lamp before me,
When I go down the long steep Road of Darkness,
I shall not fear the everlasting shadows,
    Nor cry in terror.
If I can find out God, then I shall find Him,
If none can find Him, then I shall sleep soundly,
Knowing how well on earth your love sufficed me,
    A lamp in darkness.

A Prayer

Until I lose my soul and lie
    Blind to the beauty of the earth,
Deaf though shouting wind goes by,
    Dumb in a storm of mirth;
Until my heart is quenched at length
    And I have left the land of men,
Oh, let me love with all my strength
    Careless if I am loved again.

The Cloud

I am a cloud in the heaven's height,
The stars are lit for my delight,
Tireless and changeful, swift and free,
I cast my shadow on hill and sea—
But why do the pines on the mountain's crest
Call to me always, "Rest, rest"?
I throw my mantle over the moon
And I blind the sun on his throne at noon,
Nothing can tame me, nothing can bind,
I am a child of the heartless wind—
But oh the pines on the mountain's crest
Whispering always, "Rest, rest."

The Answer

When I go back to earth
And all my joyous body
Puts off the red and white
That once had been so proud,
If men should pass above
With false and feeble pity,
My dust will find a voice
To answer them aloud:
"Be still, I am content,
Take back your poor compassion,
Joy was a flame in me
Too steady to destroy;
Lithe as a bending reed
Loving the storm that sways her—
I found more joy in sorrow
Than you could find in joy."

The Mystery

Your eyes drink of me,
    Love makes them shine,
Your eyes that lean
    So close to mine.

We have long been lovers,
    We know the range
Of each other's moods
    And how they change;

But when we look
    At each other so
Then we feel
    How little we know;

The spirit eludes us,
    Timid and free—
Can I ever know you
    Or you know me?

The Treasure

When they see my songs
    They will sigh and say,
"Poor soul, wistful soul,
    Lonely night and day."

They will never know
    All your love for me
Surer than the spring,
    Stronger than the sea;

Hidden out of sight
    Like a miser's gold
In forsaken fields
    Where the wind is cold.

The Storm

I thought of you when I was wakened
  By a wind that made me glad and afraid
Of the rushing, pouring sound of the sea
  That the great trees made.

One thought in my mind went over and over
  While the darkness shook and the leaves were thinned—
I thought it was you who had come to find me,
  You were the wind.

The Wanderer

I saw the sunset-colored sands,
  The Nile like flowing fire between,
  Where Ramses stares forth serene,
And Ammon's[325] heavy temple stands.
I saw the rocks where long ago,
  Above the sea that cries and breaks,
  Bright Perseus[326] with Medusa's snakes
Set free the maiden white like snow.
And many skies have covered me,
  And many winds have blown me forth,
  And I have loved the green bright north,
And I have loved the cold sweet sea.
But what to me are north and south,
  And what the lure of many lands,
  Since you have leaned to catch my hands
And lay a kiss upon my mouth.

Stars

Alone in the night
  On a dark hill
With pines around me
  Spicy and still,

And a heaven full of stars
  Over my head,
White and topaz
  And misty red;

Myriads with beating
  Hearts of fire
That eons
  Cannot vex or tire;

Up the dome of heaven
  Like a great hill,
I watch them marching
  Stately and still,

And I know that I
  Am honored to be
Witness
  Of so much majesty.

The Voice

Atoms as old as stars,
Mutation on mutation,
Millions and millions of cells
Dividing yet still the same,
From air and changing earth,
From ancient Eastern rivers,
From turquoise tropic seas,
Unto myself I came.

My spirit like my flesh
Sprang from a thousand sources,
From cave-man, hunter and shepherd,
From Karnak, Cyprus, Rome;
The living thoughts in me
Spring from dead men and women,
Forgotten time out of mind
And many as bubbles of foam.

Here for a moment's space
Into the light out of darkness,
I come and they come with me
Finding words with my breath;
From the wisdom of many life-times
I hear them cry: "Forever
Seek for Beauty, she only
Fights with man against Death!"

Peace

Peace flows into me
    As the tide to the pool by the shore;
    It is mine forevermore,
It will not ebb like the sea.
I am the pool of blue
    That worships the vivid sky;
    My hopes were heaven-high,
They are all fulfilled in you.
I am the pool of gold
    When sunset burns and dies—
    You are my deepening skies;
Give me your stars to hold.

D. H. LAWRENCE
1885-1930

Pax

ALL THAT MATTERS IS TO BE AT ONE WITH THE LIVING GOD
To be a creature in the house of the God of Life.

Like a cat asleep on a chair
at peace, in peace
and at one with the master of the house, with the
mistress
at home, at home in the house of the living,
sleeping on the hearth, and yawning before the fire.

Sleeping on the hearth of the living world,
yawning at home before the fire of life
feeling the presence of the living God
like a great reassurance
a deep calm in the heart
a presence
as of a master sitting at the board
in his own and greater being,
in the house of life.

Shadows

And if tonight my soul may find her peace
in sleep, and sink in good oblivion,
and in the morning wake like a new-opened flower
then I have been dipped again in God, and new-created.

And if, as weeks go round, in the dark of the moon
my spirit darkens and goes out, and soft strange gloom
pervades my movements and my thoughts and words
then I shall know that I am walking still
with God, we are close together now the moon's in shadow.

And if, as autumn deepens and darkens
I feel the pain of falling leaves, and stems that break in storms
and trouble and dissolution and distress
and then the softness of deep shadows folding,
folding around my soul and spirit, around my lips
so sweet, like a swoon, or more like the drowse of a low, sad song
singing darker than the nightingale, on, on to the solstice
and the silence of short days, the silence of the year, the shadow,
then I shall know that my life is moving still
with the dark earth, and drenched
with the deep oblivion of earth's lapse and renewal.

And if, in the changing phases of man's life
I fall in sickness and in misery
my wrists seem broken and my heart seems dead
and strength is gone, and my life
is only the leavings of a life:

and still, among it all, snatches of lovely oblivion, and snatches of
    renewal
odd, wintry flowers upon the withered stem, yet new, strange flowers
such as my life has not brought forth before, new blossoms of me

then I must know that still
I am in the hands of the unknown God,
he is breaking me down to his own oblivion
to send me forth on a new morning, a new man.

Song of a Man who Has Come through

Not I, not I, but the wind that blows through me!
A fine wind is blowing the new direction of Time.
If only I let it bear me, carry me, if only it carry me!
If only I am sensitive, subtle, oh, delicate, a winged gift!
If only, most lovely of all, I yield myself and am borrowed
By the fine, fine, wind that takes its course through the chaos of the
    world
Like a fine, an exquisite chisel, a wedge-blade inserted;
If only I am keen and hard like the sheer tip of a wedge

Driven by invisible blows,
The rock will split, we shall come at the wonder, we shall find the
 Hesperides.[327]

Oh, for the wonder that bubbles into my soul,
I would be a good fountain, a good well-head,
Would blur no whisper, spoil no expression.

What is the knocking?
What is the knocking at the door in the night?
It is somebody wants to do us harm.

No, no, it is the three strange angels.
Let them come in.

Mystery

Now I am all
One bowl of kisses,
Such as the tall
Slim votaresses[328]
Of Egypt filled
For a God's excesses.

I lift to you
My bowl of kisses,
And through the temple's
Blue recesses
Cry out to you
In wild caresses.

And to my lips'
Bright crimson rim
The passion slips,
And down my slim
White body drips
The shining hymn.

And still before
The altar I
Exult the bowl
Brimful, and cry
To you to stoop
And drink, Most High.

Oh drink me up
That I may be
Within your cup
Like a mystery,
Like wine that is still
In ecstasy.

Glimmering still
In ecstasy,
Commingled wines
Of you and me
In one fulfill
The mystery.

WILLIAM ALEXANDER PERCY
1885-1942

Overtones

I HEARD A BIRD AT BREAK OF DAY
   Sing from the autumn trees
A song so mystical and calm,
   So full of certainties,
No man, I think, could listen long
   Except upon his knees.
Yet this was but a simple bird,
   Alone, among dead trees.

Song

O singing heart, think not of aught save song;
   Beauty can do no wrong.
Let but th' inviolable music shake
   Golden on golden flake,
   Down to the human throng,
And one, one surely, will look up and hear and wake.

Weigh not the rapture; measure not nor sift
   God's dark, delirious gift;
But deaf to immortality or gain,
   Give as the shining rain,
   Thy music pure and swift,
And here or there, sometime, somewhere, 'twill reach the grain.

Soaring

   My heart is a bird to-night
That streams on the washed, icy air.
   My heart is a bird to-night
'Twixt the stars and the branches bare.

My heart is abroad to-night
Rushed on by the fierce, crystal air.
   No nest will it seek to-night
In the branches, ice-brittle and bare.

Wide-wingèd my heart to-night
With joy on the surge of the air.
   What matter that spirits of night
Make shudder the trees, lean and bare!

Autumn Tune

Sweeter than spring, sweeter than spring,
These brown and blue and lingering
   Soft days that wing
Like flimsy dreams across the world,
One by one unfurled, unfurled,
Where the ripe fields slumber and glitter and swing.

Sadder than song, sadder than song,
The choral drowse with madness strong
   That all day long
The locusts lift to their god the sun,
For joy of the life that is almost done—
Raptured and shrill and regretless throng.

Wilder than wings, wilder than wings,
The flight of the golden leaves when springs
   The fear that flings
Them swirling and shining up from the bare
Dark branches that reach to the calm of the air
Where death is a-dream on azure wings.

A Sea-Bird

I cry, I cry
Into the night.

Along the waves
I gleam and fly
A haunted flight;
A cry, a cry
Into the night.

Lone, alone,
And the sea is mad.
Mourning, mourning,
Broken and strown,
It nurseth the dead,
The dead alone—
And my heart that is mad.

Ecstasy
(After Verlaine)

The moon shines now
White in the woods;
From every bough
Cometh in floods
A voice divine ...
O love of mine!

The pool of jet,
Deep mirror sees
In silhouette
The willow trees
That moan and gleam ...
O hour of dream!

Tender and vast,
A peacefulness
Drifts downward past
The shadowless
Star-purple night ...
Hour of delight!

EZRA POUND
1885-1972

An Immorality

Sɪɴɢ ᴡᴇ ꜰᴏʀ ʟᴏᴠᴇ ᴀɴᴅ ɪᴅʟᴇɴᴇꜱꜱ,
Naught else is worth the having.

Though I have been in many a land,
There is naught else in living.

And I would rather have my sweet,
Though rose-leaves die of grieving,

Than do high deeds in Hungary
To pass all men's believing.

The River Merchant's Wife

While my hair was still cut straight across my forehead
I played about the front gate, pulling flowers.
You came by on bamboo stilts, playing horse,
You walked about my seat, playing with blue plums.
And we went on living in the village of Chokan:
Two small people, without dislike or suspicion.

At fourteen I married My Lord you.
I never laughed, being bashful.
Lowering my head, I looked at the wall.
Called to, a thousand times, I never looked back.

At fifteen I stopped scowling,
I desired my dust to be mingled with yours
Forever and forever, and forever.
Why should I climb the look out?

At sixteen you departed,
You went into far Ku-to-Yen, by the river of swirling eddies,
And you have been gone five months.
The monkeys make sorrowful noise overhead.

You dragged your feet when you went out.
By the gate now, the moss is grown, the different mosses,
Too deep to clear them away!
The leaves fall early this autumn, in wind.
The paired butterflies are already yellow with August
Over the grass in the West garden,
They hurt me.
I grow older,
If you are coming down through the narrows of the river Kiang,
Please let me know beforehand,
And I will come out to meet you,
As far as Cho-fu-Sa.

MARIANO BRULL
1891-1956

To the Mountain

JUST AS SOON AS MASS IS OVER,[329]
Put our pious airs away;
And with luncheon in our baskets,
To the mountain! To the mountain!
To the mountain for the day!

Hark, the bells of glory ringing
From the belfries of the Spring!—
Sun and sky!—oh, what a blessing
After gloomy days, they bring!

How the water o'er the mill-wheel
Rumbles furious and fast,
Bursting through a thousand echoes
Until—there—'tis gone at last!

For the woods our hearts are hungry;
Every bird hears us reply;
Incense seems to sweep our bosoms—
To the mountain! To the mountain!
To the mountain, let us hie!

Every grotto holds a secret;
Every cleft its creed and rite;
On the slopes is scattered grandeur—
Hawthorn flowers and crags in sight!

On the peaks the wind is hymning,—
Heaven is nigh—the town, far down;
Ah, why should not human dwellings
All the free-world mountains crown?—

At the nightfall—with our baskets
Empty—to the town we haste;
All the mountains fill with shadows,—
Spirits of the dreaded waste!—

EDNA ST. VINCENT MILLAY
1892-1950

Journey

AH, COULD I LAY ME DOWN IN THIS LONG GRASS
And close my eyes, and let the quiet wind
Blow over me—I am so tired, so tired
Of passing pleasant places! All my life,
Following Care along the dusty road,
Have I looked back at loveliness and sighed;
Yet at my hand an unrelenting hand
Tugged ever, and I passed. All my life long
Over my shoulder have I looked at peace;
And now I fain would lie in this long grass
And close my eyes.
Yet onward!
Cat birds call
Through the long afternoon, and creeks at dusk
Are guttural. Whip-poor-wills wake and cry,
Drawing the twilight close about their throats.
Only my heart makes answer. Eager vines
Go up the rocks and wait; flushed apple-trees
Pause in their dance and break the ring for me;
And bayberry, that through sweet bevies thread
Of round-faced roses, pink and petulant,
Look back and beckon ere they disappear.
Only my heart, only my heart responds.
Yet, ah, my path is sweet on either side
All through the dragging day,—sharp underfoot
And hot, and like dead mist the dry dust hangs—
But far, oh, far as passionate eye can reach,
And long, ah, long as rapturous eye can cling,
The world is mine: blue hill, still silver lake,
Broad field, bright flower, and the long white road
A gateless garden, and an open path:
My feet to follow, and my heart to hold.

Mariposa

Butterflies[330] are white and blue
In this field we wander through.
Suffer me to take your hand.
Death comes in a day or two.

All the things we ever knew
Will be ashes in that hour,
Mark the transient butterfly,
How he hangs upon the flower.

Suffer me to take your hand.
Suffer me to cherish you
Till the dawn is in the sky.
Whether I be false or true,
Death comes in a day or two.

God's World

O world, I cannot hold thee close enough!
    Thy winds, thy wide grey skies!
    Thy mists that roll and rise!
Thy woods this autumn day, that ache and sag
And all but cry with color! That gaunt crag
To crush! To lift the lean of that black bluff!
World, World, I cannot get thee close enough!

Long have I known a glory in it all,
    But never knew I this;
    Here such a passion is
As stretcheth me apart,—Lord, I do fear
Thou'st made the world too beautiful this year;
My soul is all but out of me,—let fall
No burning leaf; prithee, let no bird call.

PEDRO REQUENA LEGARRETA
1893-1918

Idyl

THE OPAL-BREASTED MORNING OF THE SPRING[331]
Scarce o'er the meads her luminous urn can swing.[332]

When from the nests the tremulous light flute
Of songs comes thawing, and the echoes mute

Awake and mingle with the distant brawl
Of lowing cattle and the shepherds' call:

'Twould seem that, falling from the morning's urn,
Each ray of light would into singing turn.

Alone amid the pasture's splendid breast
There stands a tree, a shadowy poem blest.

Among its prescient leaves there lurks a trace
Of old-world sadness and of pastoral grace;

And bending o'er the field, the green gargoyle
Of one long branch from out the trunk would coil.

A-straddle on the branch a maiden rides,
As though a nymph some haughty centaur guides;

Blonde is the maid, and naked, tall and fair,
With glow transparent as the morning air.

A sudden breath along the meadow grass
Stirs with a kiss the branch ere it would pass.

And she, whom hasty breaths of fever seize,
Grips the bough tighter with her snowy knees.

The while the icy jewels of the dew
Send a sharp chill her silken body through.

Her locks float back in airy coronal
Above her shoulders, as the dawn rain's fall;

And green and rose the shifting boughs appear
Like some great butterfly her lips a-near.

She sways a moment, then, as some divine
Young nymph that Jove enamored would entwine,

Her scarlet kisses all the green bough cover,—
And the tree trembles—as it were her lover—

e e cummings
1894-1962

o sweet spontaneous

O SWEET SPONTANEOUS
earth how often have
the
doting

fingers of
prurient[333] philosophers pinched
and
poked

thee
, has the naughty thumb
of science prodded
thy

beauty   . how
often have religions taken
thee upon their scraggy knees
squeezing and

buffeting thee that thou mightest conceive
gods
          (but
true

to the incomparable
couch of death thy
rhythmic
lover

thou answerest

them only with

spring)

ANONYMOUS

The Maid A-Bathing

Upon a Summer's day,[334]
'Bout middle of the morn,
I spied a Lass that lay
Stark naked as she was born;
'Twas by a running Pool,
Within a meadow green,
And there she lay to cool,
Not thinking to be seen.

Then did she by degrees
Wash every part in rank,
Her Arms, her breasts, her thighs,
Her Belly, and her Flank;
Her legs she opened wide,
My eyes I let down steal,
Until that I espied
Dame nature's privy Seal.

I stripped me to the skin,
And boldly stepped unto her,
Thinking her love to win,
I thus began to woo her:
Sweetheart, be not so coy,
Time's sweet in pleasures spent,
She frowned, and cried, away.
Yet smiling, gave consent.

Then blushing, down she slid,
Seeming to be amazed,
But heaving up her head,
Again she on me gazed;
I seeing that, lay down,
And boldly 'gan to kiss,

And she did smile, and frown,
And so fell to our bliss.

Then lay she on the ground
As though she had been sped,
As women in a swoon,
Yield up, and yet not dead:
So did this lively maid,
When hot blood filled her vein,
And coming to herself she said,
I thank you for your pain.

The Enjoyment

Gods! the raptures of that night!
What fierce convulsions of delight!
How in each other's arms involved
We lay confounded, and dissolved!
Bodies mingling, sexes blending,
Which should most be lost contending,
Darting fierce and flaming kisses,
Plunging into boundless blisses;
Our bodies, and our souls on fire.
Tossed by a tempest of Desire;
Till with utmost fury driven,
Down, at once, we sunk to heaven.

The Tapir

O little cleft of coral
Grown about with daffodils;
Fountain of porphyry[335]
Where the waters of Helicon[336] gust,
I would drink at your waters,
Entwining my tongue
About the clitoral erubescence[337]
Of your most secret passion.
Winding in and out

352

Draining, drawing,
Curving about the sardonyx[338] mouth
Of the sacred urn;
Drinking, O delicious!
O thirsty devouring of viscous moon-beams,
Of mucilaginous[339] starlight.
I gather your two rosebuds
And strip their petals
While eating your thrice extracted honeycomb,
NOW
O falling stars …
Bathed in your liquid loveliness
Anointed with your adorable essence.[340]

JACK HEITNER
b. 1931

Lost Melody

WHAT IS THIS MYSTIC FLUTE WHOSE NOTE[341]
Balanced between dream and waking
Sends the sound that seems to float?
Sends the sound that leaves me shaking?
As I vibrate to that tune—
Echoes of lost melody.

The trees are rustling with the name,
Their branches reaching in the rain.
To fail to sing it gives them pain.

The rocks try hard to hum the words;
I climb them and I feel their urge
To make their rumblings sound as birds.

The crags, they want to cry it out,
To blare it from volcano mouths
Like titan tubas brazen shouts.

Try subtle songs of birds to read
Like cries of lovers long years dead
Like mantras whispered by the gods.

Love is the mystic flute whose note—
Caught in the wind of spirit wings—
Translates us far beyond our sun
Higher than all galactic rings,
As I vibrate to that tune
Echoes of lost melody.

Arsonists

A prophet called me to my work on Earth,
And told me of a love that fired the stars.
My sacred Being, he said, transcended birth,
Seeking the planes beyond the reach of wars.

My eye could not confront the master's gaze,
So mind refused to reconcile his tongue,
Yet now I know true prophets never lie,
And masters show the path beyond the sun.

One universe afire with knowing's flame
Set other universes to the torch:
Wild fire in the blackness spreads untamed—
Firecstasy to realize God's touch.

A master or a prophet is the torch,
God's Arsonist who lights the seeker's search.

SUSANNA RICH
b. 1951

Dancing with Wide Skirts
—For Larry, longing to be

IT'S NOT THAT YOU CAN EVER NOT BE[342]
dancing so—even tucked in a tux,
legs braced by satin stripes;
or holding still as a window
shuttered to the waltz of days.

It's true—there is in all of us
a stem needing its blossom,
a clapper wanting its bell,
a sun held to its course
by an orrery[343] of planets.

It's not crinolines[344] I slip down
over my body, but tiers of angels
holding hands around my sorrows.
And the silks you think you see
are dolphins of joy surfacing.

You don't need a tutu, kilt, or Sufi's
tannoura;[345] broomstick gauze, jangling coins,
hoops, pleats, or culottes. A dancing skirt is
the mystery of sweep—the emptiness, the eye,
the vacuum at our core—made and unmade

by a tugging on our waists. To find your skirts
just turn and turn and turn. Toss your
pebble of desire into a universe
infinitely spinning, infinitely rippling,
infinitely dancing, dancing, dancing.

Applause

What else would it be, this rush
in the trees—veined leaf
brushing leaf as you sit like a maple,
old in its bark, limbs spreading?

That rain pattering the roof of your sleep
is your ovation, as is
the infinite blinking
of beetles, asps, whales.

Dearer and sure is the
unbidden and unbought—
a planet rapping melodies of itself
in the pulse of need and excess:

bees busy in the mint;
waterfalls and dripping caves;
blood, wind, wings; gills and sphincters;
dawn rubbing fog.

What little the tap of human tongue
and hand to this circuitry—
a universe rising into itself
in gratitude to our breathing.

Come to the Dance
With thanks to Ping Sun Chun

Come to the dance, beloved—
the villagers dressed for a wedding,
ribbons leaping in their hair,
lace caressing their throats.

They are waiting for you by the bridge—
horses decked with poppies,
hands heavy with bread,
children with bright hats.

357

Leave your corners and your arrows,
for they cannot cross this bridge,
nor can your questions or your money,
your luggage or your news.

Bring the sweet flute of your longing,
the drum, drum of your grief.
Slip your feet into the boots of desire;
don the wide skirts of joy.

They have swept the cobbles
with brooms of light,
dropped plums of love
under your heels.

Come to the dance; come
to the fountain at the village core.
Someone is waiting and ever will—
The hand reaching for yours is yours.

ALEX GRAY
b. 1953

Bless Your Eyes

YOUR EYES ARE BLESSED OPENINGS,
Taking in whatever light brings.
Treat eyes kindly, feed them well,
They excitedly glisten and lovingly swell.
Show them the worst all over again,
They shrink into hollows of mortal skin.
Bathe your eyes in images Divine,
All Heaven unfolds, the opposites combine.
Your eyes become temple domes for the Pleiades,
Crystalline mandalas inhabited by Deities.
Blessing every moment you see
As glimpses of eternity.

Praise Be the Song of Art

To praise the Creator,
We sing our songs.
God of Gods, Source of Sources,
Moving atomic and kosmic forces.
Hearts are pumping bloody praise
Through our veins.
Your nameless name
And boundlessness
Echo in each beating breast,
Drumming your eternal song.

Meaning counters meaninglessness,
And dreams make sense uncommonly deep.
Your fury most mysterious,
Your voice we hear in every breath.
I can't be worth your trouble, Lord,
I have such flaws and qualities bad.

359

Can't concentrate and remain with you.
Mind wanders away,
Finds things to do.
God help me hear your song.

Only You can write a poem.
Only You can paint a masterpiece.
Only You radiate from works of genius.
The artist becomes transparent to God.
An empty grail filled with God's light,
Nectar of the Arts.
A single secret drop
Can change the course of Art History.
Entire Cultures change overnight from one drop.

To see through a drop of spiritual light
Makes infinity visible
And is the consolation of the Soul
In its painful task of flight and descent
From Heaven to Earth to Hell and back.
The soul dreams itself awake,
And what strange dreams you artists make.
Culture is our collective dream.
God's promise of union with the All
And History's nightmare of our fall
Echo from unconscious ground
Through poet's tongue
And musician's sound.
The painters touch and smell the vision
While millions doze, watching television

Forgive us all our ignorance.
Wake us now
To dance your dance and hear your drum.
Help us fix this mess, Thy kingdom come.
Don't desert us now as we have You.
I call for all who never call,
Shock us awake!
Allow us to see You, feel You,
Never separate from You.

Let us love You with all our creative heart
And sing You through our Song of Art.
Praise, Praise be the Song of Art.

Guardian of the Endless Smile

Praise laughter,
From the slightly upturned mouth,
To the painful sideache.
Gasping for breath,
May we hear the cosmic joke
And see the ridiculousness
Of life and the world.
When the tragic overwhelms,
Infect us with your
Preposterous happiness.

DANIEL WEEKS
b. 1958

The Blue Morning Glory: My Rebel Emblem

1

IT ISN'T BECAUSE I LOVE
      life, any more than the
      bee loves the peonies
        or their color or thinks about
          the beauty of the August air,
but because I don't know
        any other thing to know,
      to be, to do.
Yet, I shall not go as the bee goes,
        by rote visiting each
        bursting aureole,
      and not yet in despair
        as does one with bruised
          appetite and ruined mind—
but in hope—and singing,
        as full of the world as the world
      is pregnant with me, with an eye full of
      morning glories or with their memory
at the least.
      At the least—
how else might one outface
        a waning August afternoon,
          when all the shadows lie longer on the lawn,
            with all the dogwoods cast
            in amber light,
and all the headstones that once
seemed white now aglow in a gold
        that washes out the names and dates as they
      were never there?

2

Somewhere this hour someone is dying,
      and somewhere this day someone is being born—
         a cycle of force.
    Though there shall be grief enough between
        the dawn and dawn,
grief enough, and remorse,
      and deep-stinging bitterness to stop the heart
      or lodge like lead
        behind the eye,
               and all who breathe or ever breathed
shall lie down dead—I promise you—
      we shall not be forlorn. This
        is a race to beauty,
              and I
am an engine quick
      with fire. I have no time
for hearts sprung from the strangling vine
      unless that vine be strung upon a lyre
      and teach the heart to sing
        a song aflame—
           a fine blue burning.

3

Star of the morning,
      my rebel emblem,
        stand bluely toward the light.
Like the burst face of dawn,
      defy all summer long
        the canker's blight,
kiss the gusting air,
      seek a new radiance,
        dance with the dancing sun,
          do all that might be done,
and then
      close tight
        against the warm oblivion of the night.

Clarissa among the Bovines

The cows, munching placidly,
hardly noticed Clarissa
coming barefoot through
the timothy just this side
of the long, long strands
of barbed wire.
Had John Coleman, the farmer,
not been off planting
Chinese vegetables
in the north field,
he would certainly have
pulled off his old Reds cap,
holding it by the peak,
so as he could scrape
his blackened nails
across a sweaty forehead.
But there was no one
to see Clarissa bounding
barefoot through the
timothy conducting unseen
symphonies with a single strand of straw—
a strand that ran as far
as fence wire in her mind.
No, no one saw except the
cows, who didn't seem to care.
One rolled a big moon eye Clarissa's way the first time
she passed wildly by, her bare bottom peeking out
from beneath her nightgown's hem.
But even the cows,
as observant as they seemed to be,
couldn't hear
what Clarissa's fingers
were bringing forth
under that late June sun. Oh, it was
music in her soul.
Old John Coleman, had
he been there, would
certainly have sensed

scandal once Clarissa
tore off her linen
gown and flung it
to the not-so-tender
mercies of the brambles,
cavorting with her
considerable charms one last time
close by the silent beeves before skipping away into
the golden touch of
afternoon sun.

GREG BROWN
b. 1963

Slaves of Glory

THE VERY ASTONISHING HOUR HAS COME.[346]
The very astonishing hour indeed!
Green Heinekens, jade brain and rose-coral vodkas
    —Exhausted! In one final, fantastic evening.

Hosannahs[347] invade the empty windows,
    spurs of blacks, mysterious
As the tender invitation of the body.

        Bright, alcoholic after-haloes sift
        Timid ash upon stale, upraised lips.

        Sobriety has entered us
        As mourners enter a white church.

Enough of this pathetic quietness!
This simpering, dog-like wish for "temperament,"
The madness of faces full of "sound judgment."
I forgive all disasters, all accomplishments,
Every disguise that announces "I am finished!"
Choking its inhabitant as a mirror chokes beauty.
Songs of sporadic intensity, wicked verses,
The poem of flayed skin, blind eyesight,
Mutes imagining laughter, I forgive you!

        Pathetic quiet!
        Bring tympans, wild sibilants,[348]
        Drunken elephants of sound, mists,
            the harsh clangor of brass.

New eyes, new hearts, new senses!
Bring a speech of bloods, the invention of Angels!

Why was one ever afraid of waking?
Eh! a little daydream I had in the hay pile.

But now the new era has arrived—this moment!—
Let us revenge the sky for an hour!

Let us run out, muds of new births upon us,
And seize in hands of ice the very flowing waters—
Dreams of incorporeal perfection!

Dawn-leaves splinter in my eye
Enacting the death of Satan.

Vertiginousness in the closet!

Very astonishing!

ANONYMOUS

The Border

Waves of bliss crash against the craggy shore
Of my innermost heart, dissolving me.
As I gaze gently on the mysterious horizon,
I see sea-birds of joy flying from some dark, distant land
On the opposite side, where you are, my tender one.
Singing songs in an exotic tongue,
They herald you and your coming.
I feel you looking back at me, searching the same horizon
With those entrancing, dancing, devil's-eyes.

Imagine a point beyond the briny sea-spume,
Beyond the horizons of life, love, and pain,
Somewhere unknown to you.
I, too, my love, will reach and stretch.
With my whole soul, I will rise up
And venture out towards you.
To find one another, we must imagine
The life far beyond the border.
Darling, I will meet you there.

NOTES

1. Elisabeth Kubler-Ross, *The Tunnel and the Light* (New York: Avalon, 1999), 57.

2. Allan Kellehear, *Experiences Near Death: Beyond Medicine and Religion* (New York: Oxford UP, 1996), 62.

3. I discuss this personal experience only after having received permission to do so from the student.

4. I quote this with his permission, of course.

5. Adam Potkay, *The Story of Joy: From the Bible to Late Romanticism* (New York: Cambridge University Press, 2007), 2.

6. Ibid., 20.

7. Ibid., 27.

8. See Rosemarie Taylor-Perry, *The God Who Comes: Dionysian Mysteries Revisited* (New York: Algora, 2003).

9. Ibid., 3.

10. Marghanita Laski, *Ecstasy in Secular and Religious Experiences* (Los Angeles: Tarcher, 1961), 26.

11. Cited in Laski, 51.

12. Cited in Evelyn Elsaesser Valarino, *On the Other Side of Life: Exploring the Phenomenon of the Near-Death Experience*, trans. Michelle Herzig Escobar (New York: Plenum, 1997), 32.

13. Cited in Dan Merkur, *The Ecstatic Imagination: Psychedelic Experiences and the Psychoanalysis of Self-Actualization* (Albany, NY: SUNY P, 1998), 114.

14. Cited in Stanislav Grof, *The Holotropic Mind* (New York: HarperCollins, 1990), 98.

15. Cited in Merkur, *The Ecstatic Imagination: Psychedelic Experiences and the Psychoanalysis of Self-Actualization*, 108.

16. Cited in F.C. Happold, *Mysticism: A Study and an Anthology* (New York: Penguin, 1990), 54.

17. Ibid., 130.

18. Cited in John G. Neihardt, *Black Elk Speaks* (Lincoln, NE: UP Nebraska, 1979), 43.

19. Abraham Maslow, *The Farther Reaches of Human Nature* (New York: Penguin, 1976), 285.

20. Emile Durkheim, *The Elementary Forms of the Religious Life* (New York: Free Press, 1915), 249.

21. Victor Turner, *The Ritual Process: Structure and Anti-Structure* (Ithaca, NY: Cornell UP, 1966), 7.

22. For a more thorough discussion, see Albert Hoffman, *LSD: My Problem Child* (Sarasota, FL: MAPS, 2005).

23. Merkur, *The Ecstatic Imagination: Psychedelic Experiences and the Psychoanalysis of Self-Actualization,* 91.

24. Ibid., 94.

25. For a considerably more thorough treatment of this issue, see Martin Heidegger, *Basic Writings,* trans. Joan Stambaugh (New York: HarperCollins, 1993).

26. C.G. Jung, *The Collected Works of C.G. Jung,* 20 vols, ed. William McGuire, trans. R.F.C. Hull (Princeton, NJ: Princeton UP, 1983), 12:60.

27. Laski, *Ecstasy in Secular and Religious Experiences,* 26.

28. Ibid., 176.

29. Mihalyi Csikszentmihalyi, *Flow: The Psychology of Optimal Experience* (New York: Harper & Row, 1990), 2.

30. Ibid., 49.

31. Ibid., 50.

32. Ibid., 49.

33. Ibid., 49.

34. Alderink, Larry, "Creation and Salvation in Ancient Orphism," *American Classical Studies* 8 (1981): 23.

35. Barbara Ehrenreich, *Dancing in the Streets* (New York: Henry Holt, 2006) 150-151.

36. Andrew Newberg, *Born to Believe: God, Science, and the Origin of Ordinary and Extraordinary Beliefs* (New York: Simon & Schuster, 2006), 200.

37. Ibid., 75.

38. Ibid., 187.

39. T.W. Kjaer, et al. "The Neural Basis of the Complex Tasks of Meditation: Neurotransmitter and Neurochemical Considerations," *Brain Research: Cognitive Brain Research* 13 no. 2 (2002): 255.

40. Thomas Lewis, Fari Amini, and Richard Lannon, *A General Theory of Love* (New York: Random House, 2000), 90.

41. Ljubomir Aftanas and Semen Golosheykin, "Impact of Regular Meditation Practice on EEG Activity at Rest and during Evoked Negative Emotions," *Neuroscience* 115 (2005): 894.

42. Ibid., 902.

43. Ibid., 894.

44. Belinda Ivanovski and Gin S. Malhi, "The Psychological and Neuro-physiological Concomitants of Mindfulness Forms of Meditation," *Acta Neuropsychiatrica* 19 (2007): 76, 81.

45. Ibid., 83.

46. Thomas Lewis, Fari Amini, and Richard Lannon, *A General Theory of Love*, 56.

47. Ibid., 69-81.

48. Gerard Huther, *The Compassionate Brain* (Boston: Shambhala, 2006), 114.

49. Ibid., 114.

50. Abraham Maslow, *Toward a Psychology of Being* (New York: D. Van Nostrand, 1968), 112.

51. Maslow, *The Farther Reaches of Human Nature*, 101.

52. Abraham Maslow, *Religions, Values & Peak Experiences* (New York: Penguin, 1970), 71.

53. Martin Seligman, *Authentic Happiness* (New York: Simon & Schuster, 2002), 31.

54. Ibid., 35.

55. Sigmund Freud, *Civilzation & Its Discontents*, trans. James Strachey (New York: Norton, 1989), 12-13.

56. Mircea Eliade, *Shamanism: Archaic Techniques of Ecstasy*, trans. Willard R. Trask (Princeton, NJ: Princeton UP, 1964), 44.

57. Ronald Hayman, *A Life of Jung* (New York: Norton, 1999), 174.

58. Trish Hall, "Seeking a Focus on Joy in the Field of Psychology," *New York Times*, April 28, 1998.

59. numinous: relating to the spiritual or supernatural, the experience of which is beyond rational comprehension.

60. pistis: faith

61. C.G. Jung, *Psychology and Religion* (New Haven, CT: Yale UP, 1938), 113.

62. Erich Fromm, *The Art of Loving* (New York: Continuum, 1956), 8.

63. Rollo May, *Love and Will*, (New York: Dell, 1969), 16.

64. William James, *The Varieties of Religious Experience* (New York: Penguin, 1985), 90.

65. Ibid., 79-80.

66. For a more complete discussion see the following works by Victor Frankl: *Man's Search for Ultimate Meaning*, (New York: Basic, 2000) and *Man's Search for Meaning* (New York: Simon & Schuster, 1984).

67. Christopher Peterson, *A Primer in Positive Psychology* (New York: Oxford UP, 2006), 6.

68. Ibid., 4.

69. Csikszentmihalyi, *Flow*, 30.

70. Ehrenreich, *Dancing in the Streets*, 11.

71. Ibid., 11.

72. Ibid., 27.

73. Daniel Pinchbeck, *Breaking Open the Head: A Psychedelic Journey into the Heart of Contemporary Shamanism* (New York: Random House, 2002), 37-38.

74. Maslow, *The Farther Reaches of Human Nature*, 103-04.

75. Timothy Leary, *The Politics of Ecstasy* (Oakland, CA: Ronin, 1998), 87.

76. Ehrenreich, *Dancing in the Streets*, 37.

77. Jung, *Collected Works*, 11:285.

78. Maslow, *The Farther Reaches*, 279.

79. Michel Foucault, *Madness and Civilization: A History of Insanity in the Age of Reason*, trans. Richard Howard (New York: Vintage, 1965), 13.

80. Marcel Granet, *Chinese Civilization* (New York: Barnes & Noble, 1957), 170.

81. Gregory Possehl, *The Indus Civilization: A Contemporary Perspective* (Alta-Mira, CA: Altimira Press, 2002), 113.

82. For a more thorough discussion, consult the following: Alain Danielou, *Gods of Love and Ecstasy* (Rochester, VT: Inner Traditions, 1992). Wolf-Dieter Storl, *Shiva: The Wild God of Power and Ecstasy* (Rochester, VT: Inner Traditions, 2004).

83. Cited in Ehrenreich, *Dancing in the Streets*, 126.

84. David Leeming, *Jealous Gods, Chosen People: The Mythology of the Middle East* (New York: Oxford UP, 2004), 125.

85. Huston Smith, *The World's Religions* (San Francisco: Harper, 1991), 289.

86. Steven Harris and Gloria Platzner, *Classical Mythology* (New York: McGraw-Hill, 2008), 265.

87. Ehrenreich, *Dancing in the Streets*, 63.

88. Max Radin, "The Kid and Its Mother's Milk," *American Journal of Semitic Languages & Literatures* 40, no. 3 (1984): 212.

89. Robert Johnson, *Ecstasy: Understanding the Psychology of Joy* (San Francisco: HarperCollins, 1997), 44.

90. Carl W. Ernst, *Sufism* (Boston, Shambhala, 1997), 13.

91. Ibid., 80.

92. Ibid., 11.

93. Ibid., 79.

94. Elaine Pagels, *Beyond Belief: The Secret Gospel of Thomas* (New York: Vintage, 2003), 30.

95. Ehrenreich, *Dancing in the Streets*, 71.

96. Ibid., 75.

97. Rosemarie Taylor-Perry, *The God Who Comes: Dionysian Mysteries Revisited* (New York: Algora, 2003), 115.

98. Ehrenreich, *Dancing in the Streets*, 81.

99. Ibid., 4.

100. Carlo Ginzburg, *Ecstasies: Deciphering the Witches' Sabbatth*, trans. Raymond Rosenthal (Chicago: U of Chicago P, 1991), 76.

101. Sylvia Brinton Perera, *The Scapegoat Complex* (Toronto: Inner City, 1986), 15.

102. Johnson, *Ecstasy*, 48.

103. Taylor-Perry, *The God Who Comes: Dionysian Mysteries Revisited*, 55.

104. Cited in Bruce C. Daniels, *Puritans at Play: Leisure and Recreation in Colonial New England* (New York: St. Martin's, 1995), 3.

105. Ehrenreich, *Dancing in the Streets*, 81.

106. Mikhail Bakhtin, *Rabelais and His World*, trans. Helene Iswolsky (Bloomington, IN: Indiana UP, 1984), xviii.

107. Ibid., 21.

108. Ibid., 4.

109. Ibid., 39.

110. Ehrenreich, *Dancing in the Streets*, 117.

111. Tim Pilcher, *E: The Incredibly Strange History of Ecstasy* (London: Running Press, 2008), 29.

112. Friedrich Nietzsche, *The Birth of Tragedy* (New York: Cambridge UP, 1999), 111.

113. Just as there were psychologists in the twentieth century who focused on positive states, so have there been literary critics who have offered accounts of such states. One example is Jack Heitner's *At the Edge of Consciousness: Transpersonal Psychology and Literature* (Edina, MD: Alpha, 1986), which uses an expressly transpersonal theoretical lens.

114. Priyadarshi Patnaik, *Rasa in Aesthetics* (New Delhi: D.K. Printworld, 2004), 51.

115. Maslow, *The Farther Reaches of Human Nature*, 74.

116. Nysa: The etymology of "Dionysus" is god (Dio) of Nysa.

117. coombe: a hollow in a hillside; a valley that leads to the sea.

119. filleted: decorated.

119. orichalc: A metallic mineral of a reddish color, known in ancient Greece, second only to gold in value, but mined out by Plato's time.

120. Cytherea: an epithet for Aphrodite, who arose fully formed and beautiful from the sea-foam on the shore of the Ionian island, Cytherea.

121. Cyllene: the mountain birthplace of Hermes and also the name of the nymph, or oread, who dwells there.

122. daughter of Dryops: Dryope, sometimes thought of as one of the Pleiades.

123. Taken from John Henry Wright, ed., *Masterpieces of Greek Literature*, trans. Edwin Arnold (New York: Houghton Mifflin, 1902).

124. From *Masterpieces of Greek Literature*, trans. Thomas Moore.

125. From *Masterpieces of Greek Literature*, trans. Dante Gabriel Rossetti.

126. Hesperus: Vesper, the evening star. Venus.

127. From *Masterpieces of Greek Literature*, trans. William Hyde Appleton.

128. All poems by Alcaeus are taken from Walter Peterson, ed., *The Lyric Songs of the Greeks* (Boston: The Gorham Press, 1918).

129. dog-star: Sirius, the rising of which signaled the beginning of Dionysian summer festivities.

130. Semele: mortal mother of Dionysus. Lover of Zeus. She is incinerated when Zeus reveals himself to her.

131. All poems by Anacreon are taken from T.R. Smith, ed., *Poetica Erotica* (New York: Crown Publishers, 1921).

132. tunned: having been placed in a large cask. tun: a large cask.

133. This and all subsequent Orphic hymns are taken from Thomas Taylor, trans., *The Mystical Hymns of Orpheus* (London: Chiswick, 1824).

134. Refulgent: radiating light.

135. Bacchanalian: Dionysus was celebrated in a festival called the bacchanalia. Bacchus: Dionysus, so called because he induces frenzy, or *bakkheia*, in his followers.

136. occultly: secretively.

137. Curetes: leaping, dancing male attendants of the goddess Rhea, or Cybele. They are also called Korybantes.

138. Bassareus: the Lydian name for Dionysus.

139. Licknitus: from *liknon*, or *liknities*, the winnowing fan, an instrument used in agriculture. As a fertility god, Dionysus was associated with agriculture.

140. Pericionius: Dionysus in one of his esoteric permutations, here associated with the muse, Urania.

141. Sabazius: the nomadic horseman and sky god of the Phrygians and Thracians, later associated and interchangeable with Dionysus.

142. Amphietus: Dionysus as an agricultural god, the annual god who perennially renews himself through the cycles of nature.

143. Telete: the *daimona* (spirit) who presided over the initiation rites of the Bacchic orgies. She was a daughter of the god Dionysus.

144. Silenus: adoptive father a tutor of Dionysus. Often depicted as old, wise, drunken, and libinous, Silenus is the leader of the Silenoi, followers of Dionysus who are usually bald and fat with thick lips and squat noses. When drunk, Silenus has the power of prophecy.

145. All poems by Sophocles are taken from William Hyde Appleton, ed., *Greek Poets in English Verse,* trans. Joseph Anstice (Cambridge: The Riverside Press, 1893).

146. Euboea: the second largest of the Greek Aegean islands.

147. Ceres and Proserpine: Demeter and Persephone, the subjects of the Eleusinian Mysteries.

148. Nine: nine Muses of inspiration.

149. Morian Jove: Zeus.

150. Pallas: Athena.

151. meed: a fitting reward.

152. Nereids: sea-nymphs. 50 daughters of Nereus, a sea god.

153. Zephyr: the gentle god of the west wind.

154. Cypris: Aphrodite.

155. Cytherea's son: Cupid, Eros.

156. Graces: goddesses of charm, beauty, nature, human creativity and fertility.

157. Croesus: Greek king who falls to the Persians. Known for his great wealth.

158. ogdoad: eight deities worshipped in Hermapolis in ancient Egypt during the Old Kingdom.

159. Markali: mid-December to mid-January in the Tamil calendar. Originally, during this month unmarried girls would take the Pavai vow and sing songs dedicated to the Pavai goddess (Parvati) in hopes of achieving bliss in marriage. Antal puts a spin on this rite, essentially making a plea for marriage to Krishna.

160. Ayarpati: lit. cowherd settlement.

161. Dark-bodied one: Krishna, the blue god.

162. Yasoda: foster-mother to Krishna, who was born to Devaki but given to Yasoda and Nanda by Krishna's father, Vasudeva, on the night of his birth for his own protection from Devaki's brother, Kamsa.

163. Nandagopa: Nanda, foster father of Krishna. Gopa: head of a tribe of cowherds, or Holy Gwals.

164. Narayana: Vishnu.

165. Padmanabha: lotus-navel. One of the aspects of Vishnu or God with a lotus issuing from his navel.

166. saranga: the bow Vishnu carries.

167. Garuda's lord: Vishnu. Garuda is a large bird-like creature, the mount Vishnu rides.

168. Hari: an appellation of Krishna or Vishnu.

169. Ravana: the evil antagonist of Rama, an incarnation of Vishnu, in the epic *Ramayana*.

170. pavai grounds: presumably the site dedicated for taking the pavai vow.

171. Madhava: Vishnu.

172. Tirumal: Vishnu.

173. enow: enough.

174. There has been considerable debate over whether Khayyam is making a plea for hedonism or operating in the well established Sufi tradition of wine symbolism, which should not be taken literally.

175. Saki: one who pours the wine. In Sufi literature the saki is often a young boy (though sometimes a girl) whose erotic qualities the poet praises.

176. Taken from Thomas Walsh, ed., *Hispanic Anthology: Poems Translated from the Spanish by English and North American Poets*, trans. H.W. Longfellow (New York: G.P. Putnam's Sons, 1920).

177. ween: v. to think, to imagine, to fancy.

178. fig and pomegranate: symbols of sexual organs and fertility. The fig tree was sacred to Dionysian worshippers.

179. Taken from Father Paschal Robinson, trans., *The Writings of Saint Francis of Assisi* (Philadelphia: Dolphin, 1906).

180. This and the following seven poems by Rumi are taken from Hadland Davis, ed., *Wisdom of the East: The Persian Mystics, Jalalu'D-Din Rumi* (London: John Murray, 1907).

181. Theophany: appearance of a god.

182. Many varieties of esoteric spirituality posit the existence of different planes of consciousness, or spheres of reality, which it is possible to access through meditative, contemplative, or yogic practices.

183. akin: alike, similar to, the same as.

184. Galen: a prominent Greek physician and philosopher.

185. Astrolabe: ancient astronomical instrument used for predicting the positions of celestial bodies and for ship navigation.

186. ewer: an open vessel with a handle and a spout for pouring.

187. This and the following three poems by Rumi are taken from R.A. Nicholson, trans., *The Augustan Books of Poetry: Persian Lyrics* (London: Ernest Benn, 1931).

188. dregs: sediment that has settled at the bottom of a liquid.

189. Gabr: Zoroastrian. Follower of the ancient Persian religion that predated Islam.

190. Rizwan: the angel in charge of maintaining paradise in Islam.

191. Ya Hu: Yahweh. Ya man Hu: O He who is.

192. Shamsi Tabriz: the famed Sufi teacher who transformed the 38-year-old Rumi from a rigid, legalist, Muslim scholar to a passionate, ecstatic whirling poet.

193. The nightingale and the rose are stock symbols in Sufi poetry, representing (respectively) the soul and divine love but with myriad other nuanced connotations.

194. Mussulman: Muslim.

195. dervish: a Sufi.

196. courser: swift-footed bird.

197. Magi: priest of the Zoroastrian religion.

198. Ruknabad: city in ancient Persia, modern-day Iran.

199. Weal: good.

200. Brahmana: In this context, a priest or holy man, though the term can also refer to religious texts by the same name.

201. Shakti: the divine feminine creative power. Most gods in Hinduism have a feminine consort, or shakti.

202. unstruck: that is, a sound heard but made by no physical world action, such as striking a drum or plucking the strings of a musical instrument. The sound referred to in Shabda yoga and other Indian teachings, as well as Eckankar, is an *inner* sound heard only by the trained ear. It emanates from the Godhead.

203. Om: a sacred mantra, pronounced "aum."

204. Sadhu: an ascetic and/or practitioner of yoga (*yogi*) and/or wandering monk.

205. Thatness: The refrain in *The Upanishads* is *tat tvam asi* (thou art that), the meaning of which is (loosely) you are the god you seek and worship.

206. vina: any of several stringed musical instruments of India.

207. Kazi: an Islamic legal scholar and judge.

208. Pir: a Sufi teacher, master, guide.

209. Bhaktas: practitioners of Bhakti yoga, the path of love and devotion.

210. Giridhar: lit. the holder of the mountains. An epithet of Krishna.

211. gopis: cow herding girls, followers of Krishna.

212. bramacharini: female who observes sexual abstinence when fertile unless intentionally procreating.

213. concent: harmony of notes, concord of sounds.

214. sepulcher: a chamber used as a grave.

215. unperplex: to free from perplexity. perplexity: a state of confusion.

216. forthwith: without delay.

217. All poems by Marvell are taken from *The Poetical Works of Milton and Marvell* (Boston: Houghton Mifflin, 1880).

218. the palm, the oak, or bays: the spoils of victory in ancient Greek competitions: palm (sports), oak (bravery in battle), bays or laurel (poetry).

219. Bartholomew: the festival of St. Bartholomew is celebrated on August 24 in the Western Church and on June 11 in the Eastern Orthodox Church.

220. Cherubim: plural for Cherub, a winged angel.

221. antepast: a foretaste.

222. Danae: mother of Perseus in Greek mythology. She was inseminated by Zeus, who turned himself into a golden shower and rained on her.

223. Ganymede: Zeus's male cupbearer on Mount Olympus and sometime beautiful lover.

224. pinks: flowers cultivated for their fragrant petals.

225. cowslip: early spring flower common in British isles.

226. hedgerow: a fence formed by a row of closely planted shrubs or bushes.

227. Oreads: mountain nymphs in Greek mythology.

228. sward: stretch of grass.

229. Muses: nine goddesses of inspiration in Greek Mythology.

230. Luna: the moon, or Selene, the moon goddess.

231. Endymion: a shepherd and/or astronomer in Greek mythology. Also the lover of the moon goddess, Selene.

232. All poems by Freneau are taken from Edmund Clarence Stedman, ed., *An American Anthology: 1787-1900* (Boston: Houghton Mifflin, 1900).

233. Thyrsis: a character in Virgil's *Eclogues*, a bucolic poem depicting rural herdsmen engaging in imaginary conversations, the subject of which is happy or unhappy love and/or change. In the Seventh Eclogue, Thyrsis loses a singing match to Corydon, another shepherd. Freneau's poem is a lyrical version of Virgil's bucolic verse form, itself rooted in the Greek pastoral tradition.

234. Mopsus: a famous seer in Greek mythology.

235. Arachnine-like: that is, like Arachne, who is turned into a spider in Greek mythology.

236. Eumenides-like: that is, like the Eumenides, another name for the Furies who punish transgressors, particularly those who harm or transgress against their own family members. In Aeschylus' eponymous play, the Furies are transformed into the peaceful Eumenides (gracious ones).

237. Phoebus: Apollo.

238. Hebe: Goddess of youth.

239. expostulation: an expression of opposition intended to persuade.

240. natural piety: mutual reverence.

241. She: the woman Wordsworth married, Mary Hutchinson.

242. Presageful: full of presages; ominous. presage: that which suggests or predicts the future.

243. stranger: "In all parts of the kingdom these films are called *strangers* and supposed to portend the arrival of some absent friend." (Coleridge's note).

244. Lute: a stringed instrument with a pear-shaped body. The eolian harp was a stringed instrument placed in a window, emitting sounds as the wind blew across its strings. Among Romantics, it was also a symbol of the poet, who served as the harp across which strings divine inspiration (pnema) blew.

245. sequacious: having a logical sequence or pattern.

246. unregenerate: Not regenerate or reformed, as in "unregenerate human nature." Notice the speaker's retreat from the ecstatic and his return to the Christian "fold." The implication is that his oceanic perception is unorthodox and thus not real.

247. Taken from: Franke Kuno, ed., *The German Classics: Masterpieces of German Literature*, 20 vols. (New York: German Publication Society, 1913-14).

248. concenter: to bring into focus or alignment.

249. Cytherea: Aphrodite.

250. Taken from *Poetica Erotica*.

251. Taken from Alfred Baskerville, trans., *The German Classics: Masterpieces of German Literature*.

252. Tmolus: the mountain god who judged the musical contest between Pan and Apollo.

253. Peneus: a river god.

254. Sileni: that is, Silenoi. See note 138.

255. Sylvans: spirits of the woods.

256. dedal: relating to Daedalus. Intricately and/or skillfully designed.

257. chaunt: chant.

258. Styx and Erebus: Styx: a river in Hades the dead must cross. Erebus: a personification of darkness and shadow. In later tradition, also a river in Hades.

259. See Genesis 28:11-19, the story of Jacob's dream for the allusion.

260. insphere: to place in a sphere.

261. Taken from Henry Bromwell, ed., *Translations from Poems of Schiller, Schlegel, Uhland, Schwab, Schneckenburger, Chamisso, Freiligrath, and Others* (Denver, CO: Unknown Publisher, 1919).

262. All poems by Blackie are taken from D.H.S. Nicholson and A.H.E. Lee, eds., *The Oxford Book of English Mystical Verse* (Oxford: Clarendon, 1917).

263. Thales: a revered, pre-Socratic Greek philosopher.

264. Trimurti: The three major divinities in later Hinduism—Brahma, Vishnu, Shiva.

265. porphyry: n. igneous rock with crystals embedded in a finer matrix of minerals. Here used as an adjective.

266. Danaë: see note 216.

267. Seik: Sikh, an adherent to the Indian religion of Sikhism.

268. Taken from Earle Goddard Pliny, trans., *The Masked Dancers of the Apache* (Washington: Holmes, 1916).

269. Gan: In this puberty rite masked dancing males represented the gods, or Gans. The rite was performed for girls.

270. Taken from Earle Goddard Pliny, trans., *A Mescalero Apache Ceremony* (New York: Putnam, 1909).

271. kelson: alt. sp. "keelson." A beam connected to the keel of a ship to strengthen it.

272. engirth: to surround or wrap around.

273. hautboy: a slender double-reed instrument.

274. bole: the main stem of a tree.

275. All Pueblo poems taken from Herbert J. Spinden, trans., *Songs of the Tewa* (New York: Exposition of Indian Tribal Arts, 1933).

276. Shipap: home of the dead.

277. Spheres: a reference to the ancient Pythagorean teaching that the movement of the celestial bodies created a beautiful music that one could hear through mystical attunement.

278. dram: one eighth of an ounce.

279. heft: to compare by placing side by side.

280. vair: squirrel fir.

281. fleurs-de-lys: flowers of the lily. the crest of the French monarchy.

282. Shiva, the Hindu god who dances in a ring of fire.

283. Taken from *The Oxford Book of English Mystical Verse*.

284. reck: heed.

285. unsundered: not torn apart.

286. Taken from *The Oxford Book of English Mystical Verse.*

287. All Innuit songs are taken from "Eskimo Tales and Songs," trans. Franz Boaz, *Journal of American Folklore* 7 (1894).

288. According to Boaz, this song was composed by a young man, Utitiaq, who got lost for a whole week while hunting for seals.

289. reck: see note 278.

290. rod: cross.

291. bleared: dimmed, as in to be bleary-eyed.

292. dappled: colored or streaked with blotches of different shades. pied: having differently colored sections or patches.

293. brinded: having either a gray or brown streak or a pattern, or a patchy coloring.

294. stipple: v. to make a pattern with dots. Here used as a noun.

295. fold, fallow, and plough: farming implements.

296. Selve: v. to become distinct. The concept relates to Hopkins's ideas on *inscape*, the unique, differentiating aspect of every entity in the universe. The recognition of *inscape* is *instress*, of which his poetry is intended to be a form.

297. scanted: supplied meagerly or *scantly*.

298. wimple: headdress of cloth worn by medieval women. wimpling: presumably draped.

299. sillion: the thick, shiny soil turned up by a plow.

300. abele: a poplar tree.

301. sallow: willow tree.

302. stook: a collection of sheaves, or wheels of rolled-up hay.

303. Taken from Sister Mary Paulina Finn, *John Bannister Tabb: The Priest-Poet* (Washington, D.C.: Pub. for Georgetown Visitation Convent, 1915).

304. lissome: gracefully slender; or moving with ease or grace.

305. Taken from *Poetica Erotica.*

306. Taken from *The Oxford Book of English Mystical Verse.*

307. Pierian daughters: the muses lived in Pieria, also the region in which Mount Olympus is located.

308. Evoë: the cry of Dionysian revelers.

309. Iacchus: an appellation of Dionysus. The term can also refer to a hymn (Iakchos) sung in the god's honor.

310. Maenads: the wild, female followers of Dionysus.

311. Shinar: an ancient region including modern Kuwait, associated with the old Babylonian empire. Likely a corruption of Sumer.

312. All negro spirituals are taken from: http://www.negrospirituals.com/song.htm.

313. These are the lyrics of an early, African-American "ring shout," a call-and-response song and circle-dance that often took place after a Christian sermon. Participants would repeat the same phrase over and over, sometimes for hours, while moving in a counter-clockwise circle and beating time on the church floor with broomsticks. The dance bears a striking resemblance to the Gnostic "round dance of Jesus," although it is, no doubt, a vestige of similar call-and-response circle-dances that slaves brought to the Americas from West Africa, where such dances were (and still are) widely practiced.

314. Taken from *The Oxford Book of English Mystical Verse*.

315. Wakan'tanka: a reference to the sacred or divine. Among the Sioux, it means "great mystery."

316. Taken from *Hispanic Anthology*, trans. Salomón de la Selva.

317. lave: to wash or cleanse with soap and water.

318. Primaveral: Spanish and Portuguese for spring or spring-like.

319. "May Is Building Her House" and "The Second Crucifixion" are taken from *The Oxford Book of English Mystical Verse*.

320. Bartimaeus: a man Jesus heals in the "Gospel of Mark" in the New Testament.

321. diadem: crown.

322. Presage: to fortell; to predict; to indicate what is to come.

323. The original reads "whose," presumably a typographical error I have taken the liberty of correcting.

324. houri: a beautiful, dark-eyed virgin who lives in the Islamic version of Paradise.

325. Ammon: the Libyan Jupiter (Zeus).

326. Perseus: son of Danae, mythical founder of Mycenae and the Perseid dynasty. The maiden he frees is Andromeda, whose father chains her to a rock and exposes her to the sea-beast, Cetus, in order to appease the wrathful Poseidon. Perseus slays the beast and then frees Andromeda, whom he later marries.

327. Hesperides: nymphs who guarded the golden apples that Gaia gave as a wedding gift to Hera. The reference may also be to the blissful garden they tend in the west.

328. votaress: a female votary: priestess; one who is devoted to a cause with religious zeal.

329. Taken from *Hispanic Anthology*, trans. Roderick Gill.

330. mariposa: Spanish for butterfly.

331. Taken from *Hispanic Anthology*, trans. Garrett Strange.

332. idyl: a short, pastoral poem, usually depicting an *idyllic* (happily carefree) setting.

333. prurient: lustful, characterized by lust.

334. All poems in this section are taken from *Poetica Erotica*.

335. porphyry: see note 259.

336. Helicon: Mt. Helicon, where the Muses dwell. The "waters" referred to are probably the two springs, Aganippe and the Hippocrene, which are sacred to the Muses and serve as sources of inspiration.

337. erubescence: variant of *erubescency*, the act of becoming red, in this case, blood-engorged.

338. sardonyx: a deep orange-red variety of *onyx*, a mineral.

339. mucilaginous: glue-like; sticky.

340. tapir: a nocturnal mammal with a long, fleshy snout and a long tongue. Get it?

341. All poems by Heitner are taken from *Songs of the Spirit* (New Haven: Connecticut River, 2004).

342. See the bibliography for citations.

343. orrery: planetarium.

344. crinolines: hoops used to stiffened a skirt.

345. tannoura: relating to *tanoura*, a Sufi whirling dance. The reference seems to be to the colorful skirts Sufis wear during the dance.

346. An original composition published for the first time in this anthology.

347. Hosannahs: "Hosannahs" is used in both the Jewish and Christian sense. In the Jewish sense as a plea to God and the more modern, pagan Beyond to "save me now" from this state of exhausted disconnection. And in the Christian sense of praise and excitement that "the One" has come—as is evidenced in the rest of the poem. "Hosannahs" sit at the fulcrum of the poem. But this second sense of "Hosannahs" hasn't fully dawned on the speaker yet. We are to accompany the speaker on this journey to ecstasy. Right now there is a wary sense that something new has entered his consciousness, something not necessarily easily distinguished from the "blackness" of the windows looking out on nothing. (author's note).

348. tympan: n. drum. sibilant: adj. characterized by a hissing sound or whistling. Here probably used as the sibilant cries of ecstatic revelers, or the sound produced by a percussive instrument.

BIBLIOGRAPHY

"The Acts of John." In *The Apocryphal New Testament*, translated by M.R. James, 94-97. Oxford: Clarendon, 1924.

Adams, Sarah F. *Nearer, My God, to Thee.* New York: F.A. Stokes, 1888.

Addison, Joseph. *The Miscellaneous Works of Joseph Addison.* Edited by A. C. Guthkelch. London: G. Bell, 1914.

Aftanas, Ljubomir and Semen Golosheykin. "Impact of Regular Meditation Practice on EEG Activity at Rest and during Evoked Negative Emotions." *Neuroscience* 115 (2005): 893-909.

Alcott, Louisa May. *Louisa May Alcott: A Collection of Papers, 1865-1884.* New York Public Library Archive.

Alderink, Larry. "Creation and Salvation in Ancient Orphism." *American Classical Studies* 8 (1981): 1-96.

Aldrich, Thomas Bailey. "Song from the Persian." In *Yale Book of American Verse*, edited by Thomas R. Lounsbury. New Haven, CT: Yale UP, 1912.

Alighieri, Dante. *The Divine Comedy.* Edited by John Ciardi. New York: New American Library, 2003.

Antal. *Antal and Her Path of Love.* Translated by Vidya Dehejia. Albany, NY: SUNY Press, 1990.

Appleton, William Hyde, ed. *Greek Poets in English Verse.* Cambridge: Riverside, 1893.

Arnold, Matthew. *The Strayed Reveler and Other Poems.* London: B. Fellowes, 1849.

Auden, W.H. *Collected Poems.* Edited by Edward Mendelson. New York: Modern Library, 2007.

Bakhtin, Mikhail. *Rabelais and His World.* Translated by Helene Iswolsky. Bloomington, IN: Indiana UP, 1984.

Barlow, Jane. *Between Doubting and Daring: Verses.* Oxford: Blackwell, 1916.

Baudelaire, Charles. *The Poems and Prose Poems of Charles Baudelaire.* Edited and Translated by James Huneker. New York: Brentano's, 1919.

Berceo, Gonzalo de. "The Praise of Spring." In *Hispanic Anthology: Poems Translated from the Spanish by English and North American Poets*, edited by Thomas Walsh, translated by H.W. Longfellow. New York: G.P. Putnam's Sons, 1920.

Blake, William. *The Prophetic Books of William Blake.* Edited by E.D. Maclagan and A.B. Russell. London: A.H. Bullen, 1907.

Bradstreet, Anne. *The Poems of Mrs. Anne Bradstreet.* Edited by Charles Eliot Norton. New York: The Duodecimos, 1897.

Bromwell, Henry, trans. *Translations from Poems of Schiller, Schlegel, Uhland, Schwab, Schneckenburger, Chamisso, Freiligrath, and Others*. Denver, CO: Unknown Publisher, 1919.

Bronte, Ann. *Poems: by Currier, Ellis, and Acton Bell*. London: Smith, 1846.

Bronte, Charlotte. *Poems: by Currier, Ellis, and Acton Bell*. London: Smith, 1846.

Bronte, Emily. *Poems: by Currier, Ellis, and Acton Bell*. London: Smith, 1846.

Browning, Elizabeth Barrett. *Sonnets from the Portuguese*. Edited by W. J. Rolfe. Boston: D. Lothrop, 1886.

Byrom, John. *The Poems of John Byrom*. Edited by Adolphus William Ward. Manchester, UK: Chetham, 1912.

Byron, George Gordon Lord. *Childe Harold's Pilgrimage: A Romaunt*. New York: T.Y. Crowell, 1889.

Campion, Thomas. *Songs by Dr. Thomas Campion*. Edited by A.C. Curtis. Guildford, UK: Astolat, 1902.

Carman, Bliss. *April Airs: A Book of New England Lyrics*. Boston: Small & Maynard, 1916.

Cather, Willa. *April Twilights*. Boston: Gorham, 1903.

"Chippewa Music." Translated by Frances Densmore. *Bureau of American Ethnology* 45 (1910).

Coleridge, Samuel Taylor. *The Poems of Coleridge*. Edited by Ernest Hartley Coleridge. New York: J. Lane, 1907.

Conrad, Joseph. *Heart of Darkness & The Secret Sharer*. New York: Bantam, 1969.

Cowper, William. *The Poems of William Cowper*. Edited by J.C. Bailey. London: Methuen, 1905.

Crashaw, Richard. *Poems*. Edited by J. R. Tutin. New York: Routledge, 1905.

Csikszentmihalyi, Mihalyi. *Flow: The Psychology of Optimal Experience*. New York: Harper & Row, 1990.

cummings, e e "o sweet spontaneous." *The Dial* 68.5 (1920).

Davis, Hadland, trans. *Wisdom of the East: The Persian Mystics: Jalalu'D-Din Rumi*. London: John Murray, 1907.

Daniels, Bruce C. *Puritans at Play: Leisure and recreation in Colonial New England*. New York: St. Martin's, 1995.

Danielou, Alain. *Gods of Love and Ecstasy*. Rochester, VT: Inner Traditions, 1992.

Delacroix, Henri. *Etudes d'historie et de psychologie du mysticism: les grandes mystiques Chretiens*. Paris: Felix Alcan, 1908.

Dickinson, Emily. *The Single Hound: Poems of a Lifetime by Emily Dickinson*. Edited by Martha Dickinson Bianchi. Boston: Little, Brown and Company, 1914.

Donne, John. *The Poems of John Donne.* Edited by Herbert J. C. Grierson. London: Oxford UP, 1912.

Dowden, Edward. *Poems.* Toronto: J. M. Dent, 1914.

Drane, Augusta Theodosia. *Songs in the Night and Other Poems.* New York: Catholic Publication Society, 1887.

Dryden, John. *The Poetry of John Dryden.* Edited by Mark Van Doren. New York: Harcourt, 1920.

Duclaux, Agnes Mary Frances. *The Collected Poems, Lyrical and Narrative, of A. Mary F. Robinson (Madame Duclaux).* London: T.F. Unwin, 1902.

Durkheim, Emile. *The Elementary Forms of the Religious Life.* New York: Free Press, 1915.

Ehrenreich, Barbara. *Dancing in the Streets.* New York: Henry Holt, 2006.

Eliade, Mircea. *Shamanism: Archaic Techniques of Ecstasy.* Translated by Willard R. Trask. Princeton, NJ: Princeton UP, 1964.

Emerson, Ralph Waldo. *Essays and Poems of Emerson.* Edited by Stuart P. Sherman. New York: Harcourt-Brace, 1921.

Ernst, Carl W. *Sufism.* Boston: Shambhala, 1997.

"Eskimo Tales and Songs." Translated by Franz Boaz. *Journal of American Folklore* 7 (1894).

Finn, Sister Mary Paulina. *John Bannister Tabb: The Priest-Poet.* Washington, D.C.: Pub. for Georgetown Visitation Convent, 1915.

Foucault, Michel. *Madness and Civilization: A History of Insanity in the Age of Reason.* Translated by Richard Howard. New York: Vintage, 1965.

Frankl, Victor. *Man's Search for Ultimate Meaning.* New York: Basic, 2000.

____. *Man's Search for Meaning.* New York: Simon & Schuster, 1984.

Freud, Sigmund. *Civilzation & Its Discontents.* Translated by James Strachey. New York: Norton, 1989.

Fromm, Erich. *The Art of Loving.* New York: Continuum, 1956.

General Social Survey. Chicago: National Opinion Research Center, 1989.

Ginzburg, Carlo. *Ecstasies: Deciphering the Witches' Sabbath.* Translated by Raymond Rosenthal. Chicago: U of Chicago P, 1991.

Goethe, Johann Wolfgang von. *Poems and Ballads of Goethe.* Translated by A. Edmondstoune and Theodore Martin. London: Blackwood, 1907.

____. *Goethe: Poetical Works.* Translated by John Storer Cobb. Boston: Francis A Niccolls, 1902.

Gosse, Edmund. *The Collected Poems of Edmund Gosse.* London: W. Heinemann, 1911.

Granet, Marcel. *Chinese Civilization.* New York: Barnes & Noble, 1957.

Gray, Alex. *Art Psalms.* New York: COSM Press, 2008.

Grof, Stanislav. *The Holotropic Mind.* New York: HarperCollins, 1990.

Hafiz. *Odes from the Divan of Hafiz.* Translated by Richard Le Gallienne. Boston: L. C. Page, 1903.

Hall, Trish. "Seeking a Focus on Joy in the Field of Psychology." *New York Times*, April 28, 1998.

Happold, F.C. *Mysticism: A Study and an Anthology.* New York: Penguin, 1990.

Harris, Steven and Gloria Platzner. *Classical Mythology.* 5th ed. New York: McGraw-Hill, 2008.

Hayman, Ronald. *A Life of Jung.* New York: Norton, 1999.

Heidegger, Martin. *Basic Writings.* Translated by Joan Stambaugh and Edited by David Farrell. New York: HarperCollins, 1993.

Heitner, Jack. *Songs of the Spirit.* New Haven: Connecticut River, 2004.

____. *At the Edge of Consciousness: Transpersonal Psychology and Literature.* Edina, MD: Alpha, 1986.

Herrick, Robert. *The Poems of Robert Herrick.* New York: H. Frowde, 1919.

Hoffman, Albert. *LSD: My Problem Child.* Sarasota, FL: MAPS, 2005.

Holland, Norman N. *Literature and the Brain.* Gainesville, FL: PsyArt Foundation, 2009.

Hollenback, Jess Byron. *Mysticism: Experience, Response, and Empowerment.* University Park, PA: Penn State UP, 1996.

The Homeric Hymns. Translated by Hugh G. Evelyn-White. Cambridge, MA: Harvard UP, 1914.

Hopkins, Gerard Manley. *Poems of Gerard Manley Hopkins.* Edited by Robert Bridges. London: Oxford UP, 1930.

Hughes, Langston. "The Negro Speaks of Rivers." *The Crisis* (1921).

Huther, Gerard. *The Compassionate Brain.* Boston: Shambhala, 2006.

Huxley, Aldous. *The Perennial Philosophy.* New York: Harper, 1944.

Hyde, William, ed. *Greek Poets in English Verse.* Translated by Joseph Anstice. Cambridge: Riverside Press, 1893.

Iser, Wolfgang. *The Act of Reading: A Theory of Aesthetic Response.* Baltimore, MD: Johns Hopkins UP, 1978.

Ivanovski, Belinda and Gin S. Malhi. "The Psychological and Neurophysiological Concomitants of Mindfulness Forms of Meditation." *Acta Neuropsychiatrica* 19 (2007): 76-91.

James, William. *The Varieties of Religious Experience.* New York: Penguin, 1985.

Johnson, Robert. *Ecstasy: Understanding the Psychology of Joy.* San Francisco: HarprCollins, 1997.

Jonson, Ben. *Volpone; or, The Fox.* Edited by John D. Rea. New Haven, CT: Yale UP, 1919.

Juan de la Cruz. *The Dark Night of the Soul.* Translated by Fr. Benedict Zimmerman. London: Thomas Baker, 1916.

Jung, C.G. *The Collected Works of C.G. Jung.* 20 vols. Edited by William McGuire, Translated by R.F.C. Hull. Princeton, NJ: Princeton UP, 1983.

___. *Psychology and Religion*. New Haven, CT: Yale UP, 1938.

Kabir. *Songs of Kabir*. Translated by Rabindranath Tagore. New York: Macmillan, 1916.

Katz, Steven T. *Mysticism and Religious Traditions*. New York: Oxford UP, 1983.

Kellehear, Allan. *Experiences Near Death: Beyond Medicine and Religion*. New York: Oxford UP, 1996.

Khayyam, Omar. *The Rubaiyat of Omar Khayyam, the Astronomer-Poet of Persia*. Translated by Edward Fitzgerald. London: Bernard Quaritch, 1872.

Kjaer, T.W., et al, "The Neural Basis of the Complex Tasks of Meditation: Neurotransmitter and Neurochemical Considerations." *Brain Research: Cognitive BrainResearch* 13, no. 2 (2002): 255-59.

Kubler-Ross, Elisabeth. *The Tunnel and the Light*. New York: Avalon, 1999.

Kuno, Franke, ed. *The German Classics: Masterpieces of German Literature*. 20 vols. New York: German Publication Society, 1913-14.

Lalla. *Lalla-Vakyani, or The Wise Sayings of Lal Ded*. Translated by George Grierson. London: The Royal Asiatic Society, 1920.

Laski, Marghanita. *Ecstasy in Secular and Religious Experiences*. Los Angeles: Tarcher, 1961.

Lawrence, D.H. *The Collected Poems of D. H. Lawrence*. 2 vols. London: Martin Secker, 1928.

Leary, Timothy. *The Politics of Ecstasy*. Oakland, CA: Ronin, 1998.

Leeming, David. *Jealous Gods, Chosen People: The Mythology of the Middle East*. New York: Oxford UP, 2004.

Lewis, Thomas, Fari Amini, and Richard Lannon. *A General Theory of Love*. New York: Random House, 2000.

Ludwid, Theodore M. *The Sacred Paths of the East*. Upper Saddle River, NJ: Prentice Hall, 2001.

Maslow, Abraham. *The Farther Reaches of Human Nature*. New York: Penguin, 1976.

___. *Religions, Values & Peak Experiences*. New York: Penguin, 1970.

___. *Toward a Psychology of Being*. New York: D. Van Nostrand, 1968.

May, Rollo. *Love and Will*. New York: Dell, 1969.

Merkur, Dan. *The Ecstatic Imagination: Psychedelic Experiences and the Psychoanalysis of Self-Actualization*. Albany, NY: SUNY P, 1998.

Milarepa, Jetsun. *The Message of Milarepa*. Translated by Humphrey Clark. London: John Murray, 1958.

Millay, Edna St. Vincent. *Second April*. New York: Harper, 1921.

___. "God's World." In *The Second Book of Modern Verse: A Selection from the Work of Contemporaneous American Poets*, edited by Jessie B. Rittenhouse. New York: Houghton Mifflin, 1919.

Mirabai. *Mirabai: Saint and Singer of India*. Translated by Anath Nath Basu. London: George Allen, 1934.

Morrison, Toni. *Beloved*. New York: Random House, 1987.

Naidu, Sarojini. *The Golden Threshold*. New York: John Lane, 1916.

Neihardt, John G. *Black Elk Speaks*. 1932. Lincoln, NE: UP Nebraska, 1979.

Newberg, Andrew. *Born to Believe: God, Science, and the Origen of Ordinary and Extraordinary Beliefs*. New York: Simon & Schuster, 2006.

Nicholson, D.H.S. and A.H.E. Lee, eds. *The Oxford Book of English Mystical Verse*. Oxford: Clarendon, 1917.

Nicholson, R.A., trans. *The Augustan Books of Poetry: Persian Lyrics*. London: Ernest Benn, 1931.

Nietzsche, Friedrich. *The Birth of Tragedy*. New York: Cambridge UP, 1999.

Novalis. *Rampolli: Growths from a Long-Planted Root: Being Translations, New and Old, Chiefly from the German*. Translated by George MacDonald. New York: Longman's Green, 1897.

Pagels, Elaine. *Beyond Belief: The Secret Gospel of Thomas*. New York: Vintage, 2003.

"Papago Music." Translated by Frances Densmore. *Bureau of American Ethnology Bulletin* 90 (1929).

Patmore, Coventry Kersey Dighton. *The Rod, the Root, and the Flower*. London: G. Bell, 1914.

Patnaik, Priyadarshi. *Rasa in Aesthetics*. New Delhi: D.K. Printworld, 2004.

Percy, William Alexander. "Overtones." In *The Second Book of Modern Verse*, edited by Jesse B. Rittenhouse. Boston: Houghton Mifflin, 1920.

___. *Sappho in Levkas and Other Poems*. New Haven, CT: Yale UP, 1915.

Perera, Sylvia Brinton. *The Scapegoat Complex*. Toronto: Inner City, 1986.

Peterson, Christopher. *A Primer in Positive Psychology*. New York: Oxford UP, 2006.

Peterson, Walter, ed. *The Lyric Songs of the Greeks*. Translated by Walter Peterson. Boston: Gorham, 1918.

Pilcher, Tim. *E: The Incredibly Strange History of Ecstasy*. London: Running Press, 2008.

Pinchbeck, Daniel. *Breaking Open the Head: A Psychedelic Journey into the Heart of Contemporary Shamanism*. New York: Random House, 2002.

Pliny, Earle Goddard. *The Masked Dancers of the Apache*. Washington: Holmes, 1916.

___. trans. *A Mescalero Apache Ceremony*. New York: Putnam, 1909.

The Poetical Works of Milton and Marvell. Boston: Houghton Mifflin, 1880.

Po, Li. *Li Po: The Chinese Poet*. Translated by Shigeyoshi Obata. New York: Dutton, 1922.

Pound, Ezra. *Lustra*. London: Elkin Mathews, 1916.

Possehl, Gregory. *The Indus Civilization: A Contemporary Perspective*. Alta Mira, CA: Alta Mira, 2002.

Radin, Max. "The Kid and Its Mother's Milk." *American Journal of Semitic Languages & Literatures* 40, no. 3 (1984): 209-218.

Rich, Susanna. "Dancing with Wide Skirts." *Mainewoods* 70.3 (2007): 9.

____. "Come to the Dance." *Mainewoods* 54.3 (2003): 6.

____. "Applause." *Porcupine* 10.2 (2007): 19.

Rilke, Rainer Maria. *Poems: Rainer Maria Rilke*. Translated by Jessie Lemont. New York: Tobias Wright, 1918.

Robinson, Father Paschal, trans. *The Writings of Saint Francis of Assisi*. Philadelphia: Dolphin, 1906.

Rossetti, Christina. *A Pageant and Other Poems*. Boston: Roberts, 1881.

Rossetti, Dante Gabriel. *Poems & Translations: 1850-1870*. New York: Oxford UP, 1913.

Rougemont, Denis de. *Love in the Western World*. Translated by Montgomery Belgion. Princeton, NJ: Princeton UP, 1983.

Russell, Geroge William. *Half-Lengths*. New York: Duffield, 1913.

Rydberg, Victor. "Heaven's Blue." Translated by Ernest Nelson. *Poet Lore* 27 no. 3 (1916).

Sappho. *Sappho: Memoir, Text, Selected Renderings and a Literal Translation*. Translated by J.H. Merivale. New York: Brentano's, 1920.

Schiller, Friedrich von. *The Poems of Schiller*. Translated by Edgar A. Bowring. New York: Hurst, 1872.

Scott, Duncan Campbell. *Beauty and Life*. Toronto: McClelland & Stewart, 1921.

Seligman, Martin. *Authentic Happiness*. New York: Simon & Schuster, 2002.

Shelley, Percy. *Poems of Shelley: An Anthology in Commemoration of the Poet's Death*. London: R. Cobden-Sanderson, 1922.

Smart, Christopher. *Christopher Smart: Poems, on Several Occasions*. London: Strahan, 1752.

Smith, Huston. *The World's Religions*. San Francisco: Harper, 1991.

Smith, T.R., ed. *Poetica Erotica*. New York: Crown, 1921.

"Songs of the Tewa." Translated by Herbert J. Spinden. New York: Exposition of Indian Tribal Arts, 1933.

Stedman, Edmund Clarence, ed. *An American Anthology: 1787-1900*. Boston: Houghton Mifflin, 1900.

Storl, Wolf-Dieter. *Shiva: The Wild God of Power and Ecstasy*. Rochester, VT: Inner Traditions, 2004.

Symonds, Arthur. *Nature's Way*. Concord, NH: Rumford, 1910.

Tagore, Rabindranath. *Gitanjali*. New York: Scribner, 1913.

Taylor, Thomas, ed. *The Mystical Hymns of Orpheus*. Translated by Thomas Taylor. London: Chiswick, 1824.

Taylor-Perry, Rosemarie. *The God Who Comes: Dionysian Mysteries Revisited*. New York: Algora, 2003.

Teadale, Sara. *Rivers to the Sea*. New York: Macmillan, 1915.

____. "Joy." In *Anthology of Magazine Verse for 1915*, edited by William Stanley Braithwaite. New York: Gomme & Marshall, 1915.

Tennyson, Alfred Lord. *In Memoriam*. London: Edward Moxon, 1850.

"Teton Sioux Music." Translated by Frances Densmore. *Bureau of American Ethnology* 61 (1918).

Traherne, Thomas. *Traherne's Poems of Felicity*. Oxford: Clarendon, 1910.

Tukaram. *Village Songs of Western India: Translations from Tukaram*. Translated by John S. Hoyland. London: Allenson, 1934.

———. *An Indian Peasant Mystic: Translations from Tukaram*. Translated by John S. Hoyland. London: HR Allenson, 1932.

Turner, Victor. *The Ritual Process: Structure and Anti-Structure*. Ithaca, NY: Cornell UP, 1966.

Underhill, Evelyn. *Mysticism: The Nature and Development of Spiritual Consciousness*. 1911. Oxford: Oneworld, 1994.

Valarino, Evelyn Elsaesser. *On the Other Side of Life: Exploring the Phenomenon of the Near-Death Experience*. Translated by Michelle Herzig Escobar. New York: Plenum, 1997.

Vaughan, Henry. *The Tercentenary of Henry Vaughan*. Edited by H.W. Wells. New York: Hudson, 1922.

Walsh, Thomas, ed. *Hispanic Anthology: Poems Translated from the Spanish by English and North American Poets*. New York: G.P. Putnam's Sons, 1920.

Weber, Max. *The Religion of China and the Spirit of Capitalism*. New York: Routledge, 1992.

Weeks, Daniel. "Clarissa among the Bovines." In *Virginia: A Sequence of Narrative Poems*. Cliffwood, NJ: Blast Press, 2008.

———. "The Blue Morning Glory." In *Poems*. Lewiston, NY: Mellen Poetry Press, 1999.

Wesley, Charles. *Charles Wesley: Seen in his Finer and Less Familiar Poems*. New York: Hurd and Houghton, 1867.

Whitman, Walt. *Leaves of Grass*. Philadelphia: David McKay, 1891-92.

Whittier, John Greenleaf. *Voices of Freedom and Other Poems*. New York: Caldwell, 1909.

Wordsworth, William. *Wordsworth: An Anthology*. Edited by T.J. Cobden-Sanderson. New York: Knopf, 1920.

Wordsworth, Jonathan, M.H. Abrams, and Stephen Gill, eds. *The Prelude: 1799, 1805, 1850*. New York: Norton, 1979.

Wright, John Henry, ed. *Masterpieces of Greek Literature*. New York: Houghton Mifflin, 1902.

INDEX OF FIRST LINES

392

This is Love: to fly heavenward; 105
This is the female form, 245
Thou fair-haired angel of the evening, 173
Thou, Lord, hast lifted from mine eyes 134
Thrice holy night! O hallowed rising moon! 109
Through Love bitter things become sweet; 104
Through orchard-plots with fragrance crowned 64
Through that pure virgin-shrine, 148
'T is so much joy! 'T is so much joy! 271
To be resolved to abandon selfishness is joy. 97
To praise the Creator, 359
To tell the Savior all my wants, 165
Trimurti, Trimurti, 229
True joy is not Beyond, 135
Under the flaming wings of cherubim 282
Unfold! Unfold! Take in His light, 150
Until I lose my soul and lie 328
Upon a Summer's day, 351
Up! Up! my Friend, and quit your books; 188
Wakan'tanka 314
Waves of bliss crash against the craggy shore 368
Whate'er work I did, that was my worship. 113
What else would it be, this rush 357
What is this mystic flute whose note 354
What is to be done, O Moslems? For I do not recognize myself. 106
What powerful Spirit lives within! 153
What's that, which, ere I spake, was gone! 266
Whenas in silks my Julia goes, 137
When Bacchus here is present, 80
When by repeated practice of yoga the whole expanse of the visible 113
Whence these twelve peaks of Wu-shan! 84
Whenever Bacchus, son of Zeus, 80
When first my songs became, 242
When I go back to earth 329
When I heard the learned astronomer, 247
When my soul touches yours a great chord sings! 324
When the earth was made; 241
When the sun disappeared, then came the moonlight; 113
When they see my songs 330
When thou commandest me to sing it seems that my heart
  would break with 308
When with closed eyes in autumn's eves of gold 255
Where is the need of words, when love has made drunken the heart? 116
Where, like a pillow on a bed 128

DONALD "D.J." MOORES, PH.D., is an Assistant Professor of English and Program Coordinator at Kean University's Ocean campus. He is the author of numerous scholarly articles and conference papers, as well as three critical books—*Mystical Discourse in Wordsworth and Whitman* (Peeters 2006), *The Dark Enlightenment: Jung, Romanticism & the Repressed Other* (Fairleigh Dickinson UP 2010), and *The Ecstatic Poetic Tradition* (forthcoming). In addition to compiling *Wild Poets of Ecstasy: An Anthology of Ecstatic Verse* (Pelican Pond 2011), he is currently collaborating (with James Pawelski) on two other edited volumes—*Literary Studies in Human Flourishing* and *Winged Words: The Poetry of Human Flourishing*. His current research is a critical exploration into the mysteries of rapture and ecstatic states. He teaches courses on (1) British, American and transatlantic Romanticism, (2) mystical/ecstatic poetry, (3) world literature, and (4) critical theory. An interdisciplinarian, he approaches these subjects holistically from a variety of critical perspectives. He lives near New York City.

You may contact D.J. Moores via email: dmoores@kean.edu

Made in the USA
Charleston, SC
06 January 2012